# Take Back Your Family

**Rev Run**—aka Joseph Simmons—is one of the founding members of the major pioneering hip-hop group Run DMC. Born in Queens, New York, he is the younger brother of legendary hip-hop mogul Russell Simmons. Along with his wife and family, he stars in MTV's top-rated reality show *Run's House*.

**Justine Simmons** is his wife and costar of *Run's House*. She is also the designer of the Brown Sugar Jewelry Collection for Simmons Jewelry. She and Rev Run live in Saddle River, New Jersey, with the four youngest of their six children.

**Chris Morrow** is also the coauthor of Russell Simmons's *Do You! 12 Laws to Access the Power in You to Achieve Happiness and Success*. He lives in Brooklyn, New York.

# Take Back Your Family

## How to Raise Respectful and Loving Kids in a Dysfunctional World

### REV RUN AND JUSTINE SIMMONS

*with*

### CHRIS MORROW

GOTHAM BOOKS

GOTHAM BOOKS
Published by Penguin Group (USA) Inc.
375 Hudson Street, New York, New York 10014, U.S.A.

Penguin Group (Canada), 90 Eglinton Avenue East, Suite 700, Toronto, Ontario M4P 2Y3, Canada (a division of Pearson Penguin Canada Inc.); Penguin Books Ltd, 80 Strand, London WC2R 0RL, England; Penguin Ireland, 25 St Stephen's Green, Dublin 2, Ireland (a division of Penguin Books Ltd); Penguin Group (Australia), 250 Camberwell Road, Camberwell, Victoria 3124, Australia (a division of Pearson Australia Group Pty Ltd); Penguin Books India Pvt Ltd, 11 Community Centre, Panchsheel Park, New Delhi–110 017, India; Penguin Group (NZ), 67 Apollo Drive, Rosedale, North Shore 0632, New Zealand (a division of Pearson New Zealand Ltd); Penguin Books (South Africa) (Pty) Ltd, 24 Sturdee Avenue, Rosebank, Johannesburg 2196, South Africa

Penguin Books Ltd, Registered Offices: 80 Strand, London WC2R 0RL, England

Published by Gotham Books, a member of Penguin Group (USA) Inc.

Previously published as a Gotham Books hardcover edition.

First trade paperback printing, September 2009

10  9  8  7  6  5  4  3  2

Gotham Books and the skyscraper logo are trademarks of Penguin Group (USA) Inc.

All photos courtesy of the family's private archive

The Library of Congress has cataloged the hardcover edition of this book as follows:
Simmons, Joseph.
Take back your family: a challenge to America's parents /
Rev Run and Justine Simmons; with Chris Morrow.
p.  cm.
ISBN 978-1-592-40381-3 (hardcover)   ISBN 978-1-592-40501-5 (paperback)
1. Family—United States.  2. Marriage—United States.  3. Communication in the family—
United States.  4. Parenting—United States.  5. Parent and child—United States.
I. Simmons, Justine. II. Morrow, Chris. III. Title.
HQ536.S499 2008
204'.41—dc22      2008017398

Printed in the United States of America
Set in Electra with Diotima Display    Designed by Elke Sigal

*This book is dedicated to families all around the world*

# CONTENTS

# Take Back Your Family

# Introduction

When my wife Justine and I first decided to write a book about our keys to raising a productive and happy family, I was so excited that I immediately sat down and started working on the book's cover. Granted, the cover is traditionally the very *last* thing you worry about when writing a book. But as anyone who knows me can tell you, I don't always go about things the traditional way. So before putting together any chapter outlines, or even any general notes for the book, I jotted down some thoughts for the cover:

*The cover should be a big photo of me hiding behind one of my cars with a water balloon in each hand and a big old grin on my face. My sons JoJo, Diggy, and Russy are hiding behind some bushes and trying to throw their balloons at me. My daughters Vanessa and Angela are laughing and screaming while trying to get away from us. Justine, as old as she is, is ducking behind another car while she throws a balloon at the boys. You should see busted balloons all over the driveway and the cars. And we should all have big smiles on our faces, like we're having the time of our lives.*

As you might have noticed, our publisher didn't exactly share my enthusiasm for that cover. But even though that cover never made it off the drawing board, it's very telling that a scene of pure joy and happiness is the first thing that popped into my mind when I started brainstorming about this book. Not everyone thinks of

1

laughter and hijinks when they think of family. Because as anyone who's ever done it can tell you, raising a family can be challenging, confusing, exasperating, exhausting, expensive, and even tragic. But while I have experienced all those scenarios, at the end of the day I view raising a family as *fun*. That's why hopefully the image of my family soaking wet and grinning from ear to ear will never stray too far from your mind. Because if there's one theme that's central to my life and to this book, it is that nothing will bring more fun and fulfillment to your life than your family.

Obviously, I'm not the first person who has suggested that raising a family is a great way to spend your time—the positive power of family is a truth that humans have understood since the beginning of time. But it's also a truth that we have just as long a history of forgetting. As much as we all pay lip service to the importance of family, it's very easy to lose sight of it in the pursuit of money, fame, sex, and adventure. As a society, we tend to celebrate the people who run big companies, hit a lot of home runs, star in movies or, yes, even sell a lot of records. But we don't pay as much attention to the people who simply do a great job raising their kids. In short, as important as we all say family is, it just isn't considered that cool anymore.

Take for instance the story behind *Run's House*, my reality show on MTV. The concept was very simple: Let's follow a family where the mother and father have a great relationship and all the kids stay out of trouble and do well in school. Sounds great, right? But initially we had a very difficult time convincing television people to take a chance on it. The conventional wisdom was that audiences prefer watching dysfunctional over functional families on reality TV. That audiences find TV compelling when the kids are struggling with drinking, drugs, and promiscuity instead of getting good grades, staying out of trouble, and going to church every Sunday. That viewers would be more interested in watching parents who scream and yell at each other than parents who kiss and say, "I love you" each night before they go to bed.

I'm not trying to suggest that the network suits were the only ones who had trouble believing that America would care about a functioning family. I was also hearing talk that some of the TV executives were skeptical about whether our wholesome lifestyle would interest enough people. "I don't know, Rev," an African-American friend of mine told me after he looked at some of the footage we shot. "I'm just having trouble connecting with your reality." Because while my friend understood that the footage reflected *my* reality, that reality didn't feel real *to him*. Like too many people, he grew up without a father. His mother did an incredible job raising him, but he was never able to experience the warmth and security that comes from having both a mother and father running things under the same roof. He never knew what it was like to sit around the dinner table every night and have two parents talk to him about the importance of doing well in school. He didn't have a father who could come to his ball games and on the way home tell him how well he played. He never had a father who would give him a stern lecture about staying away from knuckleheads, but then at the end still kiss him on his head and say, "I love you, son." So when my friend and others like him saw those scenes of our life, they felt very outside their experience, as if they were closer to a fairy tale than how people really live.

Thankfully, with the help of our team—my brother Russell, Sean "P. Diddy" Combs, and the legendary TV producer Stan Lathan—we were able to convince the doubters that while they might have never experienced that kind of lifestyle personally, it was still important to give the world an example to look up to and emulate. So in time we were able to convince MTV of that value, too. And I'm very proud to say that thanks to the hard work and vision of our executive producer Jason Carbone and his incredible team, *Run's House* is one of the most popular shows on MTV and just launched its fifth season on the air as I write this. And while we always believed in the show's potential, Justine and I never dreamed that people would connect with our reality so deeply. Whenever we're on the street, we're always approached by people who want us to know that they watch the show and appreciate its values. "Oh, your family reminds me so much of mine," someone will tell us. Or another person will say, "I saw the episode last night and I have to tell you, we're dealing with the exact same issue with our daughter. Thanks for letting us into your world and then talking about it." It's very humbling to get that sort of feedback and to know that you're helping promote something as important and lasting as the positive power of family.

That powerful reaction to *Run's House* has convinced me that promoting the value of family life is what I was put on this earth to do. I might have earned my reputation as a rapper, but when all is said and done, I hope what I'll ultimately be remembered for is being a good dad. I truly believe that God has intended for me to provide African-Americans specifically (and all people in general) with an example of a better way to raise their families. I believe God wants me to use my TV show (and this book) to remind folks that even though raising a family is a struggle, your family can always conduct itself with class and dignity. To remind people that when they put their heart and soul into their family, it's an investment that will always pay tremendous dividends. I really hope that the success of *Run's House* is just the beginning, and that God will keep blowing his breath through Justine and me and we can continue to be his instrument, singing the world a song about family.

## SHARING OUR IMPERFECTIONS

I understand it might sound very arrogant when I start talking about God using my little TV show as his instrument. So I want to stress that nothing Justine or I will say in this book is fueled by any sense of being holier than thou or perfect. Just the opposite, in fact. I suspect one of the reasons people have connected with *Run's House* is because Justine and I have been soooo willing to share our *imperfections* with world. If you've watched the show, then you've seen that we aren't bothering to even act like we have it all together. We talk freely about our mistakes, our doubts, and how we have to constantly pray for guidance. Besides, we both look busted half the time, with me walking around in pajamas, or Justine sitting in bed with a scarf on her head. No way do we think we're better than anyone else! Even when I send out my inspirational *Words of Wisdom* e-mail at the end of every episode, I'm composing it while sitting in a pink bubble path! Trust me, no one is taking themselves too seriously in *Run's House*!

Still, I worry that the down-to-earth attitude that comes across so clearly on the TV screen won't be as obvious in the pages of a book. On TV, you can see me strutting around my kitchen imitating silly characters like "Kato Mattee," or twisting up my face when I say, "whatchugonnado?" That part of my personality doesn't come out as easily in the written word. So if the goofy, upbeat persona that you see on TV suddenly seems a little more serious in this book, please understand that it isn't my intention. The language and the tone might appear a little more formal, but believe me, I'm still the same fool you see on TV.

And no matter how high the ratings get on *Run's House*, or how well this book might do, I never want to lose that sense of humility and humanity. Besides, I know that as soon as I start believing that I have a tight grasp on my life, God won't waste any time reminding me just how weak my hold really is. As Justine and I will discuss later, in 2006 our daughter Victoria Anne died at birth. And let me tell you, when she passed, I didn't feel like "father knows best." I felt like a lost child whose world was turned upside down. Yes, I was strong for my family on the outside, but on the inside part of me just wanted to scream, "Why is this happening to me? I've tried to do the right things! I go to church! I don't cheat on my wife! I spend quality time with my children! Why is this happening?" Thankfully, as we'll also discuss later, both Justine and I were able to pull ourselves out of that despair and make some sense of our loss. But even so, it was a very painful reminder that as hard as I might try, I'll never have all the answers as a father.

Similarly, while I'm always humbled when people approach me

and tell me what an important example I'm setting with my marriage, the truth is that I haven't always been the perfect husband, either. It's still painful for me to talk about, but my first marriage, to Vanessa, Angela, and JoJo's mother, Valerie, ended in divorce. So while I do feel I'm setting a positive example with my marriage today, my behavior hasn't always been something to emulate.

That's why I'll be the first to admit that I'm a hypocrite. I'll admit that I contradict myself too much. And that there are too many inconsistencies between what I preach and what I practice. So while this book represents the best of what I have to offer as a father and a husband, most of the time, I actually fall far short of that. I'm just trying to do the best that I can.

In light of those shortcomings, I need to stress that the goal for this book is to share the experiences of our family, not to judge and criticize anyone else's. This book is a conversation about some of the things that have worked for us, not an indictment of anyone else's methods.

I should also add that we're not claiming to be breaking any new ground with this book. The practices we're promoting in this book are no different from what people have been suggesting for thousands of years. We might use different language, or come at the issues from a different perspective, but essentially we're promoting the same kind of values that you've heard in a church, or in a synagogue, or maybe just sitting around on your grandparents' porch back in the day. It's really nothing new. That's why I believe that if this book has any value for you, it most likely will be as a refresher to help bring those values back into focus. Rather than give you a radical new outlook on raising a family, this book might simply remind you how to bring a situation that's gotten a little out of whack back into balance. And "balance" is going to be a key word in this book. To be a successful parent, we believe you must always look to create a balance between your dreams and reality, between your faith and your doubts, between strengths and weaknesses. This search for balance colors everything we do as parents and as people.

## BUILDING *RUN'S HOUSE*

While I've already talked about *Run's House* a bit, I don't want to operate under the assumption that everyone reading this book is a fan of, or familiar with, the show. Maybe you've come to these pages because you remember me from Run DMC. Maybe you're a fan of Justine's children's book *God, Can You Hear Me?* Or maybe you don't know much about me or my family, but had this book recommended to you by someone who does. So before I go any further, let me first take a small step backward and share a very brief description of my journey and how my wife and I came to write this book.

The son of Daniel and Evelyn Simmons, I was born and raised in Queens, New York. I would describe our situation as lower middle class: My father was a public school administrator and my mother worked for the New York City Parks Department. While they ended up divorcing when I was older, I have only fond memories of growing up in their house. They set strict rules and had high expectations, but they were also very loving and fair. Most of how I approach being a parent is based on their example.

As a teenager, I fell in love with a new kind of music that was sweeping my neighborhood called hip-hop. For a while I pursued it as a hobby, until I got a break DJ'ing for the rapper Kurtis Blow, who was managed by my older brother Russell. Yet as much as I loved spinning records for Russell, I was a rapper at heart and eventually I formed a group with my friend Darryl "DMC" McDaniels. We later added our friend Jason "Jam Master Jay" Mizzell to the group as a DJ, and called ourselves Run DMC. With Russell's help, we were able to land a record deal and within a few short years we had made the jump from rocking parks in Queens to selling out Madison Square Garden. During the eighties, we were sitting on top of the world. We rode around in limousines, flew in private jets, saw our faces on the covers of magazines, and got our videos played on MTV (which was unheard of for rap groups at the time). I don't want to overstate our impact, but I think it is fair to say that Run DMC helped put hip-hop on the map in a very big way.

But despite that impact, our success didn't last forever. Even though we continued to sell records at a very respectable pace, by the late eighties we could no longer match our initial popularity. Maybe all that success had gone to our heads. Maybe it was all the drugs and the drinking and running around. Or maybe it was because after so many years on top in the competitive world of hip-hop, it was the natural order of things for someone else to take our spot. Whatever the reasons, we found ourselves going from being the hottest act in the game to feeling like we were standing out in the cold.

At first, our fall hit me very hard. I had been so caught up in winning—in being the dopest rapper, in selling millions of records and making all the girls scream—that when we finally began to lose, it felt like my world was falling apart. I became severely depressed and shut myself off from my friends and my family. I even questioned if I wanted to live anymore. But in the depths of my despair, I was brought back to life by a preacher named Bishop Jordan, who healed me by reminding me of all the power and potential that I still possessed. And after being pulled back from the brink, I became very active in Bishop Jordan's church, starting off as a deacon and eventually becoming a reverend in his Zoe Ministries.

With the presence of God restored in my life, things began to turn around very quickly for me. The most important change occurred when I reconnected with Justine (she'll share our crazy story later on). When we first began spending time together, I was worried whether Justine would really be interested in me. I thought that there was no way this dynamic person—she was an incredible singer, an entrepreneur, and even a private eye for a while—would be interested in a man who already had three children. But Justine immediately took all her passion and showered it on my children without any hesitation. We fell very deeply in love, decided to get married, and soon after started working on making some additions to the family.

With my family life going strong, things began to improve for me professionally, as well. The biggest break came after Russell convinced me to help him launch Run Athletics, a sneaker division of his Phat Farm clothing company. Even though I was hesitant at first about becoming a businessman, it turned out to be a very smart move, as our Phat Farm Classic sneaker ended up selling over $200 million worth of sneakers.

So in 2003, with both my family and my finances finally back in order, I took the whole family on a well-deserved vacation to the Caribbean island of St. Bart's, where Russell likes to hang out with all the big-time players. One night our whole family was at this incredible party by the ocean. There were many celebrities in attendance, but it seemed like our kids were the center of attention. At one point, when Diggy was out on the dance floor doing his thing with Mary J. Blige and Uma Thurman, Andre Harrell, the music-industry legend and my longtime friend, came over and sat beside me. "Run," he told me, "I've been watching you and your family all night. You guys are so unique, so interesting. You guys definitely need your own reality show." I had never thought about doing a reality show before, but the concept sounded right to me, so we pitched the idea to Russell, who absolutely loved it. In turn, Russell helped take the concept to ABC Family and eventually to Puffy and MTV. And the rest, as they say, is history.

Now that you know a little bit about my story, I want to change gears a bit and introduce you to my wife, Justine. I need to stop hogging the pen and not only let her speak about her goals for the book, but also give her an opportunity to introduce you to our children, who will obviously play a major role here, too.

But before I do, I want to discuss the "voices" that we'll use in this book. When we first started working on this project, Justine and I wanted to write in one voice. We handle our marriage, our family, and our careers as a team, so why should we approach this book any differently? But when we started writing in the royal "we," something didn't quite feel right. Instead of sounding like a combination of our voices, the "we" ended up sounding like neither one of us. So the decision was made to write most of this book in my voice (hey, if you've watched *Run's House* then you already know that I like talking the most in the family), with Justine jumping in frequently to add her perspectives and insights. Having said that, I don't want anyone to interpret that literary imbalance as in any way reflecting a larger imbalance in our relationship. This book is as much Justine's as it is my own. I might do most of the talking, but the truth is that any strategies I might promote, or any suggestions that she might make in her section, are ones that we've developed together. I want to make that very clear. Here's Justine.

## YOU CAN DO IT TOO

While I plan to talk a lot about the experiences I've had as a parent, at the core I have one simple message that I'd like to share throughout this book: You can do it, too. In other words, if you watch our family on TV and say to yourself, "Wow, I wish our house could function like that," then stop wishing. Because everything we have you can have, too, if you make God your mentor and family your focus. I won't lie and say it doesn't take a lot of work, because it does. And I won't even try to imply that we have the best instructions on how to get there, because we don't. As my husband's already said, we're very far from the perfect parents. You might want to digest some of this advice, while some of it you might want to spit right back out. Either way is cool with us, because we've really been through too much as a family to ever think that everything we touch is golden, or everything that we say is the truth. But I do believe we're committed to the journey toward being better parents, and hopefully this book will let you take part of that trip with us.

Since Joey already gave you some background about the two of us, I'd like to say something about our children, whom we'll refer to constantly in this book. And as I tell you about each of them, I'll try not only to list those qualities that make us so proud, but also share some of the qualities that make them such a unique challenge from a parenting perspective. Because while we love all of our children unconditionally, the truth is that all of these kids can wear us out!

Let me start off with Vanessa, who at twenty-five is our oldest child. Vanessa is a very creative, energetic person filled with positive energy. She's really focused on living an active life—she's appeared on *The Guiding Light*, she models, she co-founded the Pastry shoe line with Angela, and she also acts (along with Angela) as a spokeswoman for the Girl Scouts of America. Her father says she reminds him of Ivanka Trump, and I can see why. They're both young women who have been blessed with beauty and brains. And the wonderful thing about Vanessa is that she's not one of these people who are so ambitious that they don't have time for anyone else. Even though she's not my biological daughter, she reminds me of myself in that she's always conscious of other people's feelings. She's an easy young woman to parent; she's very respectful to us and, as the oldest, is also very protective of her brothers and sisters.

Having said that, there are times when I have to remind Vanessa that it's not enough to just be protective of her brothers and sisters. She has to be proactive in helping us out with them too. She does her part, but it's not her first instinct. Even though Vanessa is the oldest, we'll still call Angela or even JoJo first if we need someone to help us with Diggy and Russy. In Vanessa's defense, she'll help whenever she's asked, but we'd like to get to a point where we don't have to ask. And to be fair, that's true for all of the kids (except for maybe Russy, as I'll explain later).

Next up is Angela, who is twenty-one. Like Vanessa, Angela is a real go-getter: In addition to working on Pastry, she runs her own magazine called *Angela's Rundown*, studies fashion in college, and overall is very tied into the entertainment business. Joey likes to call her a "young Run," and I can see why. She's got the same drive and hunger for success that he had at that age. She's also got a little bit of his outspokenness and swagger, too. Whereas in most situations Vanessa will always try to be polite and not offend anyone, if Angela is not feeling something, she is not going to bite her tongue. She always speaks her mind and tells you exactly how she feels.

But while we appreciate her honesty, sometimes we still have to remind her to be conscious of other people's feelings. Because in most situations with Angela, it's definitely "me first." If Vanessa and Angela are going to share an apartment, Angela is going to make sure that she gets the biggest room. If they're out shopping and find some good deals in a bargain bin, Angela's going to make sure she gets first dibs. So we have to help her find a balance between getting what she wants and not stepping on other people's toes as much.

Another issue with Angela is that even though she has a tough exterior, there's a very sensitive soul there beneath the surface. I can still remember when she was little, she'd cry at the drop of a dime. If you said, "Angela honey, you forgot to clear the dishes," the tears would just start flowing. Obviously she doesn't do that anymore, but situations still affect her more than one might suspect. I think she gets so caught up in making sure that no one tries to get over on her that her real feelings get hidden. So we encourage her to work at letting people see her sensitivity and want her to realize that it's one of her strengths, not a weakness.

After Angela comes nineteen-year-old Joseph, aka JoJo. Like his sisters, JoJo is very ambitious (are you noticing a trend here?). His main goal is to follow in his father's footsteps as a rapper, and so far he's making real strides, having already signed a record deal with his group Team Blackout. He's also getting a degree in audio engineering so that he'll have even more skills to help him make it in the music business.

Like Angela, JoJo is more sensitive than he lets on. To the

world, he acts very confident and sure of himself, but as his parents, we know when he's feeling like he's in over his head. And we believe the less he relies on that cool exterior, the better off he will be. We remind him that it's natural for a young man to sometimes feel unsure about things. And ultimately people will respect someone who's honest about those feelings more than someone who puts on such a confident exterior.

And like a lot of teenagers, there have been times, especially when he was fifteen or sixteen, when JoJo has struggled to figure out how he fits into the dynamic of our house. Whereas growing up he was very tight with us (especially his brothers), there have been times lately when we've sensed that he's begun to pull away from the family a bit. It's as if he's trying to figure out what lane he should be in. So more so than any of the other kids, his father and I really have to stay on top of JoJo and push our way into his world. Because he's at a stage where he's not going to let us in on his own.

We also have to stay on top of another bad habit he's developing, which is going from being cold and distant to extra warm and loving when he wants something from us. I find that very hurtful, because while of course I want him to be happy, I also want his affection to be sincere. I think deep down JoJo understands that, so we just have to push him to be a little more thankful and a little less manipulative.

After JoJo comes Daniel, aka Diggy, who is thirteen. We call Diggy the "superstar" of the family because he's got so much going on for himself. He's a great dancer, an amazing skateboarder, a gifted basketball player, and a talented actor. Plus, in a family where everyone thinks they can dress, Diggy by far has the flyest clothes. Not surprisingly, he's also becoming very popular with the young ladies. He's just one of those kids everybody likes and everybody wants to be around.

If anything, I worry that maybe we've gone a little overboard in telling Diggy how fly he is. I say that because Diggy has begun acting up in school lately. My husband will talk about this in greater detail later on, but we want Diggy to see that he doesn't need to be the class clown when he can be the class winner. And we stay on Diggy because he's already starting to think that he knows more than his parents. For real!

Next up is our eleven-year-old, Russell, aka Russy. We must have been onto something when we named him after his uncle, because Russy is definitely a little mogul in training. Whereas all the other kids have difficulty handling their finances, even as the youngest, Russy has his money right! Through his weekly allowance and doing extra chores around the house, Russy has managed to put away a nice chunk of change. And instead of blowing what he makes on video games or clothes, all of Russy's earnings go right into a bank account he set up. In fact, just the other night at dinner Russy asked if he could go to the mall. "Sure, but I'm not giving you any money," my husband told him. "No problem," replied Russy. "I've saved up $600 in my bank account." Well, every jaw at that table almost hit the floor. The rest of these kids probably didn't have $20 saved up between them, but Russy had all that money sitting on his card.

But while it's great that Russy is able to be so focused at such a young age, sometimes he lets that drive get the best of him. We've been noticing that in any sort of competitive situation, Russy gets too angry when he loses. If Diggy beats him in basketball, Russy will take the ball and throw it. Or if JoJo beats him at a video game, Russy will grab one of the controllers and try to break it. We don't like that, and we're working very hard to nip it in the bud before it becomes a major issue.

The main thing we're noticing with Russy is that he's just a little bit different from everyone else in the house. He definitely marches to the beat of his own drummer. Sometimes he gets a little self-conscious about his quirks, but we encourage him to embrace his uniqueness. When he is able to do that, I think he's really going to come into his own.

Last but not least is Miley, the most recent addition to our family. As fans of *Run's House* are probably aware, in 2006 Joey and I lost our daughter Victoria at birth. Despite our intense grief, we still wanted to bring another baby girl into the house, and after a lot of prayer we decided to try the adoption process. (I'll discuss that whole process in much greater detail later on in the book.) And thankfully, almost exactly a year after losing Victoria, we welcomed two-month-old Miley into our home.

When I started thinking about this section, I didn't initially plan on saying much about Miley because I thought it would be too early to have any insights into her personality. But the truth is that even after just a few months of being around her, I really feel like I'm getting to know her a bit. And the biggest thing I'm noticing is that she's a very strong-willed baby. I know a lot of mothers say that about their babies, but I really feel the force of her personality. For instance, if someone tries to take a bottle away from her before she's ready, she'll look at them like, "Are you crazy?" and then start screaming her head off. She's already very sure of what she likes and dislikes (luckily one of the likes is snuggling and kissing), which will definitely serve her well in this crazy house. Also, everyone says that even though she's adopted, she looks so much like Joey (but I think that's just because they're both bald)!

So there they are, our six wonderful children. Six kids who sometimes drive us up the wall with their attitudes and their antics, but also a group that we wouldn't trade for any other six kids in the world. That's why I really hope over the course of reading this book you'll get to know them even better and come to share some of our appreciation for them.

## WE'RE CHRISTIANS, BUT THIS IS NOT
## A "CHRISTIAN" BOOK

I want to end this chapter by addressing the role that religion will play in this book. Even though I'm a reverend and my wife is a very devout Christian, this isn't intended to be a "Christian" book. This is a book about a family that happens to be written by Christians. Our goal is to speak not only to Christians, but to Jews, Muslims, Hindus, Mormons—whoever feels like they might learn something from our example. I'm certainly not going to be shy about the fact that I have a very close relationship with Jesus Christ and that I'm very careful to follow what I consider to be his laws. But I believe that more so than any sort of specific doctrine, the best way to promote my beliefs is through demonstrating the positive effect that my faith has on my family. So if you're a non-Christian, maybe this book will inspire you to learn more about the Church. And if you are a Christian, then you will probably recognize that all my principles, all my beliefs, and all my faith is rooted in the teachings of Christ. So while I might not quote scripture and verse in this book as much as I do in daily conversation, it'll suffice to say that the teachings of Christ are never far from my mind.

I also want to take this opportunity to address a question that I've heard some people ask about me: "Is Run a *real* reverend?" Well, the answer is yes. I underwent a very intense period of Bible study, which led to me officially being ordained as a reverend. But I'll also be the first to admit that while I'm definitely a "real" reverend, I'm a funny kind of reverend too. Yes, I read the Bible every day, but you're just as likely to find me reading Yogic scriptures, or Jewish philosophies. I'm very inspired by all kinds of spirituality, and I don't like to paint myself into a corner when it comes to God.

And while it's true that I don't preach out of a physical church every Sunday like most reverends, I don't believe that makes me any less legitimate. I might not lead a physical church, but I still feel like I have a verrrry strong calling. My family is my ministry, and *Run's House* is my pulpit. (And in some ways, this book will be my pulpit too.) So instead of sharing parables in a church every Sunday morning, I'm sharing my life's examples every Thursday night on MTV. I know that approach might seem a little unorthodox to some, but I'm excited to be reaching so many families with my message. Besides, I feel closer to God than I have at any other point in my life, and I wouldn't change a thing about the relationship we have right now.

And while we're talking about what this book isn't, I should also state that this isn't an African-American parenting book, either. It's true that I mentioned earlier in this chapter the difficulties that many black families face, and I don't in any way want to overlook just how important it is for our community to refocus on family. Twenty-two years ago I helped write a song called "Proud to Be Black," and that's a message I still make sure all my children hear very clearly today. But as much as I teach them to be proud of their heritage, I also teach them to be part of the universal family. I tell my children that the most important thing they can do is surround themselves with kind, positive people. At the end of the day, I don't really care where those people are from, or what language they speak, or what color their skin is. If a person is positive and kind, then they're always cool with me and my family. So while our experiences as an African-American family might resonate most loudly with families from a similar background, I happen to know that all sorts of families connect with our message. The fact is that just as many white people come up to me on the street and tell me, "Run, our family loves your show," as do black people. So I don't want anyone reading this book to think for a moment think that it's not meant for them.

In fact, we subtitled this book "A Challenge to *America's* Parents" precisely because taking back your family is an issue that affects all of us, Christians or Jews, rich or poor, black or white, gay or straight. No matter what race you claim, or faith you practice, or class you belong to, you've probably felt like you've lost a bit of your grip on your family to the distractions of the world. Maybe it's materialism that's causing the distraction. Maybe it's greed. Or envy. Or

drugs. Or desire. Or television. Or competitiveness. Or just plain ex-
haustion. Or apathy, or any other of the countless forces out there
that we constantly find ourselves in competition with over our family. But whatever it is that seems to have bewitched your family and
tried to pull it apart, this book is designed to help you bring it back
together. In fact, you'll see that at the end of every chapter we've in-
cluded a small section called "Run's Take Back," in which I'll suggest little steps to help you regain some of that control you might be
missing.

And why is taking back your family such an important part of
parenthood? Because, as I like to say, "If you don't have 'em, then
who's got 'em?" In other words, do Justine and I have Diggy's attention, or is it that $350 hooded sweatshirt he keeps asking us to buy
him? Are we teaching JoJo what is right and wrong in this world, or
do the dudes he meets on the street have that power? Are we helping Angela feel good about herself, or is she trying to find that confidence in a bottle of booze? Or in emulating a magazine cover? As
parents, we have to ask ourselves every day, "Who has our kids?" If
the answer isn't us, then we need to go get them. We need to take
them back.

If this book can serve any purpose in your life, hopefully it will
be as a reminder that there's truly nothing out there that you can't
take your family back from. Nothing has a grip so strong that together you and God can't break its hold on your family. Drugs aren't
that strong. Drinking isn't that strong. The TV isn't that strong. The
video games aren't that strong. The peer pressure isn't that strong.
The rappers, the rock stars, and the cover girls aren't that strong.
The dudes on the corner aren't that strong. Your family's dysfunctional history isn't that strong. And as we learned firsthand, even
death isn't that strong.

The fact is that you can take back the time that your family
needs together! You can take back your family from silence and misunderstanding and fill it back up with communication and sympa-
thy. You can take back your family from values that you don't agree

with! You can take back your family from a lack of faith! And a lack of fun!

I don't want sound like too much of a cheerleader here. The truth is, there will be times when life deals you a hand that seems too much to bear. Where your weight seems so heavy that you can't conceive of ever getting back up again. I know this because as a family, we've been there. We've felt that terrible weight, the worst weight that any parent can bear. But the truth is also that you can get back up, no matter what has happened. You might have to lean on your spouse a bit. You might even have to lean on your kids a bit, too. And you'll definitely have to lean on God. But no matter what weight has staggered you, or no matter how off course you might have stumbled, you can take back your family from whatever or whoever has gotten too much control over it. And when you are finally back in the driver's seat, and God is your navigator, there's no limit to how far your family can go, and how much fun you can have along the way!

## CHAPTER 1

# Making Your Marriage
# Work First

I know that when most people picked up this book, they were probably looking for some insight into how my husband and I go about raising our family. And while we definitely have plenty to say on that subject, any discussion of our family has to begin with our marriage. Because any happiness that we've experienced as a family is rooted in the happiness we've experienced in our marriage. Which is not to say that our marriage has been a walk in the park—like all couples, we've encountered plenty of stormy weather. But learning how to weather those marital storms also gave us the confidence to weather the tornadoes and hurricanes of parenthood.

Before we even get into talking about our marriage, I do want to make one point clear: In no way are we suggesting that you can't be a great parent without having a spouse. Everywhere my husband and I go, we're stopped by single mothers who tell us, "Thanks so much for the show, because y'all are really helping us." I know how much *Run's House* means to those parents, and I need them to know we're not suggesting that they have to have a man in their lives in order to make things work. The fact is, we applaud and have an incredible amount of respect for all the single mothers (and single fathers, too) doing their thing out there.

After I talk to single mothers about their experiences, I always find myself asking, "What would I do if Joey wasn't here? How could I ever make this situation work?" I'm very aware that when my kids act up, I have the luxury of telling them, "Just wait until your father gets home!" But these women don't have that luxury. They're forced to deal with the situation then and there! While Joey and I both have someone to lean on, these women have to shoulder the burdens of parenthood themselves. They're literally holding up their homes themselves.

What's truly incredible is that they're doing more than just holding their homes up—they're also creating an environment in which their children can soar. I'm so inspired by a woman like Kanye West's late mother, Dondra, or Diddy's mother, Janice, or even Barack Obama's late mother, Ann Dunham, women who didn't always have the benefit of relying on a husband, but still found the strength to not only protect their children, but to prepare them for greatness. And I know that can't be easy.

Just the other day I was on the phone with an old friend I hadn't spoken with in a long time. She told me that a little while back her husband, who had been her high school sweetheart, decided that he needed to pursue his dreams of making it big in the entertainment business. So one day he packed up his stuff and moved to Atlanta, leaving her responsible for three kids, a mortgage, car notes, tuition, and everything else that comes with raising a family. While it's been very difficult for my friend, somehow she's making it work. She's got her son in college, her daughter in high school, and she's holding down her job, too. And when I heard her talk about juggling all those responsibilities, and paying all those bills without the benefit of someone to lean on emotionally and financially, I was in awe of her strength. I was amazed by her power. And her story made whatever complaints I had about raising a family seem very trivial in comparison.

In fact, when Joey and I began working on this chapter, I

didn't even want to use the word "marriage" in the title, because I was afraid it might make single mothers feel left out. Ultimately, we decided to keep the title because *our* marriage is such a fundamental part of who we are as parents. So even though we'll be speaking from the perspective of a married couple, if you're a single parent reading this, we believe that these principles can still apply to your experience.

But before Joey breaks down the strategies that we've employed to help make our marriage work better, I want to take a minute and explain how we came to be husband and wife in the first place. As Joey said in the introduction, we don't want to assume that everyone reading this book is familiar with our television show. And even if you are a fan of *Run's House* and know a little something about our marriage, you still probably don't know how we embarked on this journey together. Besides, I think it's a cute story (even though Joey thinks it's too mushy), so bear with me for a moment.

## TELEPHONE LOVE

It all started one day back in the late 1970s when my friends Nita, Deetra, and I went to see Kurtis Blow (rap's first "superstar") perform at a roller disco near our town on Long Island. Kurtis was a very big deal back then, so when he hit the stage with his sexy voice and nice little Afro all the girls started screaming their heads off. But while my friends were yelling for the headliner, I kept my eye on his sidekick, a young guy who seemed to be around fifteen or sixteen like us and went by the name of "Son of Kurtis Blow." I loved that when it was time for this skinny kid to say his raps, he would just stand there in one spot and never move. He was trying to act like he was hard, but I could tell he wasn't moving because he was so nervous. I thought it was the cutest thing I'd ever seen.

After the show, my friends waited around for Kurtis's

autograph, but I really wanted one from his "son." Finally, I got up some nerve and asked one of the promoters to get "the Son" to come out and meet us. My friends were annoyed and couldn't understand why I wanted that scrawny kid's autograph. But I was adamant about it, so we waited. And after a few minutes, out strode the Son of Kurtis Blow. He introduced himself as Joey and then immediately tried to tongue-kiss all three of us! (He hates it when I tell this part of the story, but it's true!)

Of course we freaked out and ran into a bathroom to get away from him. But while my friends were kicking trash cans over and screaming about what a jerk he was, I had to admit there was something I liked about him—not the kissing bandit part, but the shy part I had seen on stage. So I took one of the flyers from the show and wrote my number on it with a note that said, "Hi Joey. I'm the girl in the light blue pants and the checkered shirt that you tried to kiss. You can call me." I handed it to one of the guys working the door and said, "Can you please give this to the Son of Kurtis Blow." And the next day when I came home, my stepmother said to me, "Hey Justine, some-body named Joey called for you."

For at least three months after that, we would talk on the phone all the time. Or Joey would write me letters, saying that he loved me and we should get married one day. But while I loved talking to him, it was difficult for us to physically see each other. I lived on Long Island and he lived in Queens, which for fifteen-year-old kids without a car seemed like living on differ-ent coasts. Plus at the time I also considered Queens to be a very scary place and I wasn't trying to go over there even when I did have a ride. So in those three months of "dating," we actu-ally only saw each other once or twice. After a while, I started thinking, "This doesn't make any sense. Why am I dating some guy that I never see?" So I broke up with him.

Joey was very hurt by my decision (or at least he says so), but we agreed to go our separate ways. A couple of years later, however, I was showing a friend my scrapbook when suddenly he looked at a picture of Joey and said, "Hey, how do you know that guy?" "Oh, that's Joey from Queens. We used to date," I answered. And he said, "Justine, don't you know who that is? That's Run from Run DMC. He's famous." I was shocked, because even though I'd heard the group's music, I'd never watched any of their videos and didn't know what they looked like. I was glad to connect the dots, though. Even though we'd broken up, I was happy for Joe, because I knew how serious he was about hip-hop. I didn't try to get back in touch with him and congratulate him, but from then on, whenever I'd see him on TV, I'd smile inside.

Fast-forward to the mid-nineties, when my little sister Michele was going to high school in Long Island. One day, a guy named Pep who worked at the school started bragging to her that his cousin was Run from Run DMC. Michele had heard me talk about Joey before, so she shot back, "Oh yeah? Well, my big sister Justine used to date him!" Pep had never heard Joey talk about me, so the next time he bumped into him, he said, "Hey, this girl at my school says you used to date her sister Justine back in the day. Is that true?" And Joey said, "Justine from Long Island? Man, that's the girl that broke my heart right before I became the 'The Man.' I've always wanted to reconnect with her. Think you could get me her number?"

Soon my sister was calling me and said, "Hey, Run wants to talk to you. Can I give his cousin your number?" And to be honest, I hesitated at first. I wasn't as into hip-hop as I used to be (house music was my new thing), and as much as I had liked Joey as a teenager, I figured by then he was just some rapper who probably said, "Wassup," every five minutes. It didn't sound like my cup of tea, but my memories of the young Joey won out and I finally said, "Sure, give him my number." He called a few days later and from the moment he said, "Hi," in that cute little voice of his, all my hesitation evaporated. He still sounded like that shy kid I had fallen for all those years earlier. Soon we were talking on the phone for hours at a time, just like the old days. And just like in the old days, I found myself falling for Joey from Queens.

At first, things went pretty slowly. Joey was going through a drawn-out divorce from his first wife and needed to get that squared away. Also, he was deeply into Zoe Ministries, and he wanted me to immerse myself in the church before we went any further. At that time, I was more into dancing on Saturday nights than going to church on Sunday mornings, but I started showing up because I wanted to share that part of his life.

Over time, I began to fall deeply in love with the feeling I got at church, just as I was falling deeply in love with Joey and his young children. Whereas a few months earlier my only thoughts had been about making money and partying, suddenly I was feeling passionate about spending time with Joey, his children, and his church. It was not a lifestyle I had ever envisioned for myself, but I had to admit it was fitting me like a glove. And before I knew it, Joey was my husband, his family was my family, and his church was my church. And that's the story of how we got together.

I hope that now when we talk about our marriage, and the beautiful family that's grown out of it, you'll have a better understanding of where we're coming from. Our relationship might not have developed like most couples' (I don't know many couples who dated as teenagers, stopped speaking for almost fifteen years, and then fell in love all over again as adults), but it's working pretty good for us. And again, I really believe that any success we enjoy as parents is directly tied into the strength of our marriage. That's why before we begin delving deeply into the philosophies that guide us as parents, it would be best to let Joey share just a little bit of the philosophies that guide our marriage.

## HANDLE WITH CARE

Let me start by saying that I really love hearing Justine talk about our relationship—meeting at the roller disco (I don't know what's she talking about with that kissing, though!), the excitement and nervousness I felt when we reconnected, and then ultimately starting our own family together. But while I love reminiscing about those times, I'm also very careful not to depend too heavily on them when it comes to maintaining our current relationship. Because a marriage that leans too heavily on old memories probably doesn't have much of a future.

One of the biggest challenges couples face is maintaining that energy they feel at the beginning of their marriage. It is very, very dangerous to assume that just because your marriage started out great, you're going to be able to effortlessly maintain that energy. As most couples can tell you, there are all sorts of influences and situations that can derail your marriage. They won't be on your radar as newlyweds, but they *are* out there. That's why I believe that if you want to keep your marriage *strong*, the first thing that you need to accept is that your marriage is *fragile*.

Too many people, especially some of the men out there, treat their marriage the same way budget airlines treat your luggage: They toss it around haphazardly, throw things on top of it, and don't seem to care if it gets a little banged up. But if you keep tossing your marriage around like that, sooner or later your wife is going to start thinking about switching to another airline, if you know what I mean! So rather than treating your marriage like some cheap luggage, treat it like a delicate vase that you bought for your wife on a business trip and want to ship back home: Wrap it up in tissue paper, gently cover it with bubble wrap, put it in a sturdy box, and mark it "Handle With Care." In other words, accept that if you're not gentle and careful and conscientious about your marriage, there's a good chance it's going to crack and break.

While bubble wrap, tissue paper, and a sturdy box are great for protecting a vase, it's not always as easy to figure out what you can use to protect your marriage. In my opinion, the first way to protect it is to focus on not being so selfish. That might seem like very obvious advice, but you'd be surprised how after a few years of being with someone, it can be very easy to become totally wrapped up in yourself again. When you're single, you only have to think about yourself—where do *I* want to go, what do *I* want to eat, what do *I* feel like watching on TV? Then, when you get married, you automatically start asking your spouse those same questions. "What do *you* want to do tonight, honey?" "Hey baby, where would *you* like to go for dinner?" "What do *you* want to watch on TV, my love?" It's very easy to think like that at first. Your passion is so strong, and your enthusiasm for that person is so deep, that you couldn't imagine *not* putting their needs first.

The trouble is that after a few years of marriage, many of us tend to slip back into that "single" mind-set. Instead of focusing on what our spouse would enjoy, we revert to worrying about what's going to make *us* happy. I've found this is especially true of men after they start to feel the financial pressures of supporting a family. That extra responsibility makes them start to feel a little sorry for themselves, to the point where soon they feel justified in putting their own needs first again. I've been guilty of this in my own relationship, especially when it comes to being sociable. On the show it probably seems like I have a pretty active social life, but the truth is if left to my own devices, I would spend most of my time within these four walls. I've got my family in this house, plus an indoor basketball court, a recording studio, a movie room, a hot tub, and a pool out back. So my attitude is, "What good thing could I possibly get out in the world that I don't already have here?" But I think Justine would prefer that I loosen up a bit and become more engaged socially. While neither of us wants to spend a lot of time out in any clubs, she would probably like it if every once in a while we went out to a party. Or instead of always suggesting that we eat at home, she'd probably like it if I suggested we go out to dinner with some friends every once in a while. Or instead of watching most of my movies down in the basement, she'd like it if we actually went out to see a flick on an occa-sional Friday night. Or better yet, go see a Broadway show together. So even though the thought of socializing outside of my house often feels like a drag to me, I have to remember to stop being so selfish and start thinking about what my wife might enjoy. These are just small examples, but they reflect the kind of mentality that can put a real strain on a relationship.

That's why I always advise my buddies that in order to have a happy marriage, it's very important to get your mind off "you." Whether you've been married for five days or fifteen years, you have to remember to put your spouse's interests on the same level as your own. And I've learned that an effective way to maintain that balance is by finding a common activity to share with your spouse.

## DO IT TOGETHER

No matter how busy you get with your career or your children or whatever else seems to be eating up your time, as a couple you must always try to find activities that the two of you can do together. For instance Justine and I enjoy going to open houses together. Whether we're looking to buy a new house or not, we still love to jump in the car on a Saturday afternoon and go check out what's new on the market. For Justine, visiting these houses indulges her passion for interior design. She loves to get design inspirations for our house from how other people have hooked up their kitchens and bed-rooms. For me, checking out the designs is definitely cool, but I've also found that walking around these incredible homes inspires me on a professional level. While I am very proud of the house we live in, I've found that when I walk around some of these $10 million cribs (yes, we like to go to the very nice ones! And you can too— that's the beauty of open houses. They're open to anyone!), I'm in-spired to try even harder to create a similar environment for my own family. These homes remind me that no matter how much I've achieved, and no matter how far I've come, there's always more to accomplish. Since we're both inspired, open houses have become a great joint activity for us. They don't cost a cent, and we have plenty to discuss together afterward. We'll talk about what we liked about a kitchen, or what we didn't like about the bathrooms, or whether we liked the neighborhood or not. It's nothing too deep, but it does allow us to converse about something we experienced *together*.

We share a similar bond with hip-hop music. While I'll talk about the role hip-hop plays in our family in greater depth later on in the book, right now I do want to acknowledge the important role it plays in our relationship. Even though we're both in our forties, we still rock to hip-hop just as hard as we did back when we were teenagers. (Don't worry, I helped pull Justine out of that house music phase.) Amidst all the talk about finances, the children, or our careers, Justine will still pull me aside and say, "Joey, did you hear that new Ne-Yo song? I've been playing it all afternoon." Or if I hear something new on the radio that I like, or if I just finished working on a new track for myself, I'll always play it for Justine to get her opinion. Because I know that instead of telling me, "Joey, you're too old to be messing with that kids' music!" Justine is more likely to tell me, "Oh, that song's hot. Turn it up, baby!" Being able to listen to and enjoy hip-hop together is one of the ways we've kept our relationship fresh.

Open houses and hip-hop work great for us, but at the end of the day, it doesn't really matter what sort of activity you share, as long you're sharing *something*. That's really the key. Your spouse doesn't only want to hear about what a crappy day you had at work, just like you probably don't want to only hear about how the kids are driving her crazy. It's important that you two share a common activity that you can discuss, analyze, laugh about, or even argue about together. Even if it's only something as banal as talking about the type of tile someone used in their bathroom, or a new song on the radio, being able to share that experience will actually make your relationship feel much more energized and alive.

## RETYING THE KNOT

Another key to protecting your marriage is acknowledging that it will occasionally need some maintenance. While in the last section I suggested trying to look at your marriage like a fragile vase, now I want you to try looking at it like a car. When you first buy a car, it usually runs very smoothly. But after you put some serious miles on it, you're probably going to want to change the battery after a few years. Marriage is the same way—things generally run smoothly at first, but after a couple of years under the same roof and a few kids, it's normal if your relationship feels like it needs a little recharging. And I've found that a great way to recharge those marital batteries is by renewing your wedding vows. Justine and I have done it three times now, and I've found that each new trip down the aisle has had an incredibly positive, refreshing effect on our relationship. Each time we tie that knot again, it forces me to refocus on our marriage and remember just how blessed I am to have a wife like Justine. It's especially important for me to refocus, because like too many people, I'm sometimes so busy worrying about what might be around the corner that I don't appreciate what I've already been blessed with. I can get so caught up stressing about money or our kids or my career that I forget to tell my wife how grateful I am that she's my partner in my life. Renewing our vows is a way for me to articulate those sentiments to hear very loudly and very clearly.

I realize that some men find the notion of having a second wedding unnecessary at best—and incredibly annoying at worst. But fellas, I am here to tell you it is actually one of the *most* necessary things you can do in your marriage. First of all, I promise you that nothing—and I mean nothing—will make your wife melt like butter more than taking her shopping for a wedding gown for the second (or third!) time. When you're standing in the shop, and your wife is trying on the dress and telling all the salespeople that it's for a second wedding, you will feel yourself winning her heart all over again. You will feel how happy she is, and you'll know that you're refreshing and reenergizing the love that you two share. (And if you can afford to say your vows in a place like Hawaii or Las Vegas, then you'll get a nice little vacation out of the deal, too.) The bottom line is that when you celebrate what you have, instead of taking it for granted, you're definitely going to win not only in marriage, but in life as well.

When some people hear me talking about renewing my vows, they're quick to say, "Wow, you really put your wife up on a pedestal." But I always tell them, "That's not really true. Because I never take my wife *off* her pedestal." My wife is always the center of my universe—in fact, I look at everything worthwhile that I have as a by-product of that union. The kids are a by-product. *Run's House* is a by-product. This book is a by-product. My home is a by-product. Everything in my life that has any value has come out of my relationship with my wife, and I try to never lose sight of that truth. I could never put Justine up on a pedestal because there wouldn't be any room—since we said "I do" the first time, I've tried to make sure she's felt like she's never come down from that spot. My entire life truly revolves around my wife.

## THE FIRST WEDDING

Since my husband just mentioned how we like to renew our vows, I want to take a moment here and say a few words about our wedding (the first one). Because while I really do love all the times we've renewed our vows, sometimes I joke that the reason we've had a second and third wedding is because our first one was so wack! But before I talk about the wedding itself, I should give some background about what was happening in our lives at the time, and why throwing a "dream" wedding proved to be such a difficult task for us.

Like many young couples, one of our major problems was a lack of money. You would think that Joey would have had plenty of money from Run DMC, but that wasn't the case. Most of the money he had made earlier in his career was already long gone, lost to bad investments or simply wasted on fast living. Plus, his divorce was taking a very long time to come through, which was draining most of whatever money he had left. At that point in his career Joey had been paying the bills by touring with Run DMC, but eventually we got so immersed in being a part of our church community that he didn't want to go out on the road. Other than going to church and being with each other and Joey's kids, we frankly weren't really pursuing anything else. So it wasn't long before we were down to our last dollar.

To compound the situation, though we weren't sleeping together, we were living together in a house Joey had in Queens. For a while I was fine with that arrangement, since I didn't feel like we were really doing anything improper or immoral. But then one day we were watching TV when this preacher came on and said, "If you're living with a man and you're not married, or a woman and you're not married, then you're living in sin and life will never go forth for you." And when he said that, it was like he was speaking directly to me. It felt like God was trying to tell me that our money issues and Joey's problems finalizing his divorce were happening because we were living in sin. When I heard that message, I turned the TV off, looked at Joey, and said, "If we want this to work, I've got to move out until we are married." He understood and agreed with me, but with not much money between us, the question was, "To where?" At first I suggested that I move in with my sister, but we decided that wouldn't work because she lived far enough away that I wouldn't get to spend enough time with Joey and the kids. So after some thought, Joey suggested that I could stay with his mother, who lived nearby in Queens. It would be very convenient, but the sad reality was that she was also dying of cancer at the time. It was a tough decision, because while I wanted to be close to Joey and the kids, moving in with my future mother-in-law, especially when she was dying, felt like a very daunting proposition.

But ultimately I did move in with her, and in the end it was for the best. Not only did I get to stay close to Joey and the kids, but I was able to support his mother a little bit, too. Even though she was already in a lot of pain and pretty out of it while I was living there, I'm still glad I got a chance to be around her every day and see what a beautiful and classy lady she was. In fact, when I was recently working on a new line for Simmons Jewelry that I thought looked very classy, I decided I wanted to call it the Evelyn Simmons line. Because in my mind Joey's mother will always be synonymous with class.

So while I'll always be thankful for that time with Joey's mom, I'll be honest, living apart made us even more anxious to get married and start our new life together. The only problem was that I quickly learned that it's difficult to put a wedding together without much of a budget. Our initial plan was to have a small service and ceremony at either a banquet hall or a hotel, but we realized that even those options were out of our price range. Thankfully, Bishop Jordan graciously offered us his beautiful home, and we decided to get married there instead.

But while the bishop's house was lovely, the rest of the wedding was definitely lacking. I had a ring and a wedding dress, but there were no fancy flower arrangements or ice sculptures or monogrammed wedding favors, all the little touches I'd always pictured having at my wedding. The food was pretty weak, too. Before the wedding, we served pigs in a blanket. We had hired a woman we knew to serve some food after the ceremony, but she showed up late and didn't bring nearly enough food. There was no DJ or dancing either, just a part of the church choir singing hymns. A couple of people even ended up getting so frustrated by the lack of food that they just left and went to a restaurant! All in all, it was not a glamorous affair.

Then there was the honeymoon. The idea was to spend our wedding night in Manhattan, then fly to Maui the next day. But even though Joey had reserved the flights on his credit card, we still didn't have enough money to cover both tickets. So our plan was to use whatever cash we got as gifts at the wedding to pay for the rest of the trip. The only problem was, we didn't get as much money as we expected we would. For a second it looked like there might not be a honeymoon, but thankfully Bishop Jordan stepped up again, this time lending us enough money to get to Maui.

Having said all that, the most important thing is that when my husband and I talk about our wedding today, we can look back and laugh about it. I'll bust his chops about the fact that there wasn't enough food, or that we didn't even have enough money to send out any invitations. And he'll tease me that if there wasn't enough food (he claims there was), it was only because he was spending so much time hustling up money for the gown and the ring that I wanted.

And the truth is, even back then we had a sense of humor about the situation and never let any of those issues get between us. We both understood that while the wedding might not have been everything we had hoped for, it was only *one day*. Our marriage was going to be for a *lifetime*, and we'd have plenty of time to get things right later on. And that's exactly what we've done with the second wedding, the third wedding, and however more weddings we decide to have.

Too many couples make the mistake of thinking that their wedding is going to be a reflection of their marriage to come. They get it twisted and think that if they don't do things a certain way on their wedding day, then their marriage is going to get off on the wrong track. Nothing could be further from the truth. I've seen plenty of people with fancy, incredibly expensive weddings wind up divorced just a few years later. And I've seen couples like us, who might not have had a glamorous wedding but have remained deeply in love long after that wedding was over.

And while I do like teasing Joey about our wedding, the

truth is that there was one incredible moment from that day that I'll always treasure. As I was getting ready for our ceremony, I started to really freak out and came down with a terrible migraine. It was so bad that at one point I was thinking I was going to have to call the wedding off. But before I could, Joey's mom came to the rescue.

Mrs. Simmons had been so ill that she couldn't get out of bed and wasn't even going to the wedding. Yet when she heard about my migraine, it was like she wasn't sick anymore. Suddenly, she was completely filled up with energy in a way that I hadn't seen since I'd moved in with her. She had me come into her room and became very animated in giving tips to get rid of the headache. Even though we were running late and everyone else in the house was basically telling me just to suck it up and get moving, Joey's mom wouldn't hear of it. "Justine, take a deep breath, then get out of your dress, and get in the tub," she told me very calmly, but forcefully. "Just lie there with some hot water until you feel better. Don't feel rushed, baby. Just take your time and everything is going to be fine." That poor woman had barely spoken in weeks, but in that moment the cancer had left her. It was as if that brief burst of love and comfort was her way of trying to say thank you for whatever help I had given her over the last few months. And of course, after I listened to her advice and took that long bath, my migraine went away and I was able to make it to the wedding after all. It was an incredible moment, one that meant much more to me than any engraved invitations or flower bouquets ever could have.

## PROTECT YOUR SPOUSE

Another key in keeping the fragile vase that is your marriage from cracking is remembering to always be your spouse's protector. And by that, I don't mean protecting your spouse from muggers, speeding cars, barking dogs, or any *physical* threat. Rather, I'm talking about protecting them from the *emotional* wounds that the world can inflict on us, or even the ones that we sometimes unwittingly inflict on ourselves.

In our marriage, Justine certainly tries to protect me not only from the world, but perhaps even more importantly, from my own insecurities. For instance, Justine knows that I'm a worrier by nature. And while I've gotten better at controlling my worries by having more faith in God, there are still times when I can feel those black clouds gathering over my head. Thankfully, when Justine senses that I'm in one of those moods, she does everything she can to scatter those clouds for me. She'll try to soothe me with encouraging words. She'll bring me comfort food that helps restore my peace. She'll remind me how much she loves me and then take my hand and pray with me. And if none of those tactics work, she'll even try to absorb a little bit of the pain for me, so that my burden won't feel quite as heavy. Whenever I start to get down, I can feel her spirit standing guard over me, doing everything within its power to protect me from all dangers. That presence gives me the courage to chase those clouds away and restore the balance in my life.

I try to play a similar role in Justine's life. But rather than protect her from worry, my main assignment is to protect my wife from giving too much of herself to the world. Don't get me wrong, I love that my wife has such a big heart. Justine's heart is *huge*—she's truly one of the most giving people I've ever met. The problem is that sometimes she gives the world too much of herself. If it were up to her, our house would be filled every day with all the people she meets and feels a connection with. My wife's the kind of person who wants to invite you over for dinner five minutes after having met you. And while I applaud her hospitality and openness, I also know that if her instincts went unchecked it might lead to our world filling up with people whose motivations might not be as pure as Justine's. I worry (see what I mean?) that she's so focused on making other people happy that without my protection, she'll end up making herself miserable. Armed with that knowledge, I try to stand in front of her with the proverbial sword and shield, beating back the world just a bit. Sometimes Justine might feel like I'm being too protective, but she understands that I'm doing it for her own good. In fact, one of our friends at church came up to her recently and said, "Justine, if it weren't for that husband of yours, the world would probably eat you alive. Without him, I don't know how you would make it." And when he said that, Justine and I both looked at each other and said, "Amen!"

The irony is that while we both go to great lengths to protect each other from the world and from ourselves, it seems at times that the biggest threat to our relationship actually comes from a different—and unlikely—source: our children. I'll let Justine explain.


## DON'T LET THE KIDS GET BETWEEN YOU

Before I go any further into this section, I want to make it very clear that my love for my children knows no boundaries. I would do anything for them and could never imagine doing anything, even for a second, that might hurt them. But having said that (you knew there was a "but" coming, right?), I also realize that there need to be some limits to how much of myself I can give to the kids. That's because I've found that if there's one thing that threatens to upset that delicate happiness my husband and I enjoy in our marriage, it is those six kids of ours.

Since they realize that my love for them is so deep, my children have become very greedy when it comes to taking from me (not so much Vanessa and Angela, but definitely the boys). They try to take my energy. They try to take my attention. They try to take my sleep. They try to take my money. They try to take my time. Sometimes, yes, they'll even take my advice. But whether they really need something or not, it seems like they always want to take. Take, take, take, take.

It might sound like I'm being a little melodramatic, but it's true. If I'm in the same room with Diggy and Russy and they sense I'm not focused on them, one of them will fake a cough just so I'll turn my head and pay some attention to them. These kids will literally fake being sick just to get me to shine some of my light on them. They know that I'll drop everything if I think something is wrong with them, and they use that knowledge to their advantage.

I wasn't as aware of it before, but in the past few years Joey has helped me become more conscious of how they're playing me. He isn't trying to stop the kids from getting attention from their mother when they really need it, but rather is trying to make sure that we still have enough time for each other. That's why if he catches Diggy sneaking in a fake cough, he'll say, "Stop acting like you're hurt, Digg! I don't want to see you trying that drama with my wife again!"

He has to take the same approach with Russy, who likes to stay up past his bedtime and then come knocking on our bedroom door around 10 P.M. talking about, "Mommm, I'm hungry." In the past, I'd get up out of bed and go downstairs to fix him something to eat. But now Joey has put a stop to it. If he hears Russ start with that "Mommm" business, he will say very firmly, "Russy, do not come in that door trying to get my wife out of bed to get you something to eat. You're not even supposed to be up right now! Go back to your room!" I'll admit that my initial reaction is still to get the child some food, but I've stopped getting in the way of my husband's protection. Because I know that as much as my instinct is to make my kids happy, I also know that it's wrong to not only let them stay up past their bedtime, but then to reward them with a snack on top of it. Joey and I agreed that Russy's late-night snack attacks had to stop, and now we're committed to enforcing that rule together.

Really, the two most important words in parenting might be "united front." It's so important that you and your spouse be on the same page about everything that concerns your children. If you lay down one set of rules and your spouse lays down another, you're going to end up with a lot of wildness and chaos in your house. If your kids ask Mommy about something and you tell them, "No," then that better be what they hear when they ask Daddy about the same thing.

For instance, I have a rule that when Diggy and Russy come home from school, they have to finish their homework before they can play any video games or get into any other activities. They're usually pretty good about it, but we got into a problem recently when Joey bought an old-school, arcade-style video game for our basement. Joey had gotten tired of the boys beating him on their Xbox or Nintendo, so he wanted to school them on games from our era like "Centipede," "Space Invaders," and "Ms. Pac-Man." It was cute seeing them all play together, but the problem was he was letting them play before they were finished their homework. Joey knew better, but he was so focused on the games that he let them break the rules I had set. When I saw what was happening, I had to go downstairs and handle that situation right away. I sat all three of them down and said, "Diggy and Russy, the rule is no video-game playing, whether it's down here or up in your rooms, until homework is done. And Joey—*you're* not allowed to play either until they've done their homework. Because if they hear you playing, then they're going to try to sneak down and play, too." I know Joey hadn't been trying to undermine my authority and had only gotten caught up in showing them the games from our era. But if he let them break my rule on that day, then every day after school it would become a battle with the kids. I'd tell them no video games, and they'd answer back with, "But we played with Daddy downstairs the other day. He said it was OK!" That's why it was so important that Joey and I get on the same page. And when I explained that to him, Joey apologized for undercutting me and said that not only wouldn't he play while they were doing their homework, but that he'd become more involved in helping them with their homework instead.

And really, doing your homework before you can play video games is a pretty minor example. For instance, I'm always telling Diggy and Russy that when they go out with girls to the movies, or see them at parties, they'd better not try to touch them in any inappropriate ways. And they understand that I'm very serious about that. I don't want any parents calling up this house saying, "My daughter says your son was trying to touch on her at the dance last night." But that message wouldn't have much impact with the boys if every time they came home from a party, my husband sidled up to them when I wasn't around and said with a wink, "So, did you guys get any tonight?" If my husband did that, they'd think that even though the rules are "no touching," maybe it'd be all right if they started acting a little fresh, and then the next thing you know, we'd have a real problem on our hands. Luckily, neither my husband nor I act that way. We're very focused on being completely in step when it comes to what sort of behavior we expect from our children. We never want them to think that we're divided or conflicted about any of the rules we've set up or decisions that we've made in this house.

That's why you'll notice that when we get firm with the kids, we never say, "Your father said this," or "Your mother told you that." Instead it's always, "My husband said this," or "My wife told you that." We make that distinction because we want the kids to view us as a united front, not as two separate individuals that they can try to play against the other. We really want to drive home the point that before we're parents, we're husband and wife. Or as Joey says, "Us first, then y'all." And I don't think that's being selfish or callous on our part. It's just our way of trying to preserve order and stability in the home.

Not too long ago this woman came up to me out of the blue and started talking to me about her marriage. I didn't know this lady from Adam, but for some reason I felt compelled to listen to her. I'll never forget what she told me—it was almost as if God was trying to speak to me through her. And what she said was, "You know, I'm getting a divorce from my husband because my daughter is leaving for college." When I asked why that would be a reason to split up, she explained that after her daughter was born, she became so wrapped up in that girl's life that she stopped paying much attention to her husband. By the time their daughter was ready to go off to college, she looked up and realized she didn't know who her husband was anymore. She was so caught up with her daughter that she hadn't noticed that she and her husband had grown apart and become interested in different things. "We don't have any problems," she told me. "And we're not mad at each other or anything like that. It's just that with our daughter gone, there's nothing to keep us together. I don't know him, and he doesn't know me." I felt very sad after hearing that, and a little scared, too. Because I can see how easy it is to get lost in your kids, especially when they're constantly demanding all that energy and attention.

## FILL UP THE SPACE WITH LOVE

Justine is right—in order for your marriage to stay tight, it's critical to find the proper balance between your kids and your spouse. Because once any kind of space—physical or emotional—starts to develop between you and your spouse, your marriage is going to face some very tough times.

When you're first married, it isn't hard to make sure there's no space between you and your spouse. You two will always want to be tight—hugging, cuddling, holding hands, and being intimate. And when you two are that close *physically*, your marriage is going to be very strong *emotionally* as well. Nothing, or no one, is going to get between you two. There literally won't be any space for negativity to creep into your relationship. But over time, it's natural for people, even those who are still in love with each other, to drift apart just a bit. Maybe first your careers will create a little space. Then the children are going to push you two a little further apart. And maybe your insecurities about gaining weight, losing your hair, and generally not feeling as sexy as you used to be are going to widen the gap even a tiny bit more. And then before you know it, negativity — infidelity, alcoholism, selfishness, you name it — is going to see an opening and try to make its move. Whereas before negativity couldn't even get a tiny little toehold in your relationship, now there's plenty of space for it to settle in and open up shop. That's why it's so critical that as little space as possible develop between the two of you. And I believe the best way to maintain that closeness is through making love.

Some people might be embarrassed to hear a reverend talking about this subject, but I'm certainly not ashamed. After all, in I Corinthians 7:2–6 it states, "Defraud ye not one the other . . . and come together again, that Satan tempt you not for your incontinency." I interpret that passage as God encouraging married couples to make love as often as possible. And that instruction is not solely for our physical pleasure (though that's certainly a nice added bonus), but because God understands that when lovemaking is *absent* in a relationship, the Devil is going to have an excuse to be *present*.

I'm certainly not the only man of the cloth who believes that regular lovemaking is crucial to a successful marriage. In fact, I've known preachers who schedule lovemaking with their wives like it was a business appointment. They'll say, "OK, dinner with the Millers at six on Wednesday, then lovemaking with my wife at nine." I can even recall my mentor Bishop Jordan looking at his watch one night and then telling me, "Aiight, Rev, I'll see you later. I've got to get home to play with the wife." He didn't say it in a disrespectful way, but in the same tone he'd use if he were going home to take his kids to soccer practice or to clean the pool. He understood that if he didn't set aside enough "playtime" with his wife, negativity would creep into his marriage. And his wife takes that commitment just as seriously. The Bishop told me that if they have a lovemaking appointment scheduled and he's working late on a sermon, his wife will slip a note under the door of his office that says, "Hey, wrap it up. We have an appointment to keep." I laughed the first time I heard that, but the longer I've been married, the more I've come to understand that sort of commitment as actually very deep.

I realize that to some of you, the idea of scheduling your lovemaking is probably going to sound comical or even way too clinical. And I agree—in a perfect world, we would never have to enforce that kind of activity. It would happen as naturally and as often as it did when you were newlyweds. But as I've said, the responsibilities of raising a family have a way of getting even the most loving couple off track. That's why you must make a real commitment to pulling yourself *out* of all your dramas and getting yourself *into* bed with your spouse. Of course there are going to be times when one of you doesn't feel like keeping up that commitment. When one of you might feel unattractive. Or tired. Or just caught up in something that's going on around the house. Still, "I'm not in the mood" should never be an excuse. Because, as I like to say, you'll be in the mood *after* you do it. Whatever sort of love was missing from your life *before* you made love will be in full bloom *after* you do it.

It's especially important to remember that commitment when you and your spouse are fighting. Making love might seem like the furthest thing from your mind when you're yelling and screaming at someone. But to me, that's the time when you should actually try to draw your spouse as close as possible. After all, they say it's a thin line between love and hate. So if you're on the wrong side of that line, just cross over! I remember a few months ago, I was snarling mad at my wife. I didn't think I could ever get that mad at her, but then at the height of my irritability, I suddenly realized, "Aha! Time to *stop* arguing and time to *start* making love." So I told my wife, "Listen, I know you're mad at me and I'm mad at you, but this is crazy. Let's stop pushing each other away and instead let's get closer to all that love we have for each other." So we did, and after we made love, whatever petty little argument had been causing us so much frustration in our relationship was completely drained of its power. Whereas before, we had let that argument push us so far apart, afterward we felt as close as we'd ever been. That's the power of love, and it's a power you must harness if you want your relationship to withstand the pressures of married life.

I want to add that making a commitment to making love doesn't just make for a better marriage, it makes for better parenting as well (although my children will probably never forgive me for writing this section). The more love you make with your partner, the more positive energy will flow throughout your house. As much as children love to say, "Gross" or "Stop it!" when they see their parents being affectionate with each other, deep down all children want love to radiate between Mommy and Daddy. When children sense that their parents are tight like glue, everything else falls into place. When the kids see Mommy and Daddy as one loving unit, they'll be *less* likely to try to play each parent against the other and be *more* likely to accept the rules of the house. They'll feel more secure about the family's future and, as a result, feel more secure about their own futures as well. And all you have to do to create that vibe in your home is to make love with your spouse as much as possible. Doesn't sound like a bad deal, does it?

## KEEPING THE FIRE LIT

Since some of you might be a little uncomfortable with us being so frank about our sex life, I just want to make it clear that we don't take the subject of sex lightly in our family. As we'll discuss later, my husband and I consider sex to be something that should only be shared between two married adults. And that's not something we just preach to our kids—my husband and I didn't have sex before we were married, either. We dated for a long time and we even lived together for a stretch. And even then, we slept in different beds every night. We feel very strongly about saving sex for marriage. However, we do believe that once you tie the knot and make that commitment to each other, then it's very important to have an active and loving sexual relationship with your spouse.

I also want to make it clear that when my husband talks about "you'll be in the mood later," he's not saying that it's OK to grab your woman by the hair or anything like that. A lot of women can get uncomfortable when their husbands start talking about having more sex, because they think he's only talking about his needs. They think he's only talking about when he's in the mood. But I'm very fortunate to be married to a man who's just as attentive to my moods and my needs as he is to his own. If I had a husband who wasn't as sensitive to me, I admit I might not be as quick to co-sign this section.

I believe part of the reason we don't have a lot of problems getting into "the mood" is because we're constantly saying, "I love you," to each other. When we wake up, it's, "I love you." When we go to sleep, it's, "I love you." When we get off the phone, we don't get off with, "Bye," we get off with, "I love you." Today alone, we've probably said, "I love you" to each other twenty times, and it's not even dinnertime yet! And while those three words might not seem that important, constantly saying "I love you" can really make it much easier to feel intimate. I won't lie—after a day of taking care of the kids and trying to run the house, I'm legitimately tired. I'm not necessarily going to feel like making love with my husband. But having said and heard "I love you" all day long usually keeps a little flame simmering. So if one of us is in the mood later that night, we're not trying to spark a fire that's been out for a long time. By sharing your love verbally during the day, it's easier to share that love physically at night.

What Joey said earlier about the importance of treating your spouse the same way fifteen years into your marriage as you did when you first got married is also particularly important when it comes to your sex lives. If something turned you guys on when you first got married, don't give up on it after a few years. A lot of people either become embarrassed or just plain lazy and stop bringing that same energy and passion to the bedroom. Don't feel like just because you're older, or you've been married a certain amount of years, that it's foolish to still be into the things that you were into earlier. Stick with what made you two happy in the first place. If you used to dress up in lingerie for your man when you were first married, then keep doing that now. Or if you booked one of those sexy hotel rooms with the heart-shaped bubble baths for your wife on your honeymoon, then you better make sure you book one for your fifteenth anniversary, too. Whatever worked in the past, keep it going in the present.

And I'll keep it real with you guys. If Joey's coming home from a trip, I'm going to try to make sure that I look extra pretty when he walks through that door. Why wouldn't I? That's my husband. I want him to feel great when he comes home. I want him to be excited to see me again. And he's the same way with me. He'll make sure he has flowers set out for me by the front door, that the house is looking neat, and anything else that he thinks will put me at ease and make me happy. Whether you're the husband or the wife, you should always want your spouse to feel great when they come home, especially from a trip. You want them to feel like it's an event when they come home, not just another day.

That excitement and happiness my husband feels when he comes home is fundamental to the success of our marriage. Because if a husband isn't excited about seeing his wife, or a wife excited about seeing her husband, they're going to start looking for that excitement in other places. It might start with them watching sexy movies and TV shows. Then it might lead to the Internet. And then the next thing you know they're looking for that spark outside the marriage. That's why it's very important not to get too passive or lazy in your love life. You must keep that fire burning for your entire marriage.

And how do we keep that fire burning in a house with six kids? Like most people, we just wait till they're asleep! I don't want people to think that we're running upstairs to get our freak on during the middle of the day. No, we believe very strongly in discretion. So even at night, if it feels like something is about to go down, then we take the extra precaution of locking our bedroom door, just in case one of the kids has a nightmare and tries to come in and tell us something (though of course they've been taught that they have to knock before they come in our room, day or night).

Again, we're very blessed to have a big house with plenty of space between rooms, and we never feel like we have to "sneak around" or put ourselves in a potentially embarrassing situation. But if you don't have the luxury of having lots of private space in your home, you should still try to create situations where you and your spouse can enjoy some undisturbed intimacy. If you can afford it, hire a babysitter and spend the night at a hotel. Or if that's too much, then try to send your kids to the grandparents for a night. If there's no family around, hire a babysitter and drive to some lover's lane somewhere (just don't let the cops see you!) Whatever it takes to keep that flame lit in your marriage, that's what you've got to do. You can't let the kids be an excuse. You can't let your careers be an excuse. You can't let money be an excuse. You can't let the fact that you've each put on a few pounds and don't feel so sexy anymore be an excuse. If the two of you are still in love, then you've really got to make as much love in your marriage as possible.

## HOW TO HANDLE ARGUMENTS

But let's be real—no matter how much love you make in your marriage, there are still going to be moments when you find yourself caught up in arguments that seem like they'll never go away. It's certainly been the case in our marriage. While on TV it might look like Justine and I have an incredibly idyllic relationship, trust me, there are still plenty of times when we go *very* hard at each other. Like all couples, we argue about careers, about money, about time, about the kids, about responsibility and what we want for the future. And even though Justine really hates it, we'll even argue in front of the kids sometimes. I know that's taboo in a lot of families, but personally I don't think it's such a bad thing. Arguments are a part of life, and I don't think it's traumatic for the kids to see Justine and me go at each other a little bit as long as they see the love, too. I feel it's OK for them to see us yelling in the living room, so long as fifteen minutes later they see me coming over and kissing her neck while she's making spaghetti in the kitchen.

I believe that our ability not to let our arguments get out of control is one of the reasons our marriage is particularly successful. Rather than let those moments of frustration or miscommunication drive us apart, we work very hard to push them aside and refocus on the love we share for each other. As I've heard it said, what counts in making a happy marriage is not so much how compatible you are, but how you deal with incompatibility. And one way we deal with those incompatibilities is by remembering that it's more important to be kind in a marriage than it is to be right.

## KINDNESS IS KING

I've seen a lot of marriages fall apart because one person starts focusing too much on what they perceive their partner is doing "wrong." I've seen husbands get overly hung up on how much money their wife spends on clothes, or wives get obsessed that their husband is a slob around the house. But before you begin to focus on those failings, or whatever it is that your spouse does to drive you crazy, you have to realize that *everyone* in a marriage makes mistakes. I don't care who you are or what you do, you're going to mess up just as much as your spouse. Personally, I've never seen a marriage where one person totally had all their stuff together, while the other person was the one who kept dropping the ball. Never assume that you're operating from a higher ground in a marriage. Your particular habits are just as annoying as your spouse's. Your wife might leave the car a mess, but you probably leave the bathroom a mess. Your husband might drive you crazy by eating with his mouth open, but you probably drive him crazy by snoring at night. And both of your hair looks jacked up and both of y'all breath stink in the morning. That's why no one in a marriage ever has the right to beat up on the other person too much.

One of the most important things you can learn in a marriage is that you don't have to go to bed the victor every night. If your spouse is messing up, trust me, they already know. If you want them to improve their game, what they need is your love and support, not your criticisms. Remember, you're not going to get a prize for constantly reminding your wife that she spent too much on that new coat she just bought. You're not going to get a reward for bashing your husband if he can't pay off his credit-card bill. The only thing you get for breaking your spouse down is the job of putting them back together again. And to waste your energy on that kind of work is pure stupidity.

Instead of pulling your spouse apart with criticism, use kindness and understanding to keep them feeling whole. One way to do that is to treat your spouse the same way you would treat a little kid. Let me be clear, I don't mean that in a condescending or belittling way. Rather, I'm encouraging you to feel so much kindness toward your partner that when they make a mistake, you'd treat them the same way you'd treat a child who'd made a mistake with their homework. Do you yell at your kid for getting their homework wrong? Of course not. You just patiently explain their mistake to them so that they'll know how to do it better the next time. Try to treat your spouse the same way. If your husband has a hard time remembering to put his clothes in the hamper when he comes home from work, instead of saying, "You lazy bum. You know you're not supposed to leave your drawers on the floor!" just tell him, "Hey, baby. I know you're tired, but would you mind throwing those drawers in the hamper? I just want to keep our bedroom looking nice." Trust me, that childlike approach will do wonders with your spouse. When you get up on your high horse, you're just going to end up trampling your spouse's feelings. That's why you need to put compassion above criticism and gentleness over judgment.

Obviously many of our arguments are about issues much more serious than whether I've put my drawers in the hamper or not. Despite my best intentions, there have been times when I have failed to speak kindly to my wife about issues that are much more important to her. There have been times when I have been guilty of letting my ego or my selfishness get the best of me. Instead of treating my wife with kindness and respect, I've disrespected her by constantly bringing up subjects that made her uncomfortable.

For example, a while back I got into the bad habit of badgering Justine about watching her weight. Every time she was about to break her diet, I'd jump in with a little comment. If she was about to have some carrot cake, I'd say, "You know there ain't no carrots in carrot cake, right? You don't need that. Stop eating fattening food!" Or if I saw her about to cheat with a peanut butter and jelly sandwich, I'd come over and say, "Put down the PB&J and put up your hands! I am the Weight Watchers sheriff!" In my mind, I was trying to take a humorous approach to helping her stay on her diet. But in her mind (and probably most people's minds), I was only being annoying. At one point, I was even going so far as to grab any fattening food she bought into the house and hide it so she couldn't eat it. Finally she had enough of my antics and wrote a little note in which she told me, "I like to eat. I'm not embarrassed of that fact and I'm tired of having to hear your comments every time I want a bite of something. You're really making me feel terrible about myself. So please stop." And when I read that note, I realized how foolish I'd been acting. When I should have been sharing kind words with Justine that gave her confidence, instead I was mocking her and making her feel bad about herself. When I should have been telling her I love her just the way she is, instead I was only fueling her insecurities. Thankfully she didn't keep that hurt inside and instead corrected me before I did some serious harm to our relationship.

Unfortunately, I still haven't completely learned from that lesson. Just recently, my wife had to put her foot down once again and tell me that instead of treating her with kindness and compassion, my behavior toward her was coming across as disrespectful and hurtful. The problem started with a party that was thrown by someone in our extended family. I wasn't able to make it, but Justine went without me. However, when she got to the party, Justine didn't feel welcome. In her mind, a few people were going out of their way to make her feel uncomfortable, to make her feel like an outsider instead of like family. To her credit, even though she felt hurt, she didn't make a big scene and stomp out of the party. Instead, she simply left quietly with her dignity intact. She felt like if she wasn't being respected, there was no need for her to be there.

I heard about the situation when someone who had been at the party called me, wanting to know where Justine had gone and why she had left so suddenly. My first reaction to the situation was that Justine hadn't handled things correctly. I felt that she had probably been too sensitive and whatever she had perceived as slights were in reality just misunderstandings. So when I finally got Justine on the phone, I told her that she was bugging out and that she should just go back to the party. I told her she was being too sensitive and that by leaving like she did, she had embarrassed both of us. Of course, hearing that just made Justine even angrier and soon she was screaming at me, reminding me that instead of criticizing her, I should be supporting her.

But even after that call, I *still* didn't learn my lesson. For the next few weeks after the party, I continued to throw fuel on the fire by bringing the incident up over and over again. Finally Justine had heard enough and told me, "Please stop talking about that party. In fact, I don't want you to ever mention it again. I was in the right, and if you can't see that, then that's something you're going to have to deal with. But I'm not going to let you add insult to injury by continuing to remind me about it. What you are doing is wrong, and you should stop."

And when she told me that, I realized that once again I'd been acting like a fool with my wife. Instead of standing up for her and supporting her in a difficult moment, I had made her pain worse by not only criticizing her, but continuing to bug her about it. When I realized the errors of my ways, I told my wife, "Baby, I'm truly sorry for how I acted and I promise that you won't see this from me again. I'm putting that attitude in the mailbox and shipping it out of here today! The last thing I want to do is hurt you." I also told her that the next time we had a disagreement about a situation like the party, I would tell her how I felt once and then leave it at that. I would get off my high horse and stop beating the situation into the ground.

So while I think it's great that Justine can tell me when she's had enough of my antics, I also know that I've got to do better. I really believe my first job as a husband and a father is to be sensitive to my wife's feelings. If I'm hurting her to the point that she has to scream at me or write me notes, then I haven't been attentive enough. To do the job correctly, I have to totally slow down *my* agenda, and listen very closely to what *she's* saying. Because all my soft and kind words won't add up to much if my actions and inattentiveness are making her scream and yell.

## MO' MONEY, LESS PROBLEMS

I want to add a final note here about an issue that many couples end up arguing about: money. Though we have our share of little spats here and there over money, I can honestly say that we've never had any major fights over it, which I know is rare among couples. And one reason we've been able to avoid those sorts of fights is because when we first got married, we decided that we were going to keep all our money in the same account.

I know a lot of ladies out there believe in keeping a secret stash in case their men start acting funny with their money, but I believe doing that sets a very bad tone for your relationship. I always say, once you have one secret, then it becomes much easier to start keeping more. So while some women might justify their actions by saying they're just "saving for a rainy day," I believe their actions are only making a rainy day more likely.

This is especially important advice to consider at the beginning of your marriage. If you start off your relationship by hiding things from your spouse, then things are probably only going to go downhill from there. Instead, create a joint account where you and your spouse can each always see what's in there, and then plan for the future together. That's how my husband and I do it—if a check comes in for me, it goes into that account. If a check comes in for Joey, then it's the same deal. And I believe that's why we don't really have fights over money, because everything's in one pot. There's no, "Could I get some money to go shopping," or "Oh, you're going to have to use your own money if you want that," because everything is coming from the same place.

I know some of you might be thinking, "That's easy for you to say, since your husband's bringing in most of the money anyway." But the truth is that while Joey does an incredible job of supporting our family, I put my fair share into that pot, too. You see, I came into this relationship as a career woman. When I met Joey I had been holding down three jobs at once for more than ten years without ever taking a sick day. I was very focused about my money! In fact, when Joey asked me to quit my jobs when we first got serious, I told him I wouldn't do it until we were actually married. Because even though I trusted Joey, I was not prepared to make that sacrifice until there was a wedding ring on my finger!

And while I love being there for my children and getting to see them grow on a daily basis, I never thought this role would fit me so well. I thought I would be a rolling stone, not a stay-at-home mom. That's why I had to laugh the other day when Russy nervously asked me, "Mom, why do women stay home, but men have to go to work every day?" I explained to him that in our home, his father and I had made a decision that I would stay home in order to be a big part of the kids' lives, but that not all families are like that. I explained that in some families the mommy works and the daddy stays home, and in others both parents work. Sometime it depends on finances. Sometimes it's a lifestyle choice. Sometimes mommies and daddies change how they feel about their setup. That it's a decision that every family has to make for themselves, but that I loved being able to be waiting when he and Diggy came home from school every day.

I really have loved being home for the kids as they get older, but I'm also happy I have been able to find more time to get back into a more entrepreneurial groove. I feel great when I'm able to contribute financially to the family through something like my children's book, *God, Can You Hear Me?*, or helping to create the Brown Sugar line for Simmons Jewelry. When the checks come in for those projects, I don't hesitate for a second to put them right into our joint account. Because I know that whether Joey's making the money or I am, it's all going to the same place. And whether I'm home with the kids or out working on a project, we're going to decide how to spend it together.

## HAPPY MARRIAGES MAKE FOR HAPPY KIDS

Ultimately, the principles I'm promoting in this chapter only represent a handful of the principles I try to follow in my own marriage. Instead of a chapter, they probably deserve their own book! More than any specific piece of advice, what I'm really trying to convey in this chapter is the incredibly crucial role our marriage plays in the overall success of our family. I can promote all the parenting principles I want, but it's not an exaggeration to suggest that my kids are only going to respect those principles as much as they see my wife and I respecting each other. If the children sense that things are healthy between their parents, then my advice will carry a heavy weight with them. After my wife and I finish preaching to them, they'll be more likely to think, "Things do seem to be good at the top of the food chain in this house. So I should probably listen to them instead of listening to 'Yo, Yo, Yo' on the corner. 'Yo, Yo, Yo' has a little flavor, but my parents seem to be more stable. So I'm sticking with them."

Conversely, if our children constantly hear Justine and me bickering, or sense that there's rough water just under our placid surface (and never forget that children are much more perceptive than we often realize), then our credibility will be diminished in their eyes. Suddenly, "Yo, Yo, Yo" will have the authority that should have been ours. Instead of learning about the world under our guidance, they'll be learning down on the corner, with "Yo, Yo, Yo" leading the way. And as a parent, that's the last thing that you want.

We'll talk much more about the importance of husbands and wives working together to run a family later in the book, but for now I just want to encourage you to make sure that your marriage is in order before you start working on your parenting skills. Ask yourself, "Am I taking my spouse for granted? Am I failing to protect her from her weaknesses? Am I being unkind to her? Have I stopped giving her all the love they need? Have I recharged our batteries?" If the answer to any of those questions is "yes," then take a step back and try to patch up those holes in your life *first*. If parenthood is a never-ending journey, then think of your marriage as the ship that will carry you on that trip. You don't want to set sail with *any* sort of leak in your vessel. Because when your marriage is strong and solid, you'll have a much better chance of accessing that strong and solid parent inside of you.

## RUN'S TAKE BACK

A great way to take back your marriage from whatever forces have started to pull it away is to always remember that it's better to "give advantage" than to "take advantage." In other words, instead of looking for ways that your spouse can make your life a little easier, look for ways to make your spouse's life better. And one way to help remember that truth is to engage in a "kindness competition." That means every day try to play a little game in which each of you attempt to "out-kind" the other. Maybe it means if it's raining and one of your cars is in the shop, you tell your spouse, "Don't worry, honey, take the car. I can take the train to the city." Maybe it's something as small as telling a spouse who's worried about their weight that they look wonderful. Maybe it's as large as treating a spouse who's been worn down by life around the house to a surprise trip to a spa while you look after the kids. Every day when you wake up, just ask yourself, "What act of kindness would that person on the other side of the bed appreciate today?" And then commit to actually doing whatever you think of at some point over the course of the day. It could be taking on a household task that you've been avoiding. It could be a kind word. It could be a gift. It could even just be a loving look. But if you can commit to that one kind act a day, over time they'll add up to a very healthy marriage.

# CHAPTER 2

# Putting Family First

Despite the love we all share for our families, parenting can often seem like a very unglamorous pursuit. When you're changing diapers, picking up after a messy teenager, or stressing over how to pay your child's tuition, it's very easy to daydream about a more glamorous lifestyle. Maybe you see yourself as a celebrity with a nanny to change those diapers, a maid to pick up those clothes, and pockets deep enough to cover any bill. But while the celebrity lifestyle certainly comes with its perks, never become too envious of it. Because even if you don't have a fancy house, or have a maid, or see your name in the news, as long as you're doing your best for your family every day, you are *already* a celebrity. I've learned that real celebrities aren't necessarily the people who sell the most albums or drive the fanciest cars, but instead are the people who do their best for their families day in and day out. Those are the people we should be celebrating, and that's the lifestyle I want to encourage you to emulate!

Now please don't get it twisted—I'm fully aware that the main reason I was blessed with a TV show like *Run's House*, or even blessed with the opportunity to write this book, is that I've already achieved a degree of "traditional" celebrity. But one of my hopes for the show and this book is that they can help change the kind of lifestyle and priorities that society thinks are worth celebrating. I might have become famous with Run DMC, but I hope that when all is said and done what I will truly be celebrated for was the part I played in helping make family "cool" with the hip-hop generation. It's like that old Huey Lewis song—I'm trying to make it hip to be square again. So if you're going to emulate *Run's House* in your own life, please don't focus on our professional or material successes. Instead, try to emulate the fact that Justine and I wake up every day thinking about not only what we can do to help nurture our family, but how to have fun doing it, too. And while it's easy to believe that the toys, or the swimming pool, or the vacations are what makes our family fun, please believe me that that's not really the case. I've been around enough "celebrities" to know that all the pools and vacations in the world won't make you happy without a real commitment to doing the best for your family. You might enjoy *Run's House* because of the fancy cars, the pool, or the indoor basketball court, but none of those things really mean a thing. I'm here to say that the reason *Run's House* is standing strong is because it was built on the foundation of family.

I should also note that when I was first talking about this section with my publisher, they wanted me to add something here about the "African-American family in crisis." And while I can't deny that there are too many African-American families struggling out there, I don't like to think of our family as an exception to the rule. I really believe that there are a lot of black people out there living with the same values and dreams that we do on *Run's House*. It just doesn't feel that way because we haven't seen that image enough on television or in the media. Sure, we hear plenty about the families that truly are in crisis, but you don't hear nearly as much about the families where everyone is living and praying under the same roof, having fun, and striving to make a living. But we're out there, and there are a lot of us.

The key now is for those families to stand up and provide an inspiration for the people who aren't doing as well. Just as I'm trying to share a greater image on MTV, we need more people to promote a greater image in their community, or on their block, or even just their building. We need to help change the basic image of black families, so that the people who are struggling will have a constant reminder of what they can achieve. So that instead of worrying about what they're trying to get out of, they can be inspired by what they're moving toward.

## YOU MIGHT WANT TO BE LIKE BRAD PITT, BUT BRAD PITT WANTS TO BE LIKE YOU!!!

As a parent, the first step toward embracing your own celebrity is to stop thinking that *other* people have something that *you* need in order to be happy. Because the truth is that as long as you have a strong family life, then *you* most likely have what *they're* looking for!

I've known this truth in my heart for a long time, but it was really reinforced recently when I heard that Brad Pitt was a huge fan of *Run's House*. It was a bit of a surprise at first, because I never pegged Brad Pitt as the kind of guy who would be that into a wholesome family show. He's talented, he's rich, and he's considered to be the best-looking man in the world—if there's one guy you'd think would want to ride the party train till the wheels come off, it would be Brad Pitt, right? But when *Esquire* magazine asked him for a list of some of his favorite things in life, *Run's House* was on that list. In fact, he even called me "a patriarch that he could really get behind." Now, we can't say what exactly it was about my life that inspired Brad Pitt, but it's safe to say that it wasn't the Bentley or the house or the famous friends. Remember, Brad Pitt has all those things, times ten! If I could guess, I'd like to believe that Brad Pitt was inspired by the sight of someone committed to doing the best he could for his family. By putting the show on his list, I felt he was saying, "My name is Brad Pitt, and I'm telling you, this Reverend Run dude is cool. He's tapped into something that feels better than the cover of *People* magazine. His life looks like fun. His relationship with his wife and kids feels balanced, it feels good. I can respect that. Maybe I want more of that in my own life." Why did it feel good to him? Because even Brad Pitt—someone who *stays* on magazine covers—understands that the only thing really worth celebrating is family. And while I'm certainly not trying to claim that *Run's House* is the reason why he's become so family oriented, if you look at Brad Pitt these days, what is he really famous for now? Not so much for his movies, but for his relationship and his kids. Which is only logical, because his family is where his focus is now. He understands that all the accolades and fame are worthless without a strong family to share them with.

So if you are sitting there wishing that you had a personal assistant to pick your kid up from basketball practice, or a maid to clean up the mess in your den, please stop wishing that your life was more like a movie star's. Because somewhere a movie star like Brad Pitt is riding in a limo and daydreaming about what it would be like to be you!

## NOTHING IS AS FRESH AS FAMILY

Some of you are probably thinking, "Whatever, Run. Give me the limo rides and the parties and I'll be just fine. No matter what you say, that lifestyle sounds flyer than changing some kid's diaper." While I hear you, please understand that I've been to the parties, have ridden in the limos, and sold out Madison Square Garden. I'm not speculating on that kind of lifestyle. I experienced all of that and more. And I'm *still* here to tell you that not one of those things felt as good as taking a slow walk in the park with Russy. None of them made me feel like I used to feel when me and Angela would snuggle up on Saturday mornings and watch *The Smurfs* together. Riding in the limos never felt as good as sitting on my couch when Diggy got home from a basketball tryout and having him run over and say, "Dad, I made the team!" Rocking *Live Aid* in front of a hundred thousand people didn't feel as special as DJ'ing Russy's birthday party in our backyard. It's not even close! So instead of trying to be the number-one rapper, or the number-one TV star, I'm very content with just trying to be the number-one dad.

I will admit that there are moments when my ego gets in the way and I'll start to feel that maybe just being a good dad isn't quite enough. I'll start to long for the days of being "Run," the cool twenty-one-year-old who weighed a buck-fifty, who always had the illest clothes, the baddest swagger, and kept the ladies screaming. And then I'll turn on *Run's House*, and instead of seeing that James Bond type of cat I was just describing, I'll see a bald guy who's twenty-five pounds overweight, could use a wardrobe update, and who most people would probably describe as "goofy" instead of cool. Man, I've actually cringed when I've watched myself on *Run's House*. It's made me a little depressed, because in my mind, I'm still that cool, young rapper. But before I get too down, I remember that I only feel bad because my ego is clouding my vision. And "ego" just stands for "Edging God Out." What God has given me is so much greater than anything I ever achieved or experienced as a rapper. That's why I have to remind myself that my family is what makes me fly, not being skinny or hearing the girls scream. So instead of edging God's blessings out of my life, I have to pull those blessings even closer. I have to remind myself that the reason people get so much happiness from *Run's House*, the reason they want to shake my hand on the street or even read this book, is because they love to see me doing the family thing. Sure, I've put on a few pounds, lost a bit (OK, all) of my hair, and am probably not as slick as I used to be, but it's all OK. Because having a family is the coolest thing I've ever done, or could ever do.

That's the essence of what I really want to promote, not only to hip-hop, but to the entire world: This family thing is hot to def! Let me say it one more time: I've already stuffed my face with all those fancy dishes people that people think will taste so delicious, but none of them—not flying on Jay-Z's private plane, not having every magazine tell me I'm the greatest, not seeing twenty thousand people hold their Adidas up in the air at my command—has tasted as good as sitting down and breaking bread with my family. It's impossible. The mistake some people make is thinking that family is a job that will take the playtime out of their lives. Or, to take the food analogy a step further, they make the mistake of thinking that family is the broccoli and spinach in their life's meal—something that has to be tolerated because it's "good" for them. But while it's true that family is good for you like broccoli and spinach, it's also true that family tastes great like steak and shrimp, or pancakes and waffles, or cookies and ice cream! It's all the "good for you" things and all the yummy things you'd ever want rolled up into one. It's the best meal ever. All you have to do is sit down with your family and enjoy it.

Like all of us, there are times when I find myself stressing over the responsibilities of parenthood. Is there enough money in the bank for me to afford the lifestyle that my family enjoys? Are my kids making the right decisions with their lives? Am I being a good parent? Or am I too caught up in making the right moves in my own career? But just when all those questions start to seem overwhelming, I've found that refocusing on the little things about my family is what always brings me back into balance. I can remember a time a few years back when my responsibilities were weighing particularly heavily on me. Just when it seemed like the weight was a little too much to bear, Diggy came running up and said, "Dad, I just learned how to roller-skate!" Simple words, but expressed with so much joy that they were like an epiphany to me. I remember thinking, "Oh my God, he went roller-skating! How could I even think about being depressed when my kid is feeling so much joy from roller-skating for the first time?" Just hearing him slowly say, "roll-er-skate-ting," the words just dripping with happiness, broke me out of my little funk and helped me start to appreciate the beauty of life again.

It's so important to recognize these truths, because the commitment to family that I'm promoting is the best foundation to build your life on. Even if it seems like sometimes the *world* is focused on other things, God really does smile on those who focus on their families first. No matter where you live, what you do, or what sort of faith you might live under, God's first plan for you is family.

And when I speak of God and family, I'm not only speaking to Christians. It seems that every religion in the world stresses family. If you're a Christian, then you've probably heard 1 Timothy 5:8, which reminds us, "But if a man makes no provision for those dependent on him, and especially for his own family, he has disowned the faith and is behaving worse than an unbeliever." If you believe in Islam, the same principles still apply—the Prophet Muhammad was reported to have said, "The best among you are those who are best to your households." Or maybe you're Jewish and have read those famous instructions in the Old Testament: "Honor your father and your mother in order that your days may be prolonged on the soil that your God is giving you." And from Buddhists to Taoists to Hindus, it's the same story—no matter what sort of faith you operate under, an emphasis on family is going to be at the heart of it.

## FOCUSING ON FAMILY CAN TAKE TIME

I feel like I've always been a family man at heart. I was as competitive as they come at rocking the mic, but I would also rush home after every show. I was trying to conquer the world, but only so I could share the spoils with my family. In fact, my desire to stay close to my family occasionally created ripples within Run DMC, especially one time when I decided I didn't want to extend a tour with Aerosmith because it would have kept me away from my family for too long. Jam Master Jay, God rest his soul, particularly had trouble understanding that decision at first. He knew more tour dates would have meant more paychecks, and we were all struggling for money at that point. But my mind was more on my family than on whatever money we would have made by extending the tour, and ultimately I think Jay and D could respect that. We were like brothers, so they knew that family was my ultimate job and the paycheck written to me by my family is the one that has the most lasting value to me.

I realize that some people might not think that it's possible to be a rapper and a "family man" at the same time, but trust me, you can be. I happen to know a lot of rappers who are also great fathers. Will Smith is one of the greatest fathers I know and is a huge inspiration to both Justine and me. Our neighbor Ja Rule is also an incredibly devoted father. As are Snoop Dogg, LL Cool J, Mike D from the Beastie Boys, 50 Cent, and so many other rappers. I've spent time around these men and their families, seen how much their children mean to them, and witnessed how dedicated they are to being a part of their lives. So please never assume that just because somebody rocks a mic, they can't lead a family, too.

But while I obviously feel very strongly about family, I also understand that it is a concept that doesn't come as naturally to some people. Maybe you weren't raised in that sort of environment, so the idea of making a complete commitment to family seems alien to you. Maybe you're so focused on your career, or your lifestyle, that you feel like you don't have the time to work on a family. Or maybe you were brought up in a strong family environment and want to build one of your own, but still feel overwhelmed by the sense of responsibility that comes with raising kids. To all those people I would say, "Don't be so quick to write off family life." I've seen firsthand how someone who never thought that family would be one of their top priorities has turned into an absolutely incredible mother. That's right, while a lot of people like to tell Justine that she's such a "natural," she'll tell you that for a very long time, motherhood was actually the furthest thing from her mind.

Ever since *Run's House* came on the air, so many people have come up and thanked me for setting such a great example as a mother. And while it's such a blessing to think that I've been able to inspire people, most of them probably don't realize that for a long, long time, I never envisioned myself as a mommy. The truth is that when I was younger, I was never into babysitting or any of the other activities that might have reflected a maternal instinct. Truth be told, the idea of raising a family never entered my head when I was older, either. I was much more focused on partying and making money than on looking after a bunch of kids. In fact, I can remember telling my mother that I was never going to have kids because I hated the idea of having to wash all those dishes! I really felt that way! But then I met Run, Vanessa, Angela, and JoJo, and suddenly the idea of dirty dishes and packing lunches didn't seem so unappealing anymore. Those kids were so cute and so loving toward me that I just had to be part of their lives. Still, I have to admit there are times that I'm still shocked when I step back and think about having all these kids.

We share that example to remind you that even if you're not convinced that you're cut out for a family life, there still can be an incredible mother or a loving father just waiting to come out. Just as we hope to show that even if you feel yourself drifting away from the family man that you truly are at heart, it's never too late to take back that part of your life. No matter how much you don't like washing dishes, or no matter how much you think children are going to slow you down professionally, or how out of control your ego gets, please understand that you do have what it takes to be a terrific parent. This is the message I want to share right now, and it's a message I want to keep driving home throughout this book. Nothing is hotter than family. Nothing is more fun than family. Nothing tastes better than family. Nothing will keep you whole and happy like family. And as long as you do your best by your family, your family will bring out the best in you!

## DOING YOUR BEST

I want to take a step back now and clarify one important point: You don't get to enjoy all that fun, bask in all that hotness, and feel all that happiness just because you *have* a family. Sorry, but I've found it takes a little bit more than that. You'll only feel that great energy I just described when you not only have a family, but you do your best by it as well. "Best" is really the operative word here. Some people think they can just "have" kids and then mail in the rest. But all the joy we've experienced as a family has only been possible because despite our shortcomings, Justine and I haven't settled for *just* being parents. Instead, we've really committed ourselves to being the best parents possible.

That obviously raises the question, How can you define doing your "best" as a parent? Ultimately, that's an answer that everyone has to meditate on and decide for themselves. What might be best for our family might not be best for yours. For some folks, "best" might mean making the most money, or buying the most toys, or throwing a big Sweet 16 for their kids. But in my experience, "best" usually means taking the time every day to do the little things that let your family know you are committed to them. And by "little things" I mean talking to your kids, showing them affection, and perhaps most importantly, just being a constant presence in their lives. These might seem like very obvious steps, but we've found that they can help you make great strides toward having a fulfilled family.

## KEEP UP THE CONVERSATION

One thing you must try to do every day is talk with your children. Obviously, most people do *literally* speak with their children every day. But when I say "talk," I mean taking it a step further than just basic conversation. Instead of just asking your kids what they want to eat or watch on TV, or reminding them to clean up their rooms, it's important to take the time to really try to find out what's going on inside your kid's heads. That's why it's so important to turn off the TV every day for a minute, put the video games away, turn down the music, and once everyone is paying attention, just ask your kids, "So, how was your day?" Admittedly, for a long time I wasn't as conscious about doing this as I could have been. I assumed that of course our kids would speak up if something important happened in their lives. But just recently we had a situation with Diggy where we learned that that's not necessarily the case.

One afternoon I saw I had a message on my cell phone from Diggy, which was strange because normally he doesn't call me while he's at school. Things got even stranger when I listened to the message, because I could tell that he had dialed me by accident. I could overhear Diggy screaming and cursing, using the type of language that I would have never believed could have come out of his mouth if I hadn't heard it with my own ears. The call eventually got disconnected, but it left me very concerned. Why was Diggy talking like that? What had gotten him so upset?

When Diggy got back from school, I gave him a hug and asked if anything had happened to him that day. "Nah," he replied very nonchalantly. "Nothing happened." "Oh, really?" I said, and then played him the message. Faced with this evidence, he admitted that yes, he had gotten into a beef with an older kid on his school bus that day. The older kid was a wrestler who had been picking on him for a long time. And even though he knew there was no way he could take this kid if things became physical, he cursed out the kid because he was tired of getting punked! So while I had to give Diggy a reminder about watching his language no matter what the situation, Joey and I were secretly proud that our son had stood up for himself. Yet at the same time, we were worried that we would have never known about this ongoing situation if I hadn't gotten that call by mistake.

That's why since that incident, we try to take a minute every day to ask each of our children very pointedly what is happening in their lives. And if one of them tries to blow off the question, or seems to be hiding something, then we ask again, and again, until we feel comfortable that we've gotten to the truth.

Because unless you repeatedly ask your children about their lives, they're not going to offer up the information you need to know. They might be hiding something as minor as a run-in with a bully on a bus, or it could be a potentially more serious issue that needs to be addressed. But you may never know unless you keep asking.

As Diggy's example showed, it's particularly important to try to become involved in your child's school life. When we get caught up in the daily dramas of the adult world, it becomes easy to write off school as a place where children go off to learn and laugh every day. And while hopefully that's the case the majority of the time, never lose sight of the fact that school is a place where children are learning a whole range of experiences. Yes, they're learning about knowledge and sharing and friendship, but they're also learning about selfishness and disappointments and even discrimination. It's very important to keep abreast of what happens every day from 8 to 3, or however long your child is away from your authority. And sometimes it's not enough to just ask your kids about school—it's also a good idea to go to your kids' school and sniff around a bit yourself. Try not to be that parent who only shows his face for parent/teacher conferences. Instead, try to find a little time every single week to hang out at their school. Get to know their teachers, get to know the principal, the crossing guards, the coaches, the other kids—whoever it is who is interacting with your children on a daily basis.

In fact, I've always liked to linger around after I drop Diggy and Russy off at school. To take a few minutes and walk around the halls before I head home, just breathing in the smell of stale milk and pencil shavings. It's great to immerse yourself in your kids' world, even if it's only for a few minutes. I don't do drugs anymore, but I definitely feel a little high when I'm in those classrooms and halls—it gives me a feeling of rising above the adult box that we tend to paint ourselves into every day and getting back into the incredible world of childhood. Spending time on their turf not only brings a new energy to my day, it also helps me better understand what my kids are experiencing. That's why when I ask them later, "How was school? What did you get into?" the conversation is taking place on common ground.

(In the spirit of full disclosure, I should add one thing: I haven't been able to spend that much time wandering around the boys' school lately because adults aren't allowed to walk around the campus unsupervised anymore. I'm not mad at the rule—they're just trying to protect the kids—but I am starting to miss that stale-milk smell.)

And while it is very important to get involved in their school lives and find out what's happening there, it's also important to remember that your children's lack of communication will not always be connected with them having "done" something. There's not always going to be a fight or an outburst or an event that you can indentify as the place where things have changed. A lot of times they might be going through the normal growing pains of childhood and just don't know how to express themselves to you. They might want to talk, but because they're confused or embarrassed, they can't get the words out. Just recently Angela told me that looking back, she can see how she really stopped communicating with me when she was thirteen and got her first period. Prior to that, she had always felt like she was "daddy's little girl" and that we had a very open relationship. But after she started to experience the physical changes of puberty and adolescence, she felt that our relationship changed too: I didn't realize it at the time, but she just stopped feeling like she could talk to me about certain things. She didn't tell me how she was feeling, so in my mind our relationship hadn't changed. We were still talking, I just didn't realize we weren't talking about *every-thing* that was troubling her. Thankfully, we're now back to having that totally open relationship, although I really do regret not doing a better job of recognizing the changes she was going through and pushing harder and digging deeper to get at all the things that were troubling her. Again, most children are not going to volunteer what's really bothering them, or the truly difficult things that are happening in their lives. As a parent, you must always keep talking with your children, not only about the things they say are bothering them, but also the things that you *suspect* might be bothering them.

## SHOW YOUR LOVE

Another way we try to do our best every day is by being physically affectionate with our kids. For some, showing affection is as natural (and necessary) as breathing. For others, showing affection can be incredibly difficult, almost as if they're allergic to touching the people they love. If you've watched many episodes of *Run's House*, then you can probably guess what category Justine falls into. She is definitely someone who expresses her love with words and hugs. But for me, showing affection hasn't come as easy.

I remember that when I first met Joey, after I would give him a hug, he would just pat me on the back. Like he was burping a baby or something. "What is he doing?" I'd ask myself. But I came to realize that it wasn't that Joey didn't feel affection for me—it was just that he just wasn't comfortable showing it. He didn't grow up in a family where they did a lot of hugging, so it felt awkward to him. But with some gentle nudging on my part, now he feels comfortable not only hugging me, but all of our children, too. I will admit that sometimes it's still a struggle with him and JoJo, since the older men get, the less comfortable they feel hugging. Even a father and a son. But they have at least reached a point where Joey feels comfortable kissing JoJo on the head and saying "I love you." Still, if Run and JoJo have a fight and one of them tries to walk away with just one of those "head kisses," I will get into both of their faces and tell them, "Hug!"

I'm glad my wife does that, because I would never want the fact that I'm a little uptight make my children feel like I don't love them.

And it's the same with the kids being affectionate with one another. Yes, it's still difficult for JoJo and the girls to hug sometimes, probably because they're older and embarrass easier. But JoJo feels fine hugging Diggy and Russell, and the more he does that, the more comfortable he'll feel down the road hugging other people that are important to him.

Again, hugging might seem like the easiest thing in the world to do, but it's really a struggle for a lot of people. That's why you must stay at it and enforce it as a habit in your household. Remember, the people who feel weird about giving hugs are usually the ones who need a hug the most. The teenage boy who's uncomfortable hugging people will turn into a middle-aged man who's uncomfortable hugging people. I've heard about so many people who lost a loved one and then said, "I never hugged my father," or "I wish I had told my mother I loved her more." That's a terrible pain to have to carry with you, especially since it's a pain that could have easily been avoided. Not wanting to have to live with that kind of regret is why, as we mentioned, Justine always says, "I love you" at the end of every phone call, no matter what the conversation was about. Likewise, if I have an argument with one of the kids, no matter what was said, no matter whose feelings were hurt, I always end the conversation by reminding the kids that "I love you."

I want to encourage you to show a little more affection toward your own family today. If you're already a hugger, then you probably don't need much pushing. You know how good it feels and how much love it spreads. But if you're like me and are not a hugger by nature, make a point of giving your kids a hug today. It doesn't have to be for a special reason, or come with a big speech. Just hug them, tell them you love them, and leave it at that, if you want. And then do the same thing tomorrow, and the day after tomorrow, and every day until it becomes second nature. I promise that soon all the awkwardness will fade away and you'll be able to experience the incredible warmth and sense of well-being that comes from being affectionate with your family.

## JUST BE THERE

Little things like communicating and showing affection are great ways to do your best by your family, but perhaps the most important thing you can do is to just be there for your family. By that, I mean commit to being a constant, unwavering presence in your children's lives. Whether you feel like you are on the right road as a parent, or whether you feel like you are lost and searching for direction, as long as you stay close to your family, things will always work out in the end. You might say the wrong words to your children, you might argue with your spouse, or you might feel like the weight of parenthood is too much to bear, but by simply being there for your family, you are already doing your best.

That's why you'll notice that I'm home a lot when you watch *Run's House*. They don't just edit the show that way—I really am a homebody. For me, being a constant presence in the home is really the key to running my family the right way. Sure, there is temptation to spend more time hanging out with the Puffys and Jay-Zs of the world, but instead I try to stay home with my family as much as I can. I've learned that when you're not around, you end up missing the little things that make being a parent so incredible. Just the other night, I had an opportunity to go to a party in the city. It would have been fun—big stars, great music, photographers taking our pictures—but I ultimately decided I'd rather stay home and chill.

That night, I was lying in bed, getting ready to watch some show on BET, when Russy came into our room and asked if he could watch a blooper show with me instead. He was probably expecting me to tell him to beat it because it was getting close to his bedtime, so when I said, "Sure," you could just see the joy on his face. "You really want to watch it with me?" he said. And we lay there together on the bed, watching some silly blooper show, laughing our heads off. To know that I had brought my son so much joy from just getting to lie there next to his dad and act silly, that made me feel so great. It made me feel so much greater than any sort of ego stroking I could have gotten from hanging out at some party in Manhattan.

It made me feel better than any drink or joint ever could have made me feel. I'm not claiming to be a saint, or holier than thou. Like everyone else, I'm pretty easy to read: I like things that make me feel good. So all I'm saying is that no other feeling, no other setting, no other activity beats the feeling I get from my family. Now that I know I've got something right here that feels better than the party, feels better than the drugs, why would I ever want to get too far away from that?

Ultimately, being a presence at home is about much more than just your own satisfaction. Even if you don't get the same satisfaction from hanging out with your kids that I get from mine, if you'd rather watch the game in your room by yourself than with your ten-year-old, or if going to a nightclub sounds better than a night reading children's books, you're still making some progress as a parent. Because your mere presence in the home is *still* going to have a very positive impact on your child's life. When a parent is away from the house, even for just a week or so, it has a very negative affect on their children. We all know this, but it still needs to be said, because the people who are hurt the most by a parent's absence usually can't speak up for themselves. A child is most likely not going to tell you how confused or hurt he feels by your absence. Instead, it's much more likely that he'll go into a shell, or express his frustrations in other ways. When you're thinking everything is OK because your child is not talking about your absence, I just want to remind you that it's *not* OK. Trust me, children feel it deeply when a parent is not around. I know this because I've experienced a parent not being "there" myself.

For the most part, I was blessed with a very happy childhood. My parents might have had their ups and downs as a couple, but I never felt anything but love and support from them. However, when I was in fifth grade, they hit a rocky stretch and my father moved out of the house for a while. Though I never said anything about it to my parents or my brothers, looking back I can see that even that temporary absence had a real impact on me. As soon as my father left, I almost immediately started getting into trouble at school. Whereas before I had been a model student with good grades, in his absence things started to slip. Instead of taking notes and paying attention in Ms. Stewart's class, I used to sit around cracking jokes and being bad as hell! I thought I was having the time of my life until I got my report card. When I opened it up, instead of seeing the As and Bs I was accustomed to, instead I saw three Fs staring back at me. In fact, I can still see those Fs, written in bright red ink, very clearly, to this day. I remember I started bawling my eyes out because it seemed like the most terrible thing that had ever happened to me. I was still upset later that night when my father called to check in on me. I can still remember him sighing over the phone and then saying, "You know he got those Fs because I haven't been around, right?" At the time, I didn't make the connection. But looking back, I can see that my father knew what he was talking about. I was acting out because I missed my father.

## WHEN YOU STAY IN THE MIX, YOU'LL ALWAYS GET MIXED UP

My personal experience is only one of the reasons that I put such an emphasis on our family sticking close together. Another is that Justine and I have seen so many other families struggle when one or, in some cases, both parents seem so focused on their professional lives that they start to drift away from what's important. While I recognize that everyone wants to provide the best possible life for their family, chasing paper should never come at the expense of spending time with the people you love. The paper might make you rich, but you're also going to pay a very high price for that so-called wealth. I have to shake my head when I hear people say, "Well, the only reason I'm working these long hours is to support my family," or "I hate to be on the road so much, but I gotta keep the food on our table." Sorry, but if you really wanted to support your family, you'd find a way to be home more. For instance, while working on this book,

Kid Rock invited me to join him on his Rock and Roll Revival. It was an incredible opportunity, a chance to not only rip the mic with Rock, but also a chance to make a nice piece of change on the side. But obviously it meant that I would have to be away from the family a good bit. Justine and I had a long talk about it, and we finally decided that I should go on the tour because the opportunity was too good to pass up. But we also decided that I would take a little bit of that money that I was getting and use it to rent my own tour bus so that Justine and the kids could go out on the road with me for part of the tour. And it's worked out great—the shows have been incredible, and my family has been able to join me from time to time. And if I have a couple of free days between shows, instead of hanging out in St. Louis or Memphis, I have the driver fill up the truck and head back to Jersey so I can see my family again. Even if I have to drive two days just to spend one day with my family, it's worth it for all of us.

I believe that when someone is constantly away from their family, it's often not because they really *have* to be away. Instead, it's because they *want* to be away. A husband who really wants to be home will find a way to be home, no matter what sort of job he has. Similarly, a husband who claims he can't be home probably doesn't *want* to be home.

I've been very blessed that my husband has managed to provide for this family while staying home as much as possible. But I've also seen a lot of women who haven't been as fortunate. Yes, their husbands are making good money. But in making that money, they also start to make a lot of excuses about why they can't be around as much. So be careful when there start to be more late meetings, more networking dinners, and more three-day road trips. I'm not saying that those husbands are looking to get into trouble, but I do know that the more you're away, the greater the chances are that you're going to eventually run into something. I don't care how faithful you claim to be—the more you stay in the mix, the better the odds that you're going to get mixed up. That's why Joey wants us out there on the road with him. He doesn't want to take any chances of getting into the wrong type of mix.

Again, I'm not trying to tell anyone not to provide for their families. I'm just encouraging you to look for ways to do it closer to home. Justine and I certainly pursue as many opportunities as possible, but never at the expense of our kids. So when I have to meet with my business partners, I try to hold the meetings here at our home, instead of somewhere on the road. When a shoe company wanted to meet with Vanessa and Angela about their Pastry sneaker line, for example, I insisted on holding the meetings here, instead of at the company's headquarters. Not that the girls couldn't have gone there, but we wanted to remind them that family and business don't have to be separate things (more about that later).

Of course, not everyone is blessed with a bus and a driver to take them home on their off days, or even a house where there are plenty of extra rooms to hold meetings. I understand that for a lot of people, it's a struggle just to have a separate bedroom for each child, let alone a home office for business meetings. But no matter what your situation is, there are steps you can take to achieve the balance we are describing. With all these handheld computers and Black-Berrys, you don't have to be as chained down to your office as you used to. Instead of working late, go home, spend some time with your family, and then answer those last few e-mails after you put your kids to bed. Instead of going out for drinks after work in order to catch up with your clients, maybe you can call them on your cell during the commute home. We know it's hard, we know that there are a lot of bosses out there who care more about the bottom line than about you spending time with your family. But if you can make an effort to find even little ways to grab an extra hour here and there with your family, it will be very rewarding for you in the long run.

## THE BEST TAKES TIME

While I encourage you to try to take some of these small steps toward doing your best, please also remember that you are going to make mistakes. Despite the love you have for your family, despite your great intentions and your desire to stay on the right path, you are going to drift in the wrong direction from time to time. There will be moments where you come up a little bit short of your best. The key is to remember that while you might not be doing your best right now, as long as you stay focused on that goal, you're already doing better.

Again, while many people admire me today for my parenting abilities, I also went through a period when I was decidedly out of balance as a family man. As a rap star with plenty of fame and temptations surrounding him, it would have been very easy for me to walk away from those responsibilities, to let my fears and insecurities build a permanent wall between my children and me. In fact, that almost did happen.

As I've alluded to, there was a time in my life when I fell out of balance and lost some of my focus on family. When Run DMC was on top of the world during the 1980s, I admit that I got too caught up in the hype. Instead of focusing on Joey Simmons, the father, husband, brother, and son, I put too much focus on being "Run," a larger-than-life figure. And because I started believing my own hype, I subsequently lost touch with my roots. I stopped making time for my brothers and my parents, which was bad. But even worse, my wife at the time and our children didn't always get the best out of me, either. Instead of understanding that my family was my greatest accomplishment, I thought what made me great was cashing checks and staying on top in the rap game. I won't say that I was a terrible father—if we did a show in New York, instead of hitting the clubs afterward with my boys, I'd rush home so I could be with the family instead. But when we were out on big national tours, I didn't want to bring the family with me. I'd make a lot of phone calls and send presents, but I didn't try to go that extra mile and make arrangements for them to physically be with me. In some ways that probably made sense—my wife and kids probably didn't need to be around a bunch of wild young rappers back then. But that decision also meant that there were long stretches where I didn't get to physically see my family, to hug my kids, to give my wife a break from watching the kids and take her out to dinner. My family was never far from my mind, but I can't truly say they were at the front of it, either. And that's where they deserved to be.

Even though my marriage wasn't able to survive my neglect during that period, I am truly thankful that my relationship with my children remained intact. And I'm thankful that even though I was doing waaaaay less than my best as a parent back then, I feel like I'm doing much better now. That's why it's so important to remember that no matter who you are, there are going to be periods in your life when you feel yourself coming up short as a parent. The key is that when those periods come, you can't let them discourage you too much. You have to fight through them and have faith that in time you will be that parent your family deserves. From big issues to small ones, we all have our moments when we feel we're not doing our best. There's nothing unnatural about it. In fact, let me let Justine share one of hers.

## BUILDING A BETTER FOOD FOUNDATION

Personally, cooking is one area where sometimes I feel like I'm doing less than my best as a mother. For the first ten years or so of our marriage, I used to cook for the family all the time. But lately, I've been ordering more and more takeout, which makes me feel like I'm shortchanging the kids, especially Russy and Diggy, who are home the most. When I do get it together and make them a meal, I can tell how much they love it. "Mommy, you're the best cook," they'll tell me. And their father will egg them on, saying stuff like, "Don't y'all love it when your mommy cooks?" And when they scream, "Yes!" I feel even guiltier.

But as guilty as I feel, my problem is that with a new baby in the house, I've just been very tired lately and can't seem to muster up the energy to cook. Another, and probably larger, problem is that I've been struggling with my weight recently and when I cook, I tend to have an even tougher time sticking to my diet. I'm one of those people who can't stop picking at the food while they're cooking. What ends up happening is that I eat while I'm cooking, then I eat the actual meal, and if the kids end up leaving something on their plate, I end up picking at that, too, while I'm cleaning up. It's really selfish, but my solution to protecting myself from all that extra eating is simply not to cook. So while I feel like I might be doing better on my diet by not cooking, I feel like I'm doing worse as a parent.

We're going to talk in this book about a lot of powerful forces that you have to try to take your family back, but I'd say that bad eating habits are as important as any of them. And it's ironic, because out of all those things, what we eat is the easiest to control. Nobody else tells you what you put in your refrigerator—only you can make that choice. Yet if you're like me, you consistently make the wrong choices. And I really don't have any excuses—I've been blessed to be able to afford expensive organic foods, and I've got an incredible kitchen that gives me plenty of space to spread out and throw down.

My inability to make better choices with food is a very serious concern for me. One of my big fears as a mother is that I'm going to pass my dysfunctional relationship with food along to my kids. Both Joey and I love to eat, but despite our best intentions, we end up eating too much food that isn't good for us. Like a lot of African-Americans, we have a weak spot for comfort foods like fried chicken, macaroni and cheese, smothered pork, fried catfish—you name it. To make matters worse, we also have a craving for fast food. So if I'm not cooking, it's not like we're picking up a healthy alternative. Instead, I'm probably grabbing an extra-large bag from White Castle. I know it's wrong, but it's just proving very, very difficult to stop eating a certain way when I've been doing it for a long time.

Joey and I have tried to do better and have found some success at controlling our own weight by following the Weight Watchers points system. But even when we're doing well and being careful to count our points, we still usually end up falling off the wagon with a chicken wing here or a piece of cake there. Hopefully at some point we'll be able to adopt a healthy diet and actually stick with it. But whether we do or not, I'm most concerned about creating an environment that will lead our kids down the same path that we seem to be stuck on.

I'd be really sad if twenty years from now Diggy is still eating KFC and struggling with his weight, or JoJo's developed high blood pressure from eating too much junk food. But so far, thankfully, the children seem to be developing a better relationship with food than their parents have. Particularly Vanessa and Angela, who over the past few years have become very conscious of their diet and have made a real effort to eat right. They'll go out of their way to avoid sweets and instead eat salads, or healthy greens like spinach, kale, and bok choy. When I see them eating that way, it makes me very proud, because I know that they're building a foundation that's going to help them a lot when they're my age. In fact, I recently joked with them that "I want to be like you two when I grow up" when it comes to diet.

They're definitely doing better with eating healthy greens than their father. Let me tell you, getting Joey to eat greens is a real struggle. He'll eat a Caesar salad, but otherwise he's not really interested. When we were first married and I tried to cook him some veggies, his little comment to me was, "My mother knew I didn't like vegetables." In fact, Joey was so bad growing up that he used to take whatever veggies his mother had cooked and hide them behind the couch when no one was looking. When she finally found that nasty, rotting pile of veggies, she just stopped cooking them for him. And frankly, he hasn't really been eating any since.

Luckily, there is at least one person on Joey's side of the family who has a good relationship with food and has gone out of his way to share it with our kids: Uncle Russell. The first big thing he did was give Angela a video called *Diet for a New America*, which apparently (I'm going off what she told me, since no one else in our family would watch it) showed all the ways that eating a lot of red meat is bad for humans and bad for the environment. It must have been a pretty powerful video, because after she saw that, she was done with beef and pork for good. She'll still eat a little chicken and fish, but she won't touch the other stuff. I think it's great, because she now feels better about herself and her weight (although as we'll discuss later in the book, we do worry that she takes the dieting thing a little too far at times).

Uncle Russell also helped Russy by educating him about the dangers of drinking too much soda. Like most kids, Russy didn't put much thought into the effects that soda would have on him, but his uncle taught him that too much soda can lead to obesity and diabetes, can cause more cavities, and can even make it more likely for you to break your bones. After Russy heard all that, especially from the uncle whom he looks up to so much, he was done with soda for good.

If there is one thing that I feel positive about when it comes to our family's diet, it's that water has become the drink of choice in our house. Really, the whole family is fanatical about drinking water. Even Miley wants in on the action—she sees us drinking so much water that she'll begin to cry if we don't give her a water bottle and let her have some, too. We might still have a ways to go with what we're eating, but at least we seem to be drinking right.

If you want to take back your family from any bad eating habits it's developed, there are any number of steps you can take. Maybe you'll follow my lead and simply focus on cooking more and eating out less, and making sure your kids drink a lot of water instead of soda and juice. Or you might want to try some steps that have worked for my friends. For example, stop buying sugar cereal—if your kids want sugar on their cereal, let them put it on themselves at home. I know that's far from perfect, but at least it's a start. And if you are going to keep getting them fast food, limit it to once a week. Make it a special occasion for your family, not an everyday occurrence. Also try to have at least one dinner a month where your husband (if Mom is the one normally doing all the cooking) and the kids actually cook for the family themselves. By cooking themselves, they'll not only have a great appreciation for all the effort that goes into making their meals, they'll also have a greater appreciation for the ingredients, too. Instead of just taking their food for granted, they'll hopefully start to really think about what's going into their bodies and as a result become a little bit more focused on making healthy choices.

Now that Miley is with us, I'm very determined to learn from some of my past mistakes and make sure she develops very strong roots when it comes to eating healthy. I know that like most children, Miley will likely want to have her share of hamburgers, pizza, potato chips, and other junk foods. And that's fine, as long as those kinds of junk aren't the foundation that her relationship with food is built on. I really want her to grow up eating healthy, so that even though she might mess around with the junk when she's a kid, she'll return when she's older to that very healthy foundation that we helped build for her. And then in turn she'll hopefully be able to build a similar foundation for her kids one day. It's a process, but it's got to start somewhere. That's why as Miley grows up, I'm committed to taking back my kitchen and my house from the bad habits that I've allowed to develop over the years. And I hope that some of you will be able to make a similar commitment to your homes and your children.

## WE CAN ALL MAKE A COMMITMENT

I think the ups and downs my wife has gone through in order to help our family eat healthier serve as a reminder that no matter what we've been blessed with, no matter what kind of lifestyle we lead, there are always going to be times both big and small where we struggle to do our best. The key is to just keep working at it, to accept that raising a family is going to be an everyday struggle, but a struggle that you will overcome with faith, love, and commitment.

Try to remember that family is the one game in life where everyone is on an equal playing field. Black or white, rich or poor, ugly or beautiful, everyone really has the same opportunity and ability to raise a happy, loving family. Whether you live in the projects with a tiny kitchenette or in a mansion with a chef's kitchen, you can do more to help your family eat healthier. Whether they go to the fanciest private school around or one of the worst public schools in the city, you can talk to your kids every day and get involved in their school life. Whether you drive a Bentley or a beat-up Hyundai, you can give your kids a hug every day and tell them how much you love them. Whether you run the company or work in the mailroom, you can make a commitment to passing up the late-night dinners or drinks after work with your buddies to make sure your kids get the most of your time. And whether you have a million dollars in the bank or nothing but lint in your pockets, you can always be there for your family. Because in your family's eyes, just having you around is worth more than all the money in the world. And that's true for all of us.

## RUN'S TAKE BACK

While I really believe that "nothing is more fun than family," it's also important to recognize that fun doesn't just happen on its own. That's why if you want to take back the joy and happiness that should come with raising a family, you must accept that one of your main jobs is to constantly *create* fun in your household.

Personally, I'm always looking for ways I can interject some fun into our home, which is why sometimes I like to call myself "Rev Fun." If I come home and feel like the energy is too low, I'm going to find the boys and make them play a game of H-O-R-S-E with me, or grab Russy and challenge him to a game of Pac-Man (of course, only after he's finished his homework), or make Angela go for a swim with me. Even if they say, "Naw, Dad. I don't feel like playing," or "I'm not going to jump in the pool, Dad. I can't get my hair wet!" I'm going to keep pushing until they give in. In fact, I recently decided to start something called "Camp Fun," where I had Diggy and Russy invite some of their friends over for a sleepover party. I put them through basketball drills, brought out my DJ equipment and taught them how to dance, had a marshmallow cookout, and even regaled them with some of my stories about touring with Run DMC. Russy and Diggy were rolling their eyes when I first told them about "Camp Fun," but by the end they admitted that everyone had a great time.

And even when money was tight and we didn't have a house with a pool and a basketball court and room for the kids' friends to sleep over, we still always found ways to have fun. Maybe it was a train ride into the city to go to a museum. Or a trip out to the beach. Or we'd hit a street fair somewhere. All those activities were free, but they were lots of fun, too.

If you feel like the fun is missing from your household, then try to set up your own version of Camp Fun. At least once a month, set aside a time for the entire family to get together in the pursuit of fun. Your kids might complain that it sounds like a stupid idea, or complain that they're not interested, but don't give in to their protests. Commit your family to having fun, even if you have to drag them kicking and screaming. Because in order to take back your family, you're going to have to show your kids where the fun is at first. Or to put it even more plainly, get off your butts, Mr. and Mrs. America, and go play with your kids!

Finally, I want to mention that it's also very helpful to create a set of rituals with your children. When your children have a certain activity that they grow accustomed to sharing with you on a regular basis, it helps create a special bond between you and them. A bond that will last long after the ritual has been replaced or even forgotten.

For instance, a few times every week Diggy and I like to take a ride to the skating rink while listening to a new album. This past week it's been Jay-Z's *American Gangster*. We've had a great time turning up the speakers full blast and just rocking out the entire way, either singing along with the album or making up our own rhymes. These sessions are our little secrets— his mother knows where we're going, but not what's happening during the trip—and it's turned into a very special time for both of us. In fact, if I'm ever out of town for a few days, one of the first things I want to do when I get back is take a drive to the skate park with Diggy.

For Russy and me, our little ritual is to get into my bed and then order movies off pay-per-view. We don't normally let the kids into our room that much, so for Russy it's really a special treat. Without any of his brothers or sisters around to steal my attention, he really likes to snuggle up in our bed and watch a movie with his father.

JoJo's too cool now to cuddle up and watch movies with

his dad, so our ritual has become hanging out together in our basement recording studio and discussing the rap game. We like to sit around listening to beats and talking about who's hot on the mic, who's not, and why. We'll also analyze the business side of the game, and I'll try to explain why advances are for suckers and how it's much more important to own your publishing rights. We'll get together for a few of these conversations every week, and they've become sessions that we both really look forward to.

Vanessa and Angela aren't around enough anymore to have set rituals with, but I still remember one we used to share when they were much younger. Around that time, I was on the road a lot and going through a divorce with my first wife. I didn't get to be around them as much as I would have liked. But every time I did come home, I used to take them to a place out on Freeport, Long Island, called Nathan's Fun House. It had lots of rides and video games, and the girls used to love spending hours eating hot dogs and going on these rides over and over again. It got to be that every time Daddy came home, that was the ritual: Go to Nathan's and play on the rides. And I believe having that constant in our relationship helped us weather a difficult time for our family.

That's why I recommend trying to institute some sort of rituals in your own family. It could be something as simple as reading a short book to your child every night before he goes to sleep. It could be taking your daughter out for a slice of her favorite pizza after each of her soccer games. Or it could be spending half an hour with your son every night reviewing his homework. Any activity is fine as long as it can help establish a ritual in your relationship with your child. Children learn from rituals. And when you create a special ritual with your children, what they're learning is that they are loved.

## CHAPTER 3

# Clean Out Your Clutter, Not Your Children

We've had a lot of memorable episodes on *Run's House*, but judging from the feedback I get, one that our fans especially loved was when I insisted that we clean out all of the junk in our pool house. Admittedly, an episode about me throwing out old pogo sticks, old fans, my wife's prized collection of *Oprah* magazines, and all the other junk (no offense, Oprah) that was sitting there unloved might not seem like particularly compelling television. So why did people love to watch us chucking all that junk? I suspect it was because most of us, whether we realize it or not, have all felt like we're losing not only ourselves, but our families as well, to the clutter we create. That's why when it comes to successfully raising a family, one of my favorite mottoes is, "Get rid of your trash, not your children!"

In other words, stop creating barriers between you and your family with things you no longer love and therefore no longer need! I realize that the threat of losing your family to trash might seem exaggerated, but it's a very real phenomenon. You won't literally have to go looking for them under a pile of old clothes, but the negative energy created by the clutter in your home *will* erect a psychological barrier between you and your loved ones. Conversely, many successful parents know that one of the most effective ways to build a *strong* family is to keep their homes clutter free. They've learned that when you unburden your home from all the things that you don't need to keep anymore, you can start to pay some attention to the thing that is the most important—your children.

Like most steps that lead toward success, clearing out your clutter is a spiritual as well as a physical process. Truth be told, the reason I was so passionate about clearing out our pool house was because I realized that all that junk in there was a manifestation of our minds. Those objects weren't filling up the pool house because we didn't have anywhere else to put them—our house is more than ten thousand square feet in size! We could have found plenty of places to store that stuff if we'd really wanted to! Instead, the pool house ended up looking like that because our minds weren't as neat and ordered as they should have been. The state that the pool house had fallen into was like an alarm to me, a warning that somehow as a family we must have lost a little bit of our direction. That episode was a reminder that when our thoughts and hearts aren't focused on the right things, that lack of clarity and order will always be reflected in our physical lives.

One of our goals for this chapter is to teach you how to make the connection between physical clutter and a lack of spiritual clarity in your own home. As you will see, we really believe that throwing out old toys is only one step in reclaiming your family from clutter. It's also important to make sure your children truly appreciate not only the physical toys, but all of the gifts they are given. In many ways, clutter reflects a lack of gratitude. And children that are not grateful for what they have been given will always block blessings that might have otherwise come their way.

I sometimes see that lack of gratitude in my own children, which is why I often have to remind them of one of my mottoes, "I'm Rich, and You're Not." In other words, they need to remember that just because my wife and I make money, they don't have a green light to spend it. Yes, our children have toys, but we also work very hard to make sure that they never feel entitled to them. And when we do see little signs of entitlement starting to pop up, we make sure to get them back in line with the quickness! A sense of gratitude, rather than a sense of entitlement, must always pervade a household in order for it to be healthy and prosperous.

## DON'T BLOCK YOUR BLESSINGS

I'm sure some of you are saying, "Wow, I bought this book to learn more about family and instead this dude is talking about throwing out old magazines? Isn't there something more serious he should be addressing?" While I can understand that reaction, I can also promise that I have learned through experience that cleaning out clutter is actually a very, very critical step toward maintaining a happy family. Why? First, there's the physical aspect. Have you ever walked into a house that's filled with clutter? I'm not talking about a house where there are a few things that need to be put away here and there. I'm talking about a house or an apartment that's nasty—really messy and filled with junk. If you have, your first thought was probably, "How can this person live like this?" But your next thought was probably one of concern for the person, because you can sense that the physical mess in front of you represents a much larger problem in the person's emotional life. And you'd probably be correct. That's because clutter doesn't just collect dust or take up floor space. Clutter actually stops good things from happening in people's lives. When God sees that you've stopped appreciating the things that he's given you, those blessings will grind to a halt. That's why you must get rid of the stuff you aren't appreciating if you want God, or the universe in general, to breathe any new blessings into your life. Think of clutter as a dam that's creating stagnation and stopping the waters of your life from flowing freely.

That stench of stagnation and decay is why I react so strongly to clutter. In fact, I dislike clutter so much that I don't even like *writing* about it, let alone living with it. Just putting these words down on paper makes me feel like I'm going to have trouble breathing, or break out in hives. It has a physical effect on me. A few years back I was just coming out of a rough period in my life when I noticed that all my cars had tinted windows. I'd had them done up that way so I'd appear to be that cool cat when people saw me. But instead of making me look cool, I realized the tint was actually creating clutter in my car. By separating me from the world, that tint was actually causing all my negative energy to stagnate while I drove. Sure enough, when I took all the tint off the windows, I immediately started feeling much better.

That's why I work so hard to make sure that everything in our home is free from the claustrophobic energy created by clutter. I can be feeling down, but when I walk into an open, uncluttered space I suddenly feel free again. Every time time I throw out a piece of junk, I feel like I'm creating more breathing space for myself in this world. I feel healthier. I see movement and possibilities instead of stagnation and dead ends. I see a bright window to the world instead of those dark tints keeping me an outsider.

I will admit that not everyone in my family shares my passion (OK, they might even call it an obsession) about clutter. It's certainly been a battle to get my kids to throw away the things they don't love anymore. If I walk into their room and see piles of clothes on the floor, or boxes of clothes stacked up in their closets, I'll scream and yell until they get rid of it. It was a particular struggle with the girls, who liked to keeps tons of clothes in their rooms even though they never intended to wear half that stuff again. But once I wore them down and made them get rid of the clothes, they admitted that they felt better without all the junk clogging up their closets and their lives.

My wife, however, is another story. We have definitely had some disagreements over throwing things out. I suspect that it's because she's a Sagittarius (who are typically sentimental and procrastinators) while I'm a Scorpio (who are typically passionate and impulsive). So while I love to see the garbage cans fill up with unloved stuff, she has a very, very difficult time letting go of certain things. I'll let her explain.

Well, it is true that I'm inclined to hold on to things more than my husband, mainly because I get very sentimental about old things and don't want to throw them away. I especially don't like to get rid of any old photos of my kids or things I associate with them—when I do that, I feel like I'm disrespecting my children in some way. I don't know if it showed or not, but I was really very upset during the pool-house episode. Every time we tossed something into one of the trash bins, it felt like I was losing something irreplaceable.

Still, I have to admit that my husband's instincts were correct. Despite my protests, at the end of that day I didn't miss any of those things. And I did feel like the house was freer and more focused with all that junk gone. So while it's in my nature to hold on to things, I'm trying to learn how to let them go. I'm making progress, and I think my last big hurdle is my magazine collection. I keep a big stack of decorating magazines next to my bed to read at night, which of course drives my husband crazy. But now I've developed a little trick—when I see something I like in *Oprah* or in *Better Homes and Gardens*, I just cut out the article that I want and put it in a folder to read later. That way I get to keep what interests me, but I don't have to have fifteen magazines piled next to my bed, creating clutter in our bedroom. Which is a room that should always feel free and open. Again, I admit that clipping out magazine articles might seem like a very small step, but I have come to believe that the more I can move toward a clutter-free home, the more time and energy I'll have for my children and my husband.

Seeing my wife make those kinds of strides (I believe they're bigger than just "steps") really makes me happy. I'm excited for what it means for our family, but also for what it could mean for yours. Because if a pack rat like Justine can come around, then I really believe that *anyone* can make that change. The big question is how. The first thing I'd recommend is looking around your home and making an honest assessment of what you really need versus what's just taking up space. Once you've done that, then look inside and tell yourself, "No matter how much attachment I feel for these things, I am going to find a mental space where I'm OK with letting them go." And once you've made that peace, then physically get rid of your clutter, even if you have to start slowly. No need to get crazy like me and start throwing things into trash bins. You can start by simply tossing an old magazine here or a beat-up pair of sneakers there, until you start to realize that letting those things go doesn't hurt so bad. That knowledge will create its own momentum, and you'll soon be cutting yourself free from the webs of clutter that have entangled you.

And if you have trouble with even those first steps, try to focus on the fact that there will be a reward for your actions. Instead of obsessing about whether you might want to wear those old sneakers again, try to focus on understanding that by tossing those old sneakers, you're allowing new things to come into your life. Maybe it will be a fresh pair of kicks to replace the old ones you'd been holding on to. Or maybe instead of a pair of sneakers to walk around in, your unclogged blessings will include something much greater, like a new car to ride in. Or a new house to live in! There's really no limit to the blessings that can flow into an uncluttered life.

If you still don't believe me, consider this analogy. If you've ever gotten a colonic, then you know that you feel much better after you've flushed all of that stuff out of your body. Your organs begin to flow better, you're less constipated, your skin clears up, your hair starts to look a little shinier, and you become more vibrant in general. Why? Because you've flushed so much unnecessary stuff out of your body. Well, getting rid of that clutter is going to be similar to a spiritual colonic (sorry if that's a little nasty, but I think clutter is nasty, too!) for your family. I promise, when you lose all that weight, the blessings for your family are going to spring open and it's going to be so rewarding.

Another benefit of clearing out clutter is that it helps free us from our obsessions with the past. Many of us get so caught up reliving the past that we never spend any time appreciating the present. I believe that when someone insists on holding on to an old shirt that they can't even fit into anymore, or an old record when they don't even own a turntable anymore, it's symptomatic of an unwillingness to let go of the past. I try very hard to avoid doing that, because I know that if my family perceives me as being stuck in the past, it's going to have a very negative affect on my ability to lead them into the future. It's great to reminisce and pay tribute to the past, but too many odes to the past in a house can become a form of clutter, too.

That's why if you've seen my house on TV, you might have noticed that I don't have all the gold records and magazine covers from my Run DMC days up on the walls. (There is one picture of the group up in our kitchen, put there by a producer from MTV, so I let it stay because I like that it shows me, D, and Jay together.) Almost all of those mementos are packed away down in the basement, where they belong. And if it weren't for my children's interest in them, I might even throw them away. I see those mementos as keys to doors that don't lead to anywhere I want to go anymore. Since they don't open the right doors, why bother keeping them? It's not that I'm not proud of what I've accomplished in the past, or thankful for those experiences. Rather, I don't want my family, and the world at large, to think that I'm content to live off my memories. Because when I let those memories pile up around me, taking up space not only on my walls but in my soul, too, I'll be blocking opportunities for new, exciting things to come into my life. I don't care if I sold a billion records in the past; anyone with a sense of how this world works knows that you must always stay relevant and push forward. And relevant is something I always want to be—both inside my home and out in the world. That's why if you look at the pictures in my house, you'll see that they're mostly of my lovely wife and beautiful children. Because my family is my present *and* my future.

## ADDRESSING ADULT CLUTTER

Having talked about the dangers of physical clutter, now I want to speak about the spiritual clutter that tends to build up in our lives. Because while electronic games that don't get played anymore, clothes that don't get worn anymore, and DVDs that don't get watched anymore can create obstacles in your life, that's mainly kid stuff. It's what I call "adult clutter" that's really the biggest threat to your family.

When I speak of "adult clutter," you might think I'm referring to material objects like cars, jewelry, or fur coats. But those kind of toys just reflect some of the larger problems in our lives. In my experience, the things that truly weigh down most adults are their vices, not their de-vices. I'm talking about vices like infidelity and excessive drinking and drugs. Habits that might start simply as ways to pass the time, but soon begin to take up so much space in our lives that they ultimately separate us from our families. Too often we see a one-night stand become a long-term affair, an affair that creates clutter between you and your family. Similarly, when a few drinks with your buddies after work, or a blunt with your boys before watching the game, becomes your hobby, then you're creating obstacles between you and your family. You might tell yourself that you're just looking to unwind, but what you're really doing is blocking blessings with your clutter. You don't need another woman to spice up your life—your family is all the excitement you need! You don't need to smoke a blunt to find some peace—your family will help you unwind more than that weed! Trust me, I've been there. I used to think that happiness was inside a bag of weed, or a stranger's bed, but thankfully I've healed myself by clearing all that clutter out of my life. And you can heal yourself, too, when you realize that you never need to go outside of your family to find happiness. You've already got everything you need at home.

## PROMOTE AN ATTITUDE OF GRATITUDE

In the first part of this chapter, we addressed the importance of cleansing your home of the toys and clothes that your kids no longer love. So now seems like a good time to address a larger issue that troubles many parents, which is how to teach their children to respect and appreciate the material things they've been blessed with. To help them establish an attitude of gratitude. Or to put it even more simply, how to make sure that their butts don't get too spoiled.

If you don't want to spoil your kids, the first thing you have to do is accept that the responsibility lies with you and you alone. As much as they'd like to, most kids can't buy themselves all the things that they want. Only parents can bankroll that kind of excess. And the parents who do are usually the ones who also feel guilty about their parenting. If you are one of those people, please try to get past that temptation and understand that excessive gifts will not correct the problems you have created. As much as you might wish it were so, buying your kids every present they want will not make you a better parent. If anything, it's only going to spoil your kids worse than they already are.

I realize some of you might think I'm guilty of the very things I'm preaching against. I've heard people say, "I love that show, but Reverend Run's kids are so spoiled!" And after seeing Angela and JoJo get new cars for their graduations, I can understand why people might think that. But, as I promise to explain in greater detail in the next chapter, my kids are not spoiled! In fact, far from it! And one of the reasons I won't let them get spoiled is because I was spoiled a bit myself growing up, and I can see now how it hindered my development.

When I was growing up, my father often tried to express his great love for me through gifts. I can distinctly remember a period (I think it was right after he had gone away for a while) when he started bringing home presents to me almost every night. The gifts weren't fancy—they cost maybe a buck or two each, at the most—but to me they were mind-blowing. It was as if every day was Christmas.

Unfortunately, I learned in time that there's a reason we only cele-brate Christmas once a year—when you get used to receiving things without earning them, you tend to become very spoiled.

Those gifts probably didn't do it alone, but over time I definitely developed the mentality that I deserved whatever I wanted from life. And for a while, the world didn't challenge my mentality. Run DMC was the hottest thing you'd ever seen, and it seemed like everything I touched turned to gold. But when the well eventually began to run dry, I wasn't prepared to deal with the repercussions. I was so used to getting whatever I wanted that I had no idea how to deal with failure. In fact, my father later admitted that he had made a mistake in giving me too much. "Joey," he told me, "the problem is that I made it so you never really had to pay before." My father had only wanted me to feel loved and to be confident, but I also needed to learn how to be humble, too. Now that I have struggled a bit in life, I've learned that while it's great to expect success and feel entitled to happiness, it's even more important to be grounded.

And that's a lesson Justine and I are committed to teaching our own children. While we want our children to feel loved and confi-dent, we also never want them to feel entitled to things. And for the most part, I feel we've done a good job at living in that balance. Still, there are definitely moments when we sense that our kids are just expecting a new toy, or new clothes, rather than hoping that they'll be rewarded with it for their hard work. And when those mo-ments arise, I go out of my way to remind my kids, in a very loud voice, that "I'm Rich, and You're Not!"

## I'M RICH, AND YOU'RE NOT!

Before I get into the heart of this section, I want to make it clear that I'm not trying to be arrogant or condescending by referring to myself as "rich." While there have been times that I've been blessed with considerable wealth, I've also experienced times when financial blessings were withheld from me. But no matter what my bank statements have looked like, my message to my kids has always remained the same: "I'm rich, and you're not." Because whether you have $300 or $300,000 in the bank, in your child's eyes you'll always be rich. Whether it's a toddler who wants an ice cream cone or a teenager who wants some ice on his wrist, you're going to be the person they expect to make it happen. That's why it's critical for them to understand that the money you spend on them is spent at *your* discretion. Never theirs. When it comes to how the family funds get allocated, the children should never call the shots. As soon as children start to think of *your* money as *their* money, then you've lost control of your house. It's a constant battle, and even though we feel our kids have their heads on pretty straight when it comes to money and toys, little outbursts of entitlement still pop up every now and then. Justine can tell you about one of them.

I agree with my Joey that overall our children have done a very good job at not expecting things from us. But it is also true that there are moments where they get out of line and start thinking that *our* credit cards have *their* names on them. They've all done it before, but I'm going to pick on Diggy here because his example is still very fresh in my mind.

I recently sent Diggy to the mall with Jessica, one of our babysitters. I gave her a little money for food, but that was it since I was under the impression that they were just going to hang out. So imagine my surprise when an hour or so later Diggy called me and in a very rude voice said, "How come you didn't give Jessica enough money for us to go shopping?!" His tone implied that I was totally insane for not giving Jessica enough money for him to buy stuff with. Frankly, it had never even occurred to me, because in my day, going to the mall was all about looking around and window shopping, not necessarily buying things. I guess Diggy had started to develop different expectations about what happens when you go to the mall. And

what really upset me is that I hadn't noticed that lack of gratitude in him earlier. In fact, if I had heard another boy his age
speak that way with his mother, I probably would have said to
myself, "Hmph. I know Diggy wouldn't start that nonsense with
me!" But here he was on the other end of the phone, acting very
spoiled and rude.

I really got after him when he got home that afternoon.
Dig's not a crier, but when he saw how mad I was, his eyes did
well up a bit. His attitude went very quickly from a stanky "Why
didn't you give me any money?" to a sincere-sounding "Okay,
I'm sorry, Mom! I'm sorry." While I was relieved that he seemed
to understand where he had gone wrong, I was still surprised
that he'd even gone there in the first place. That's why it's very
important to remember that no matter how hard you work to
make your children stay humble, that sense of entitlement can
still grow in them overnight.

In fact, let me pick on JoJo a little bit here too, not only to
make things fair, but also to show again how a genuinely humble and grounded kid can still lose that attitude of gratitude.
Just the other day I was thinking about him, so I picked up my
BlackBerry and sent him an e-mail. "Make sure you thank God
for your life, because you really have a nice life here. Just make
sure he knows you appreciate it," I wrote him. "You might feel
like you don't have time, but you always have time to thank
God. I do it when I lie down at night. Or if I have a really good
feeling inside my heart, I try to stop whatever I'm doing and
just acknowledge that feeling for a second. That way God knows
that at the very least I'm aware of what he's giving me." Then I
hit "send" and waited for a response. And waited. And waited. I
began to get upset, because while I figured that while the most
I'd get back was an "OK, Mom," or "Gotcha," at least then I would
know that he'd heard the message. But he never responded.
And outside of the fact that I felt it was disrespectful for him
not to reply to me, I was also concerned that he hadn't ab-

sorbed what I was trying to share with him. I got on his case
when he finally came home, but of course he gave me that old
teenage rap that all mothers hear these days, "I did write you
back, Mom. I wrote back, 'OK.' Your BlackBerry must not be
working or something. . . ." Maybe he did write me back, or
maybe he didn't. But the incident was just another reminder to
me of how important it is that we stay on these kids about having an attitude of gratitude.

I should say that I'm not only picking on Diggy and JoJo
here, because all the kids have had moments where they
wanted a certain thing and then given me the side eye when
I've said no. It is a constant battle to make them understand
that they're not going to get something just because they want
it. Or even worse, that they can bully you into getting them
something. If you let them bully or pout their way into a toy,
you are creating a monster that will become very difficult to
control. We've all seen kids throwing tantrums and causing
scenes in the mall. That's why you have to really show these
kids that they can't get everything they want. We're not saying
no to that toy because we're selfish, we're saying no because we
care about your future. It's funny—you would think that the
more you give your kids, the more it would make them happy
and grateful. But it seems that the way God made it, or the universe made it, is that the more you give a child, the more bratty
and selfish he becomes. It's like you've given him a thirst that
can't be quenched.

Sometimes I have to shake my head at our kids, because I
just don't think they realize how good they have it. For them,
it's nothing to jump on a plane and go on vacation in St. Bart's
or Las Vegas. I keep telling them that I never went on an air-
plane when I was little. For us, just driving to Hershey Park was
a very big deal. But for them, it's nothing to ride around in a
Bentley or a new Benz. I can remember Joey telling me about
how he always used to be jealous of his brother Russell be-

cause Russell used to get to sit in the back window of their station wagon. Forget a sports car—it was a big deal just to get the back window all to yourself!

That's why I think I need to keep reminding them to be thankful, and not to assume that this is "just how it is." As I like to say to our kids, we play our part and you play your part. Our part is to remind you to be thankful, and your part is to seem sincerely thankful. And if you play your part well, then you'll be happy with how we play ours. But if you're acting up in school, or taking things for granted, then we're going to be less free with what we get you.

It's true, Justine and I are constantly fretting about the kids becoming too used to getting what they want, when they want. And it's not just about getting new things—we also work very hard to make sure that they do a better job of appreciating the toys they already have. As I said earlier in this chapter, no matter how much it costs, a gift that's not being used is only creating clutter and promoting wastefulness in your home. We saw this recently with Russy, when he asked us to buy him a new digital toy called a Milo. I'm still not exactly sure what a Milo is (which was probably part of the problem), but it seemed to be some sort of device that lets you send e-mails, listen to music, chat online, and a lot of other stuff that seems very cool to an eleven-year-old. So even though I didn't know exactly how the thing worked, and even though it cost almost $600, I decided to buy one because Russy seemed so excited about it. Unfortunately, when he got home, none of us, not even our genius babysitter, could figure out how to make the thing work. Now it just sits in his room and never gets used, which really pisses me off. And I'm not upset because it was $600 down the drain. I'm upset that the thing isn't being loved and is creating clutter. I'll preach it again: Keeping clutter around the house will ultimately cost you way more than $600. Clutter will block all sorts of blessings from coming into your home.

A final example of having to remind my kids that "I'm Rich, and You're Not" was the time I sent Vanessa and Angela apartment hunting in Manhattan. I had agreed to pay the rent on their own place, but when we had our initial conversation about apartment hunting, I could tell they didn't have a sense of just how expensive it is to live in New York City. Still, instead of sending them out with a set budget, I let them go without any guidelines so they could learn just what a big difference there was between what they *wanted* and what they could *afford*.

Of course, they immediately headed out to the flyest places they could think of, even looking at a $14 million duplex at Trump Tower! In their minds, they lived in a fly house in Jersey, so why shouldn't they be able to live in something just as fly in Manhattan? It never occurred to them that the type of lifestyle we are blessed with in Jersey is basically beyond our blessings in the city. So when I shut down the Trump Tower talk and told them what I could actually afford, which was closer to $2,000 a month, their perspective changed very quickly. And when they went out with the new budget, instead of views of Central Park, they found themselves looking at places with warped floors, tiny bedrooms, and bars on the windows. The new places were in the same borough as Trump Tower, but that was about it! And while they were definitely disappointed at first, I believe the experience gave them a much greater appreciation for the lifestyle they have been blessed with. Seeing all those busted-up apartments made them more grateful for what they already had. And how hard it is to get it.

Again, I want to make it clear that I'm not knocking my children or anyone out there for enjoying the flyer things in life. That would be very hypocritical of me. God willing, there's always going to be a slick car sitting out in front of my house. And I don't see anything wrong with that, since I'm not one of these guys who buys a fancy car and then sticks it in a garage somewhere because he's afraid to get a scratch on it. My cars make me feel too good for them to sit under wraps in a garage. To me, that's just creating high-priced clutter. I'll drive a Rolls to Boston Market or to the gym because just sitting in it makes me feel happy. I believe that as long as you use and appreciate your toys, then it's fine to acquire nice things. As I say, "Nothing is too good for us. We are sons and daughters of the most high." As long as my toys don't take me away from my family, I don't feel like my toys are creating clutter or spoiling anyone.

Vanessa and Angela's trip to Trump Tower notwithstanding, one interesting thing that I've noticed is that my older kids are not quite as wasteful as the younger ones. Maybe because they grew up in the 'hood and tasted some hardships, they have a better appreciation for the value of things. With Diggy and Russy, who were essentially born into wealth, it's a little bit more of a struggle. A very small example of this, but one that really gets under my skin, is their attitude toward bottled water. Nothing, I mean nothing, drives me crazier than coming downstairs and seeing three or four half-drunk bottled waters sitting on the kitchen counter! Because I know that the next time they're thirsty, they'll come into the kitchen and, since they can't remember which bottle they were drinking from before, they'll take out a fresh one. Then they'll only drink half of it, put it down, run off and then repeat the same cycle an hour later. To me, that is pure waste! I did try to get them to write their names on the bottles they were using, but that never caught on. So my response was to make water bottles off limits for them. If they're thirsty and I see them digging in the fridge for a bottled water, I tell them, "Use cups!" Again, it might seem like a small matter, but to me it's actually a very big deal. Because wasting water, or wasting anything for that matter, is the opposite of wealth in my book. It's sheer silliness that will keep us from having a truly wealthy and wise house.

## ENFORCE GRATITUDE

Since it's so easy, especially for children, to become wasteful and spoiled, one of my main duties as a father is to enforce behavior that goes against those attitudes. Some fathers might focus on enforcing curfews, or enforcing rules or punishments, but in our house, my primary responsibility is to enforce an attitude of gratitude.

Despite being a bit spoiled growing up, gratitude has become a part of who I am. Since I come from the 'hood, it's hard to forget how bad many people still have it. And conversely, how great God has been to me. So that's why if I wake up a little grumpy because my back hurts when I bend over to tie my shoes, I snap out of it by thinking about all the people laid up in hospital beds, unable to move an *inch* by themselves. Just thinking of those people makes me say, "Thank God for my legs!" Or if I get a little upset when I open the fridge and don't see the snack I'm looking for, all I have to do is think about all those dudes in jail, fighting over cookies and cigarettes. And when I think about having to live a reality like that, I'm grateful that I even have a fridge and that I'm free to get in my car and go get food wherever I want. I know that instead of worrying about whether my snack is using up too many points, I need to be saying to God, "Thank you so much for my big fridge with the ice machine and the deep freezer and every morsel of food you've seen fit to ever put in it!"

It's important that I live up to the standard of gratitude that I expect from my children, because if I failed to do that, then my words would just ring hollow. I believe my children have generally accepted my teachings about gratitude, but what really drove it home for them was when Victoria Anne died. I don't want to go into the baby's passing too much at this moment, because Justine is going to address it in greater detail later in the book. But I do consider that day as an example of when I pushed myself to the boundaries of thankfulness and found that it was truly part of my core being. When we were sitting in that hospital room after Victoria died, the pain and the sorrow was palpable. Yet through all that sadness, I heard a little voice in my mind saying, "You still have sooo much to be thankful for. Your wife is hurt, but she made it through this alive. Be thankful for that. You children are upset, but they're still beautiful and are still going to have incredible lives. Be thankful for that.

You're unsure of how to handle this situation, but you have your spiritual mentor with you, and he's going to help you find the strength to say the right things to your family. Be thankful for that." And after I heard that voice, I turned to my wife and said, "Baby, you still have to be thankful." And while she and the kids probably thought I was crazy at the time, I was deadly serious. I wanted my family to be as deeply thankful in that moment of pure heartbreak as we'd ever been sitting by the ocean at St. Bart's. I wanted them to remember that it's easy to be thankful during the good times. But to be able to say "Thanks" during the terrible, dark moments is when you cement the culture of gratitude in your family. And sure enough, Vanessa later told me that while even she had had her doubts about the level of my own gratitude, that moment in the hospital room sealed it for her. To hear me say that, despite all the pain, made her think, "Wow, this guy is for real. He really is thankful for everything." And her appreciation of that moment meant a lot to me.

Of course, the example I just used is a very, very extreme one. In day-to-day life, it's very hard for children to see past their own wants and needs and adopt an attitude of gratitude. Since they haven't experienced as much, it is difficult for them to understand how fortunate they are, or how hard someone else has worked to make their lives easier. They simply don't have the context to appreciate their blessings yet. For instance, when my dad brought me all those toys back when I was a boy, I'm sure I didn't say, "Wow, Dad, you've been working all day and probably just wanted to go home and chill, but you still took some extra time to go to a store and pick out this gift for me. I really appreciate that." Instead, I probably just mumbled, "Thanks, Pop," grabbed the toy, and ran off. Similarly, kids whose parents always drive fancy cars aren't going to say, "You know, Mom, thanks for always having a nice car for us to drive around in. You must have worked very hard to be able to buy this car for us." They just accept it as something that's naturally part of their world, like food or a roof over their head. Just like most kids who go to expensive private schools probably never tell their parents, "I realize that the tuition you are paying is really expensive, and I want you to know that I am going to do everything I possibly can to get the most out of this experience." Instead, most kids getting sent to private schools not only never express their gratitude, they probably grumble about the dress code, or that the teachers are mean, or that they have too much homework. Gratitude is not something that comes naturally to kids. It was true for me and it was probably true for you, too. That's why it's so critical that as parents we don't just hope for gratitude in our homes—we must enforce it.

As a parent, you must keep your finger on the pulse of the level of gratitude in your house. If your kids seem relatively thankful for the sacrifices that are made for them, then it's not necessary to ride them too hard. Treat them to the things they like, indulge them a bit if that's what feels good to you—after all, family should always be fun. But at the same time, always keep your ear to the street. The moment that you hear those first rustles of ungratefulness and selfishness, act at once. The gifts might have to stop, the treats might have to go away until the kids get the message and realize that a lack of gratitude won't be tolerated.

One way we promote an attitude of gratitude in our home is by insisting that everyone answer the phone by saying, "Praise the Lord." I don't care if it's one of Angela's friends calling, the guy who cleans the pool, or the head of MTV. Every call that comes into my house is going to be answered with "Praise the Lord." And since our phone is always ringing, we're ensuring that every day we thank God for all the blessings we've been given. We might forget to thank Him when we ride in our nice cars, or sit by our beautiful pool, or even when we say our prayers. But at least by answering the phone with "Praise the Lord," even in our forgetfulness, we still remember to show a little bit of our gratitude.

I encourage everyone reading this to implement a similar policy in their own home. Maybe answering the phone "Praise the Lord" feels too intense or out of character for you. If that's the case, then try to lead a little prayer of thanks before every meal. Or if you're not comfortable with that, then look to create some other sort of ritual in your home that will instill a culture of gratitude. Maybe it's having your children make a daily list of all the things that happened during their day that they are grateful for. Maybe it means you and your spouse need to make a similar list with them. Maybe it's organizing a monthly group activity, like working in a soup kitchen, or going to an old-age home—something that will remind everyone of just how good your life is. Or maybe it's simply remembering to smile and show your child some love when you see or hear him go out of his way to say "thank you" to someone else.

Whatever ritual you create, be consistent with it. Because when you are vigilant in making sure that a culture of gratitude is present in every corner of your house, and in every inch of your family's hearts, then your family will truly prosper. It's very simple. The more your family says "thank you," the more you will have to be thankful for.

And that's really the message of this chapter. A happy, successful, and functional family is going to be the one that's thankful for what it's got. And in order to reach that mind-set, clutter must be removed, entitlement must be nipped in the bud, and gratitude must be enforced. When you can take even those small steps, you'll really be making giant strides toward taking back your family.

## RUN'S TAKE BACK

Hopefully some of these words have motivated you to purge your house of whatever is clogging it up. If so, then you can take the exact same steps we took in the pool-house episode. Pull out the trash cans and just start packing up the things you don't need anymore. And once you've got all that stuff packed up, don't just throw it away. Instead, take it all to the Salvation Army or the Red Cross or whoever accepts used clothes and goods in your area and help create a blessing for someone who is less fortunate than you are. I do this every few months with my old clothes, and it feels sooooo great. I throw them all in a big box and then drive it to my supermarket, where they take donations. And when I get back home, even though I'm empty-handed, I feel so much richer than I did at the start of the day.

And as I mentioned earlier in this chapter, it's also very important to take back your children from any sense of entitlement they might be feeling by enforcing gratitude in your household. And one way you can do that is by imposing a "new things" freeze in your home. In other words, for a fixed period of time—maybe it's a month, or, if you'd like to go really hard, even six months—let your kids know that you won't be buying them any new things. You might want to make an exception for items related to school (i.e., new sneakers for basketball, or a new calculator for math class), but otherwise they're going to have to do a better job appreciating what they already have. Instead of getting that new iPod or Sidekick, they'll get a month to appreciate just how great their old cell phone really is. Instead of getting them a new sweater, let them appreciate just how warm their old sweater keeps them. Instead of buying them the new pair of sunglasses that they want so bad, let them pull that old pair of glasses out of the closet and appreciate just how well they can block out the sun, too. And then after that month has passed, or for however long you want to go, you can start bringing new toys back into their lives. But I believe the more you can put a freeze on those toys, the more your children will begin to appreciate the toys they already have.

And speaking of toys, try to set a good example for your children by cutting back on the shiny and flashy things in your life, as well. I know I said that vices, not *de*-vices, are what creates the most clutter in adults' lives, but we still all probably have a few toys that it wouldn't hurt to cut back on. In my life, it's probably cars. As much as I love my Lamborghini, my Rolls-Royce Phantom, and the Bentley I just bought my wife, having all those fancy cars in the driveway probably isn't sending my kids the right message about spending their money wisely. It's getting harder to tell JoJo, "I'm rich, and you're not!" when he sees a Rolls-Royce in the driveway every day. So maybe this year, as much as it pains me to even write this, I've decided that I'm going to at least trade in the Lamborghini and go with something a little more sensible. Instead of paying $7,000 a month for one car, I can pay a grand (which is still a lot) and use the money I've saved to do something nice for my family.

Try to take a hard look at your own life and find some wastefulness and flash that you might be able to trim. Maybe it's trading down when it comes to your cars. Maybe instead of getting the new fur coat you've been eyeing, you take your old parka out of the mothballs for one more winter. Or instead of getting the forty-inch flat-screen TV that you've been salivating over, you stick with your old TV that's not as big but is working just fine. If you can make some of those small sacrifices when it comes to your own toys, you'll have a much easier time diminishing the power that toys and material items will hold over your children.

## CHAPTER 4

# Examples Move the World More Than Doctrine

As I alluded to in the introduction, I'm not the kind of preacher you're going to find at the front of a church every Sunday, quoting Scripture and leading the choir. I've never been quite comfortable presiding over that kind of setting. But while my ministry might not take on a physical manifestation, I'm still very conscious of tending to my flock. And as a preacher who doesn't have a church but has been blessed with uncommon visibility through a popular TV show, the most effective way for me to reach people is by living a life that inspires others. I truly believe that providing an uplifting example through *Run's House*, or my books, or my music, or whatever else I'm involved in, is what God wants me to be doing with my life. I believe that God has blessed me with such a beautiful family life because he wants me to *show* the rest of the world that it *is* possible. And notice that I use the word "show." Because the key is rather than just talk the talk about family, I really walk the walk with my actions. For example, Puffy recently called me up and told me he enjoyed watching the episode where I organized a "Simmons Family Olympics" (more on that later), and that now he wants to organize a "Combs Family Versus Simmons Family Olympics." So I like to think that's one person who's been influenced a little bit by my example. I'm using Puffy as an example because he's a friend and his personality and lifestyle is one that many of my fans look up to.

But obviously I'm not only trying to touch a Puffy or a Brad Pitt. I'm trying to touch *everyone* who can hear my message.

One of the most important strategies that I'm trying to share with the people who watch our show is the value of putting actions over words. Because I love to "run" my mouth, I've found that it's much more important to walk the walk than to talk the talk when it comes to raising a family. It's pointless to talk to your children about living a clean, healthy, and respectful life if you're not going to lead your own life in a similar manner. Nothing can drive a wedge between you and your children like the perception that you don't practice what you preach to them. As hard as it can be, we must always try to parent by example. It's critical that you not only address, but correct your own shortcomings if you want to teach your children how to stand tall.

## WALKING THE WALK

I'll be the first to admit that leading by example doesn't always come easy for me. As a rapper and a reverend, my first instinct is usually to open up my mouth and start talking. Yet while I love getting up on my pulpit and giving a good sermon to my family, my wife is always quick to remind me that kids don't like to be preached to all the time. If my kids are outside playing but Justine senses that I'm about to drop a heavy sermon on them, she'll take me aside and say, "Joey, please just go out there and play with your children instead of preaching to them. They don't want to hear a sermon when they're just trying to have fun." And she's right, because if my relationship with my kids is all preach and no play, then no matter how many jewels I think I'm dropping on them, eventually they're going to tune me out.

If I want to teach Russy about the importance of hard work, then he needs to see me busting my tail all day trying to provide for my family. If Diggy's having a problem respecting his teachers, then he needs to see firsthand how respectful I am around the people I work with. If Vanessa is considering doing a photo spread that I think will compromise her integrity, instead of telling her, "don't do it," I want her to watch how hard my wife and I work at protecting our own reputations. No matter what the issue is, my wife and I want to provide our children with an example of the right way to handle it.

And while it's not wise to preach too much to your kids, it's even worse to live in opposition to your preaching. Try to remember back to when you were a kid—probably nothing disgusted you more than adults who seemed hypocritical or phony. Especially if it was your own parents acting that way. If you suspected that they weren't following the rules they expected you to live by, then those rules probably stopped carrying as much weight with you. So don't give your kids the ammunition they need to shoot holes in your rule book. Instead, show the same respect for those rules that you would expect from your kids.

For instance, if I encourage Diggy to be honest and respectful toward women when he grows older, he's never going to live that way if he knows I'm running around in the streets disrespecting my wife. Yet if he sees that every day I treat Justine in an honest and respectful manner, he'll eventually absorb that lesson. He might not even realize that he's absorbed it until he's much older, but I believe that he will try to emulate my lifestyle instead of some of the more negative ones he might encounter. And that's really the key here— no matter what they hear in the locker rooms, no matter what they read on the Internet or see in the streets, when all is said and done, you are going to be the biggest influence on your child's life. Don't squander that power.

Understanding the impact that my actions have on my children is why I ask God every night to please keep me from doing stupid things. I know that if I ever return to some of the stupid, selfish behavior of my youth, I am going to lose whatever influence and respect I have earned from my children. That's why I put all my energy into making sure my present behavior and actions are completely

different from how I used to live. I don't want my kids to follow the
guy who used to smoke ten bags of weed a day. Who used to be
rude—even hurtful—to his friends. Who slept around and didn't
treat women the way I'd want my own daughters treated. Who was
jealous and selfish instead of kind and giving. I don't want to lay
down those kinds of footsteps for them to follow in. I want that guy
out of the picture forever.

Thankfully, my kids aren't honoring any of my past foolishness.
They're only honoring my present example. And as long as I don't
slip up and start smoking weed, or hanging out in strip clubs, or doing any of the stupid things I used to do, then my kids will respond
to how high I'm setting the bar now, not how high I used to get. As a
parent, you can never forget that you're driving the bus and your
kids are the passengers. So don't be that driver who breaks the speed
limit, runs red lights, and gets drunk during lunch. Be the one who
drives safely and slowly, and who makes sure he's always headed in
the right direction.

I'm always a little surprised to hear that Joey is so worried about
setting the right example for our kids. While it is true that sometimes I have to remind Joey not to preach so much, I feel like
the kids really look up to him, and it's as much for his actions
as for his words.

For me, the struggle has been finding the strength to discipline my kids. I don't have a problem articulating the rules I expect them to follow, but sometimes I do have difficulty enforcing
those rules. For instance, if I punish Russy by telling him to go
to his room for the rest of the day, I don't always hold him to
that. If I check on him a few hours later and see he isn't in his
room, my tendency is to let the punishment slide. I feel like I
can talk a good game about what I expect from my children in
terms of behavior, but I haven't always backed up those words
with the proper action.

That lack of toughness has caused my kids to regard me as

something of a softie. One of my assistants even told me that when Russy wanted her to buy him a toy he knew my husband wouldn't approve of, that little rascal told her, "Ask my mom instead. She's the soft one." In fact, not long ago Russy, Diggy, and I were being interviewed on a radio station in Atlanta when a listener called in and said, "Justine, you inspire me because you're so calm with your children." And when she said that, I laughed out loud and said I couldn't believe it, because I always feel like the only way I can get my kids to do something is by screaming at them. But when the host then asked the boys if I'm wild and yell a lot around the house, they shook their heads and said, "Nope, she's not that bad at all."

I was really surprised to hear them say that, but it also made me realize that all my screaming and yelling wasn't having much impact. I thought I was going hard, but I really wasn't going hard enough. Since I love my children so much, I'd rather they were outside having fun instead of sitting in a room serving a punishment. Unfortunately, that makes the kids think, "She's letting me get away with this because she's a sucker." And I don't want my kids thinking I'm a sucker. I don't think they want to see me that way, either. What child wants a parent who doesn't have a backbone? Even the greediest child secretly wants someone to stand up to them. That's why I believe that as much as they act like they don't, most kids really do want discipline, as long as the rules are enforced fairly. Which is why it's so important for me not only to stand firmer and say no to these kids, but to actually back it up.

Luckily, as much as I struggle to enforce the rules, my husband doesn't have a problem taking a hard line with the kids. For instance, I recently had a problem with Diggy where he kept bugging me about some new sneakers he wanted. I told him a couple of times to let it go, but he kept on nagging until I finally said, "Diggy, if you keep this up I'm going to tell your father." Usually the drama stops when I tell my kids that. But Diggy must have been feeling extra fresh that day, because instead of quieting down, he actually told me "I don't care. Go tell Daddy." Well, when I heard that, I picked up the phone and called my husband so he could hear what his sassy son had just said. Joey had been relaxing at a bookstore, but when he heard about Diggy's defiance, he almost went through the roof. "He's not going to be talking like that when I get home," he said. "I'm going to take that Sidekick he loves so much and put it in the sink to teach him a lesson." "Yeah, you need to do that!" I told him, even though in my mind I didn't think it would go that far. But sure enough, when Jocy came home, the first thing he said to Diggy was, "Give me your Sidekick," and then marched him into the bathroom and turned on the water. And while he held the Sidekick up in the air, he asked Diggy, "Have you lost your complete mind? You need to see where being disrespectful and selfish gets you!" And then he took that Sidekick and held it under the water until it was ruined. I know that hurt Diggy because it was a fancy Dwayne Wade Sidekick that he really loved (and I won't lie, it hurt me a little bit, too, since I was the one who bought it), but he got the message loud and clear: "My dad doesn't play and he'll come at me hard if I act this way again." I think that kids need to know that their parents are serious and will back up their rules with action. They need to know that yes, we love you, but if you get out of line, love ain't have anything to do with it!

I'm proud to report that I'm learning to get a little tougher myself now. Instead of letting things slide, I'm really beginning to take action when the kids step out of line. The most poignant example is a situation I recently had with JoJo. We were having a normal disagreement when JoJo began to get very disrespectful, speaking to me as if I were one of his friends instead of his mother. As usual I was going to let his attitude slide until he sent me over the top. What did it was when he interrupted me by pounding his fist into his palm—hard—and then saying real tough, "Yo, I'm saying, though!" as if he was about to really beef with me! He lips might have only said "yo," but his body language was saying "@#$% you!" Well, when he did that I just lost my complete fricking mind! I started screaming at JoJo, "I love you and I go so hard for you all the time and then you talk to me like this? Like I'm some dude on the street? I'm not having that! Get out of my house." And I meant it. I screamed at him to leave and then stomped around the house trying to collect his things and throw them in the trash!

After a few minutes of acting that out of control, I actually had to lock myself in the bathroom because I felt like I was having a nervous breakdown and didn't want the kids to see me that way. Once Joey heard what was going on, he tried to get me to come out of the bathroom and squash things with JoJo, but I wasn't ready yet. I really needed some time to collect myself. Meanwhile, I could hear JoJo in the hallway arguing with Joey and yelling, "But I love her, man! I love her." Hearing that only made me angrier, so I had to stick my head out of the bathroom and tell him, "Stop acting like this is only about you! If Russy and Diggy see you acting this way toward me, what do you think they're going to be like at your age? They'll be even worse. And if they ever try anything like that, I swear I'll ship them off to boarding school! Because no one is going to disrespect me in my house like that! And don't think it's because you're my stepson that I'm going to throw you out. Because Diggy and Russy are gone, too, if they ever act that way with me!" And Diggy and Russy were both watching all this and looking very scared. Like they were going to get shipped off to boarding school that night!

Eventually I calmed down and JoJo and I were able to patch things up. In fact, later that night Russy, who's a little comedian, came up to me and said, "Wow, Mommy, I didn't know you could go so hard!" I laughed, but the lesson I learned that day was a very serious one—my kids need me to set a strong example in the house. It's not just enough for me to talk about being respectful—if they step out of line, I need to go at them hard! My children need to understand that even though their mother loves them, there are certain lines that they cannot cross. JoJo crossed that line by talking to me like I was one of his boys, and I reacted. Maybe more emotionally than I would have liked, but now he knows that there are going to be repercussions if he gets out of line.

I'm very happy to say that since that incident, my relationship with JoJo is stronger than it's been in a long time. Even my husband says, "I can't believe how close you two are now." It's true—since I went at him very hard, he's been right under me. Now I'm hearing, "Mommy, let's do this," or "Mommy, I want to talk to you about something," instead of him just sulking off to his room and shutting the door. And even though he'd probably be too embarrassed to admit it, I feel that he appreciated me going at him that hard. It showed him how deeply I felt about him. If I had only said, "JoJo, you're being bad, go to your room," that would have disappointed him on a certain level. Again, I think that kids really do want that discipline. They want to know that there will be a reaction to their action. And so I have to constantly remind myself: I'm not going too hard—this is what my kids need. They don't need a friend. They need someone to lead the way! I think I've reached that level with the boys, though I still need to work on it with the girls. They need to see me more as "Mommy," not just as their homegirl Justine. Again, it's a struggle because I love my kids so much and I always want them to be open and happy around me. But I also realize that it's more important that they see me as somebody who's going to walk the walk when they get out of line.

## TAKING ACTION MAKES YOU FEEL BETTER

I want to end this section by co-signing what my wife wrote about teaching children that there will be repercussions if they cross certain lines. Not too long ago I was telling an associate about putting Diggy's Sidekick under the water, and when I was finished, she looked at me like I was a little off. "Don't you think that was a tad drastic?" she asked me. "Couldn't you have taught him a lesson without acting so crazy yourself?" I was a little surprised that she took issue with how I handled things, so I had to tell her that I didn't consider what happened in any way drastic or crazy. You see, Diggy had been acting disrespectful for quite some time, and every time the punishment would be, "give me that Sidekick." Then I'd hold it for a few days before I'd give it back to him, only to see him act up again later. So when Justine called me that day and told me how fresh Diggy was getting, I knew he needed to hear something other than, "give me that Sidekick." Diggy had to understand that instead of his usual punishment, he had really crossed a line and as a result he was going to lose his Sidekick for good. So while I admit that maybe I was a little theatrical in how I went about things, I wanted to make sure Diggy got the message loud and clear.

As a parent, I'm not afraid to make big statements in order to get my kids' attention when they keep acting up. I'll give you another example involving Diggy. We had been getting reports from Diggy's school that he had been talking during class, not handing in homework assignments, and misbehaving in general. When I first heard about what was happening, I told Diggy, "If you keep acting like a clown in school, I'm taking you off the basketball team." And believe me, that was no small punishment in Diggy's eyes. He was one of the only seventh graders to make the cut, and he was very focused on playing a big role for that team. It meant a lot to him.

After that initial call, every time I dropped Diggy off at school, I'd look him in the eye before he got out of the car and say, "Remember, don't talk in class. Because if you do, you're off the team." And for a while, there weren't any real problems. He seemed to

1. *A young Rev Run and Justine on a church date* 2. *Rev Run and Justine on their wedding day* 3. *The newlyweds in their limo* 4. *Angela, Justine's mom, Justine, and Vanessa*

5. *Young Angela* 6. *Angela in her school play, The Lion King* 7. *Angela singing* 8. *Angela playing the guitar with her music class*

9. A school picture of Vanessa
10., 11., **and** 12. Vanessa in a beauty pageant

13. *Diggy and Russy*
14. *Diggy, 2 years*  15. *Russy, 7 months*
16. *JoJo, 7 years, with Diggy at his*
*2-year birthday party*

17. Ninja JoJo  18. JoJo in
The Lion King *school play*  19. JoJo, 4 years
20. Diggy, Justine, and Russy

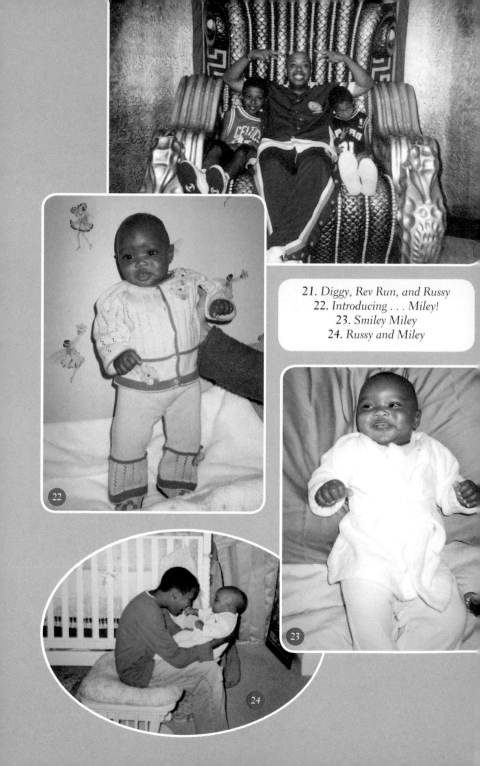

21. *Diggy, Rev Run, and Russy*
22. *Introducing . . . Miley!*
23. *Smiley Miley*
24. *Russy and Miley*

*25. Justine feeding Miley  26. Miley and Rev Run watching TV in bed*

27. *The family in Vegas, where Rev Run was getting a BMI Award*
28. *The family portrait that hangs in the Simmons' home*

have gotten the message. But sure enough, after about three weeks later I got a call from his teacher saying, "Mr. Simmons, your son was talking back in class today. He got so bad that I had to take him to the principal's office." She added that when she told him she was going to call us, at first he tried to blame the incident on his friend. When she didn't go for that, he started begging and pleading with her not to call because he had a game that night and he was terrified that I wouldn't let him play.

When his teacher first told me how upset he'd seemed, I felt a moment of hesitation, even though I knew what I was supposed to do in that situation. Yes, I had told him I'd take him off the team if I got another call, but I also didn't want my son to be miserable. While I was disappointed in how he was acting in school, I was also proud of how hard he'd worked to make the team. Part of me thought maybe I should give him one more chance. As my associate might have said, "Do you have to be so drastic?"

But the more I reflected on the situation, the more I felt I wouldn't be a good parent if I didn't follow through on my threat. So I took a deep breath and called the school and said, "Hi, this is Mr. Simmons. Please don't let my son get on the bus to leave for the game tonight. He no longer has my permission to play." And then I e-mailed his coach and said, "I really appreciate that even though my son is only in seventh grade, you gave him a shot and put him on your team. Unfortunately, he hasn't been behaving like he should in the classroom, and as a result I'm going to have to pull him from the team this year. Hopefully he can learn from his mistakes and play for you next year." Believe me, it wasn't easy to write that e-mail. I knew how hurt Diggy would be when they pulled him off that bus in front of all his teammates. But as a father, I simply couldn't let him repeatedly cross that line at school without paying the price.

Truth be told, as tough as it was to write that e-mail, I felt tremendous relief the moment I sent it off. The second I hit "send," I felt it very deeply in my soul that I was doing the right thing by my son. When I had just kept warning Diggy, I hadn't felt good about the job I was doing as a parent. I felt like I was avoiding my responsibilities. But when I finally stopped threatening and took some action, I really felt great. Not because I had hurt Diggy. But because I knew that by teaching him to be more respectful to his teachers, I was teaching him a lesson that was much more important than him playing on any basketball team.

## DO AS WE SAY, NOT AS WE DID

Another question many parents find themselves asking is, "How can I motivate my kids to lead a more responsible life than I did at their age without sounding hypocritical?" It's an especially relevant question for me, since I was far from an exemplary teenager. I drank, I smoked, I stayed out until all hours of the night, I didn't put much energy into my relationship with God—exactly the kind of lifestyle I *don't* want my kids to lead. I think the best answer is to be as direct and honest about your own experiences as possible and let your kids know that rather than being hypocritical, you're simply trying to help them avoid the same potholes (no pun intended) that tripped you up back in the day. That's the approach I've taken when I've discussed drinking and drugs with my kids.

To be honest, drinking and drugs is a subject that I don't even like to think about too much, let alone talk about, when it comes to my children. But in my heart I know that they are as big a temptation for my kids today in New Jersey as they were for me in Queens back in the day. So rather than try to ignore my own experiences with drugs and alcohol, I want my kids to hear about how destructive they can be, both physically and emotionally, directly from their daddy. That's been especially true when it comes to weed, a vice I struggled with back then and the one I consider to be the biggest threat to my kids.

The first thing I've tried to let my children know is that even though weed has a fairly harmless reputation, it does take a toll on you physically. When I was smoking too much back in the 1980s, it stopped me from living up to my abilities as a rapper. Even though I was a young man, I smoked so much that one of my lungs eventually collapsed. My children need to know that at a time in my life when I should have been onstage rocking the mic, having fun, and making money for our family, I was lying in bed like an invalid because of the damage that weed had done to my body. Back then I thought weed was spinach and I was Popeye. I thought it was what gave me my cool kid swagger, my edginess. But lying there with my lung busted, I felt like I was Superman and the weed was something like kryptonite. It had actually robbed me of my powers.

At the same time I was ruining my body with weed, my partner DMC was destroying himself with alcohol. He was drinking so many forty-ounce bottles of Olde English 800 malt liquor that he ended up with pancreatitis of the liver. The doctors told him that if he didn't quit, he'd be dead by the time he was thirty-five. I tell my children these stories because I want them to realize that even though on the *outside* it might look like rappers and rock stars are leading the good life and are on top of the world, a lot of times they're killing themselves on the *inside*.

I've also tried to teach them that there are other ways in which drugs can mess you up. For instance, my brother Russell and I get into arguments all the time. But the only time in forty years that one of those arguments actually got physical was when we were high. It was back when we were teenagers, and while I can't remember what started the fight, I know it ended with me throwing a chair at Russell. The only problem was that Russell had been studying karate, so when I threw the chair at him, he kicked it and—poof!— it flew back and hit me on the back of the neck. And for about ten years after that my neck would give me a lot of pain every winter. So not only did smoking weed have me ready to hit my own brother in the head with a chair, it also caused me a big pain in the neck— literally!

And outside of the physical issues, I want my children to know that weed wasn't healthy for me emotionally, either. I might have started smoking weed because it felt cool, but it wasn't long before I was using it as a crutch to deal with the pressures of being a big rap star. Rather than taking a step back and examining what was troubling me, I tried to ignore my problems by getting high. Instead of improving my life, that high only created a false sense of security. So while the weed was telling me that everything was fine, the truth was much different. I left money on the table because of weed. I lost respect from my peers because of weed. I became alienated from my friends because of weed. I couldn't keep my first marriage together because of weed. I want my kids to know that my lowest moments as a father, as a son, as a brother, as a businessman, and as a person in general all came when I was smoking too much weed. It's not easy for me to say that, since my kids hold me in such high esteem today and I think it's a little painful for them to think of me as that severely flawed man. But even though this conversation makes me uncomfortable, I know I have to have it. Since the streets are going to be screaming, "It's all good, try some," I have to be even louder in reminding them about the downside to smoking weed.

Sharing my personal experiences (Justine never really smoked weed or drank too much, so she doesn't have many war stories) is just one of the ways we try to teach our kids about the dangers of drugs and alcohol. Whenever we see an example in the media of someone messing up because of drugs, we always hold that up as an example to our kids. If Justine and I are watching *Cops* with the kids and we see some guy running down the street naked, or getting hauled off in handcuffs, we'll tell them, "You know that man is in all that trouble because he was messing with drugs, right? If he hadn't messed with those drugs, he'd still be home chilling with his family." Or if there's a story in the news about some young celebrity getting arrested for drugs, or a sports star getting suspended, we'll be sure to point that out to them, too. It's important that our kids realize that "Don't do drugs" isn't just one of Mommy and Daddy's rules. Instead, we want them to know that the fundamental laws of the world are going to tax them for messing around with drugs more than their parents ever could. We want them to realize that we're only trying to stop them from getting hurt, not from having fun.

Thank God, our approach seems to be working. I've heard JoJo say he'd never smoke weed because "I don't want my lungs to bust like my daddy's." If anything, it's worked *too* well on Russy. All our stories about the dangers of drinking and drugs have him terrified to even be around anyone who seems to be under the influence. When we were on vacation in St. Bart's over the holidays, we went to a party where a few people started dancing on the tables. It really wasn't that rowdy, but Russy still came running over to where we were sitting with some other parents and said, "How much did these people have to drink? Is it safe for us to be here?" The other parents thought he was joking, but we knew he was serious, so we had to tell him, "Yes, they might have had a little bit too much, but we think it's safe to stay." He had a similar reaction when we recently went out to dinner with Kid Rock. We all ordered sodas with our meals, but Kid Rock ordered a glass of wine. Not too big a deal, right? But Russy, who was sitting next to him, got so freaked out that he wanted to leave. He was kicking Justine under the table and giving her looks like, "Let me out of here before this guy starts some trouble." He got so worked up that she finally had to lean over to him and whisper, "One glass for Rock is fine. He's not going to go crazy." So it feels like our message about the dangers of drugs and alcohol have definitely reached our children.

But while I think hearing me *talk* about the dangers of drinking and drugs helps my children stay straight, my *actions* are what really seals the deal for them. For instance, when I tell Vanessa not to do drugs, right now she listens. But there's no way she'll listen if she knows that every night I'm sneaking out of the house to smoke some weed before I go to bed. Or I can tell Russy that drinking too much makes people get into trouble, but he probably won't believe me if he sees me sipping beer around the house. That's why we don't have any liquor in our house—since we don't want our kids to drink, we're not drinking, either. In fact, when Kid Rock stayed at our house recently he brought some Bud Light with him, which was fine by me. He didn't have anything to drink until the kids went to sleep, and despite his image in the media, he's really not that wild of a guy. Or at least when he's with us. The only problem was that when he left, he forgot to take the rest of the beer with him. At first, I called a few people I know who drink beer and asked them if they wanted to come over and get what he'd left behind. But when no one picked it up after a few days, I decided I didn't even want Rock's beers in our garage anymore. I had told my kids that drinking wasn't healthy, and if I really felt that way, then there was no need for me to keep any in my house. So I took all those beers out to the driveway and threw them in our trash. I know that might seem extreme to some people, but if I stress to my kids that drinking and drugs are bad news, then I don't want my actions to even hint at any other attitude.

## OUR STANDARD FOR SEX

Since I'm already discussing uncomfortable subjects like drinking and drugs, maybe now is the time to address the subject that I'm probably the *least* comfortable talking about with my kids: sex.

As you might have noticed in the first chapter, sex is not a topic that I'm particularly uptight talking about. Yet like millions of other dads around the world, when it's time to sit down and discuss sex with my own children, I still get pretty nervous. But despite my awkwardness and nervousness, I have managed to have some short talks about sex with my kids. And the reason those talks have been short is partially because I'm nervous, but also because my message about sex is really very simple: Don't have sex until you're married. That's how my wife and I did it, and it's what we think is best for our children, too.

We've based that message on the Bible, which teaches that fornication and adultery should be avoided at all costs. We've tried to help our children understand that God isn't saying don't have sex because he doesn't want them to have fun, but because he's trying to protect them. While they might not be able to see all of them yet, there are many dangers that come from being sexually active. First and foremost, we really don't want our children getting pregnant before they're married, or getting anyone else pregnant, either. And obviously, we also want to protect our children from contracting any sexually transmitted diseases.

But while we're concerned with the physical ramifications of our children having sex, we're just as concerned with the psychological impact of having sex before you're married. When you have sex with someone, you're not only giving them power over your body, but you're giving them power over your spirit, too. Basically you're giving someone else the keys to your car when neither of you are really ready to drive yet. So even though most young people think they are ready and can handle the incredible emotions that come with sex, the reality is that most can't. While some young people might feel like they're in control when a sexual relationship starts, once things change, as they inevitably do at that age, then they tend to lose control very quickly. And the result is that it's very easy for a young woman to have her world turned upside down after a boyfriend breaks up with her, or for a young man to feel like he's been broken into a thousand pieces after his girlfriend leaves him. That's why we encourage our children to hold on to that power for as long as they can. To hold on to it until they're comfortable enough with their bodies and their spirits to share it with another person. And since the Bible teaches that the right time to share yourself in that manner is when you're married, then that's the time that we encourage our children to aim for as well.

I don't want to give the impression that I'm only talking about the girls here. I've told my boys that I expect them to remain virgins, too. I'm not one of those fathers who's going to encourage their daughters to remain chaste but then look the other way when it comes to their sons. I'm very clear in teaching my boys that it doesn't make you more of a man if you've had sex with a lot of women. In my eyes, it makes you *less* of a man. In this house, a real man is someone who can control himself and wait for marriage, not someone who's going around and carelessly spilling his seed.

While "no sex until you're married" is the standard we've tried to instill in our children, I also understand that that's an exceptionally high standard these days. Mentally, I try to prepare myself that the day might come when I learn that one of my children *is* having sex out of wedlock. And when that day comes, as uncomfortable as it might be, my wife and I are going to have a talk with that child about the ramifications of what he or she is doing. It's going to be very important that we make a close inspection of the situation and find out more about why they made their decision. Because as much as I don't want my kids having sex before they're married, I also don't want my kids getting married just so they can have sex. In other words, I don't want the "no sex" rule to feel like such a heavy weight on my kids that they feel like it's easier to just get married than carry it any longer. Because a marriage that's rushed into for that reason isn't necessarily going to be any healthier than having sex outside of marriage.

But thankfully, that day hasn't arrived yet. In fact, just recently Vanessa was on Wendy Williams's radio show when this very topic came up. "I'm sorry, Vanessa, but I gotta ask you this question," Wendy apologized. "Are you a virgin?" I didn't happen to be listening, but apparently without any hesitation, Vanessa responded, "Of course!" When I heard that, it was actually a bit of a pleasant surprise. Even though I know Vanessa is an incredibly moral woman who takes her faith very seriously, I also know that there are a lot of temptations for a beautiful twenty-five-year-old woman out there. So to hear that she was so quick to say "Of course" filled me up with a lot of pride.

My wife had a similar situation with JoJo recently. JoJo was telling her how his girlfriend had called him up the night before and asked him to bring over some special type of ice cream she had a craving for. Well, when Justine heard that, her heart skipped a beat.

She thought, "When a woman demands a certain kind of ice cream at eleven o'clock at night, that can only mean one thing." And before she was able to censor herself, she blurted out, "JoJo, is your girlfriend pregnant?" When she said it, JoJo looked at her like she was crazy for even suggesting that he was having sex. "No, I'm not trying to be no father. I can't even take care of myself," he told her. "It's not even like that." So while Justine was a little disappointed in herself for even putting the possibility that JoJo was having sex with his girlfriend out there, we felt very blessed that he also seems to be living up to our standards.

I believe one of the main reasons that our kids have been able to meet those standards is the example that Justine and I have set for them. I'll be real—I didn't abstain from premarital sex before my first marriage. And Justine wasn't a virgin when I met her, either. But while we had both slipped up earlier in our lives, the truth is, we didn't have sex with each other before we were married. We did live together for a time, but as I mentioned earlier in the book, Justine got so freaked out by the idea of just living with a man out of wedlock that she moved in with my mother until we actually tied the knot. That's the kind of foundation that this house is built on. And it's that foundation that allows us to set a similar standard for our children.

I realize that to some parents out there struggling with this issue, it probably feels like our standards are impossibly high or unrealistic. To those parents, I want to say without any confusion, "This is real. And if you want to, you can hold your children to the same standard, too." I know how much temptation there is out there. I know how much sex kids are exposed to through the media. I know that in the schools and in the streets, the attitudes toward sex are waaaaay more relaxed than when Justine and I were growing up. I know it's a huge challenge to take your kids back from the pressure of being sexually active.

At the same time, I also know that I have a beautiful twenty-five-year-old daughter who listens to hip-hop and enjoys going out to clubs, seeing movies, and following the latest fashions—in short, most of the things that other young women her age are into. But I also know that unlike many of them, she's putting off having sex until she's married. Similarly, I have an eighteen-year-old son who's a rapper, who is crazy about girls, who is always dressed fly, and is into the same music, sports, and movies that most of his friends are into. And he's a virgin, too. And as I'll discuss in the very next section, I've got a twenty-one-year-old daughter who dated a famous rapper but still choose not to have sex with him (or at least that's my understanding). The point I'm trying to make is that these kids aren't living in some weird religious house that has no connection to what's going on in the larger world. Our kids are very much part of the world. It's just that they've put more stock in their parents' standard than in the world's standard.

We're living proof that you *can* take your family back from a casual attitude toward sex, if that's what you want for your children. In your family, maybe you want to set it a little differently. Maybe you're OK with letting your kids have sex as long as they're in monogamous relationships. Or maybe you feel like you can't control who they have sex with, you just want them to have safe sex. Whatever decision you make, we're not judging it. We're only suggesting that you set *some* sort of standard.

And once you set that standard, you have to commit yourself to enforcing it. Not America's standard, or the school's standards, or other parents' standards, but *your standard*. That's why in our house, we don't accept, "Why are you so mad? I wasn't doing it as much as the other kids in school were." Or, "At least I'm not getting into as much trouble as these other young actresses out here in L.A." When we start to hear talk like that, we say, "We don't care how good or bad those other people are. In our family, under our rules, you're still missing the mark."

That's a very important point not only for this section, but for the *entire* book. Your kids have to know that what matters the most is your standard. That's true for sex, it's true for drugs, it's true for good grades, it's true for how they dress, it's true for how they interact with other people, it's true for *everything*. As long as you set a standard, and then live up to it yourselves as parents, you're going to have the ability to take back your family from the world's standards and raise your children in a way that best fits your values and your aspirations.

## ANGELA AND BOW WOW

Probably the best example of our struggle to find that balance between the standards we set at home and the difficulties in asking your children to set a greater example than you did at their age has been Angela's relationship with the rapper Bow Wow.

Angela and Bow Wow ultimately broke up before things got too serious, but when I first heard that they were dating, I became very concerned. Why? Because as much as I respect Bow Wow, I didn't want my daughter dating a rapper who cultivated an image as a ladies' man. You heard me right—the man who ran amok in the world as a famous rapper doesn't want *his* daughter running around with a rapper who bragged about being with a lot of women. To most kids, that would sound like the kind of hypocrisy I was warning against earlier, right? If I ran amok when I was her age, why can't she do a little bit of the same thing? If I got to enjoy that sort of lifestyle, why is it so important to shield her from it? These were the questions I was faced with as I tried to show Angela that I was trying to protect her, not restrict her or stop her from enjoying life.

I don't want to go too deep into this story, because like any young woman, Angela probably can't think of anything worse than her father discussing her love life in public. But I will share some of it, because Angela is an incredibly mature young woman who understands that in some ways her life is now an open book. And by sharing her experiences, she's helping other young women deal with their own issues.

In fact, I think that her maturity and sophistication is probably what caught Bow Wow's attention in the first place. Angela's smart and doesn't seem like she's chasing fame or popularity. That's probably intriguing to someone like Bow Wow, who's used to girls screaming his name and chasing after his limousine. Of course he would want a girl who's successful and has her own thing going on. But that's also what worried me about their relationship. Was it just about the chase for Bow Wow? All rappers get groupies, so was he trying to be the rapper who could say he had also conquered a "good girl"? I wasn't sure, but now that you know our philosophies on premarital sex, you can understand why I was nervous.

I really did try to stay out of their relationship at first, but I felt I had to get involved when Angela told me that they were planning on walking the red carpet together at an ESPN event. When I heard that, I felt like I had to step in. While it's true that Angela's life is a bit of an open book, she still needs to watch what pages people are reading. I knew if they were photographed together, the mean-spirited people would start writing things about her on the Internet. Soon, every time Angela was seen in the same room as a singer or an athlete, people would start saying, "They must be sleeping together." Having a relationship is a lot of pressure for a twenty-one-year-old girl, especially when she's having it in public. The more I thought about that, the more I felt I should try to dissuade her from going out with Bow Wow. "Look, he travels a lot. There are going to be a lot of young girls throwing themselves at him," I finally told her. "Do you want to have to deal with that? Do you want to deal with picking up the paper one day and reading that he was out with Ciara [his ex-girlfriend]? Then you two are going to feel like you have a beef with each other, even though you're both nice girls. Basically, I want you to be free. I don't want your heart in his hand—or the public's for that matter—so it can be crushed. I'm your daddy, and I was in the business for a long time and I know how it can be. And even though it might not seem fair and it will hurt a little now, I'm really only trying to suggest what I think is best for you in the long run."

I won't lie—at first, that speech was not very well received in my house. Like any young woman, Angela resented her father interfering in her love life. She really did want to experience being Bow Wow's girlfriend, walking the red carpet with him and enjoying the limelight. She didn't want me raining on that parade. And Justine was worried I was being too strict with Angela. She pointed out that when we were Angela's age, we certainly didn't want anyone telling us whom we should or shouldn't date. Even Vanessa chimed in, warning me, "It's good to let her know that you're worried, but you don't want to chase her so hard that she feels like she has no power, no say in her own life. Because then she's going to rebel against what you tell her."

Hearing all those comments helped me realize that I needed to find a balance between giving Angela a chance to grow on her own and pushing against her dating Bow Wow. I realized that the only way to find that balance was to explain my concerns to Angela, but then to step back and be confident that she would make the right decision on her own. I had to believe that I've helped her become anchored in the universe, instead of floating adrift like I was at her age. Because—and this is the key—as long as I'm providing Angela with the right example of how a man should act in a relationship, then she's going to expect the same thing from the men in her life, too. If I'm acting a fool, then all my advice and warnings and restrictions won't have any effect on her. But as long as she looks at her parents and sees a loving, respectful, and God-fearing couple, then she's going to want to emulate that in her own life. I have to plant seeds and then be patient that the flowers will eventually bloom. So while I was too hard at first, with the help of my family, I managed to catch myself in time. I told Angela how I felt, but then I eased up and didn't push her as hard as I wanted to. I didn't cross the line, but I let my toes get real close to it.

I should also add that I shared my views on relationships with Bow Wow, because beyond his relationship with Angela, I wanted to make sure that he was on the right path, too. I didn't want my daughter dating a rapper who I perceived as a ladies' man, but the truth is

I also love Bow Wow. I appeared in one of his videos, and as much as he's already accomplished, I think he has an even brighter future ahead of him. Which is why before they broke up, I decided to have a little talk with him. "Bow Wow, you're a king. You're royal," I told him over dinner one night at a Cheesecake Factory near our home. "Now, you know in this house, we don't believe in premarital sex. So if you're truly serious about Angela, and she's truly serious about you, then we have very high expectations for how you two are going to act. But outside of this whole thing with my daughter, in the larger picture, you don't need to be spilling your seed randomly. It's too important for that. So if you're serious about Angela, then ask her to marry you and do this the right way. And if you're not, then you two can go your separate ways and still be friends. Your ultimate goal should still be to find a good girl and get married. Focus on that instead of running through as many women as you can. Because if you really want to trump the industry, that's the move to make. Any rapper can do the groupie thing for fifteen years, but how many of them can get on the Will Smith/Jada Pinkett plan? The sophisticated 'I'm so incredibly focused on my career plan that I only come down from my castle to make movies or go to the Oscars plan.' Acting a fool is for boys—you can leave all that behind and be a grown man."

And while it's not easy to sit there and hear your girlfriend's father talk about spilling seed and marriage, I think he respected what I was sharing with him. In fact, after I finished my little sermon and we were about to finish our meal, he said, "Thank you, sir." Maybe I'm a sucker, but that really made me feel great. Still—and this is at the heart of what we're talking about in this chapter—I don't think I reached him because of my sermon alone. Rather, I reached him because he sees me *living* that kind of lifestyle myself. If I get him to live right, it will only be because he's watched me living right. He sees that even though I'm a rapper, I still let my wife know that I love her every day when I come home. He can see through my example that showing affection doesn't make you weak. He sees that tending to my family—not being the greatest MC to walk the earth—is my first priority. And he sees that I'm so tied into my daughter's life, and so concerned for her future, that I'm going to sit down with her boyfriend for a man-to-man talk, even if it's a little uncomfortable for everyone. Now I can't say I'm disappointed that in the end it wasn't meant to be with Bow Wow and my daughter (though who knows, they could start dating again tomorrow), but hopefully my example will help him settle down and start a great family life for himself one day, too.

The situation with Angela and Bow Wow reflects the balance we'd like to reach between trying to control our kids' lives and letting them take risks for themselves. As much as we want to protect our children, we also realize that an important part of parenting is letting your kids make mistakes. So even though our natural reaction is to *step in* when we see a potential mistake coming, we're learning that sometimes it's better for our children if we actually take a step back. Of course, we're not talking about potentially life-altering decisions like dating an abusive boyfriend or quitting school or using drugs: We're stepping in and shutting down that sort of nonsense *immediately*. Instead, we're talking about allowing mistakes that might sting a bit in the present, but will actually help teach our kids an important lesson down the road. A good example of that type of scenario was Vanessa's decision to appear in *Maxim* magazine.

## THE PICTURE AND THE TATTOO

A few years ago, Vanessa told us that she had been selected for *Maxim's* Hot 100 list and wanted to know what we thought about her posing in the magazine. Even though our initial reaction was "No, no, no," Vanessa still tried to sway our opinion. First, she told us that she had been promised that she wouldn't have to pose for a "normal" (i.e., way too sexy) *Maxim* pose. Instead, *Maxim* had promised she could pose for a tasteful shot that wouldn't embarrass her. Second, she pointed out that appearing in *Maxim* would be a very major step in her career. She would be right next to Penélope Cruz, which might really put her on the map. How could she say no to that? She was shocked that they'd even picked her. We still had our doubts and reservations, but Vanessa seemed convinced that it would turn out OK. Therefore we told her that if she truly thought the shoot would boost her career without compromising her values, then she had our blessing.

Vanessa went ahead, did the shoot, and afterward felt like it went OK. But when the magazine hit the stands and she saw the picture *Maxim* had used, right away she felt like she had made a mistake. My wife and I have actually chosen not to look at the picture, but I'm told that they picked a shot of her in a black slip and garter belt. And even though apparently it was a fairly tame shot by *Maxim* standards and the caption noted Vanessa's "excellent moral fiber," she was still a little bummed out by how things turned out. I'll admit that whenever I've mentioned the photo, she's tried to change the subject or acted like she wasn't that upset. But I know my daughter, and I know what she's told other people in the family. She was not happy with how she appeared in that magazine.

But even though in her mind she's probably said, "Dag, I wish I had listened to my parents," Justine and I haven't given her a hard time about not following our advice. She was hard enough on herself, so if anything, we've told her not to worry about it too much. Even though we're not happy that there's a picture out there that doesn't reflect our daughter in the best light, overall we're happy that Vanessa seems to have learned an important lesson from the experience. In fact, when I heard about a story going around the Internet claiming that Vanessa would be appearing topless in the new Quentin Tarantino movie, I didn't even have to ask her if it was true or not. I knew it was a lie because after that *Maxim* shot, I knew she wouldn't be willing to do anything that might compromise her image again.

We also went through a similar situation recently when Angela announced that she wanted to get the word "Pastry" tattooed on one of her wrists. As Angela had expected, I wasn't happy about the idea. I think kids today view getting tattoos too lightly, because in reality they are a very big deal. Kids are only thinking about the moment, so they don't realize that a tattoo will leave a mark that the world will look at forever. And as Justine pointed out, what looks good now probably isn't going to look so hot in twenty years ("Your skin will be so saggy that it'll just say 'Pay,'" she joked.)

But Angela is very determined, and her stance was, "I appreciate your concern, but it's my wrist and I'm happy with it. I want to have some stories to tell when I get older." That argument still seemed weak to me, but she eventually broke me down anyway. How? The same way girls have been winning over their fathers for thousands of years: She looked up at me with her big brown eyes and said, "Daddy, pleeeeease. It will make me happy." When she said those magic words, I found myself mumbling, "OK." But I didn't cave in completely. I made her agree to let me go to the tattoo parlor with her so I could at least be there to help if something went wrong.

When we got to the parlor, I asked her one more time, "Are you sure this is what you want?" She said, "Yes," so then I asked, "Well, would you ever consider getting the tattoo somewhere else, in a place where not everyone can see it?" She then admitted that she had also been thinking about getting a small star on her foot instead of the "Pastry" on her wrist. That sounded a lot better to me, so with a little prodding, I convinced her to go with Plan B. And truthfully, she seemed a little relieved not to have gotten the "Pastry," because as tough as she was trying to appear, she probably had her own fears about marking herself in a public way.

In the end, I felt we had reached a good balance between letting Angela make a mistake and letting her feel like she was in control of her own life. Yes, we don't really approve of tattoos, but at least she got a small one where people won't see it. And if it does end up sagging or fading or simply seeming too childish to Angela down the road, at least it won't be staring her in the face every day.

More importantly, Angela saw that while we're always going to want to have a big say in her big decisions, we're not trying to control *every* aspect of her life and her body. If she feels strongly about something, we're prepared to take a step back, provided we don't think the consequences will be too severe.

And as Justine pointed out to me, the most important thing in this situation wasn't whether Angela did or didn't get the tattoo. It was that she still asked permission in the first place. We almost take it for granted, but it's really very rare that a twenty-one-year-old girl seeks her parents' approval for a tattoo. The truth is, if she had just gotten the star on her foot, she could have snuck it by us. As long as she was careful around the pool, we probably wouldn't have noticed. Or she even could have taken the "I'm twenty-one years old and I don't have to ask if it's OK" stance, like some of her friends were telling her to. But that's not how it is in this family. Our kids always come to us for advice and approval. And I believe that happens because they know that while we're going to be very strict and unbending on some issues, we're also willing to be fairly flexible on others.

The challenge for parents is finding that delicate balance in your own family. As parents, you should always tell your children, "This is what we believe. And this is what we think you should do." But after saying that, you have to give them some flexibility to make their own decisions. As much as we'd like to spare them from hurt or disappointment or embarrassment, children sometimes just have to experience those emotions themselves. Because if we continue to make all the decisions for our children, and never let them taste a little sip of that hurt now, then there's actually a greater chance that they'll take a big gulp of it later. They won't know how bad it tastes, and when they take that big swig, it'll be even worse for them.

Most importantly, if they take a step you've advised against and end up slipping, they need to know you'll always be there to catch them. So when that *Maxim* photo came out, we weren't holding it up and running around the house yelling, "We told you so." After we saw that Vanessa was discouraged, we wanted to make her feel better. Our goal was to prop her back up instead of knocking her down even more. And we tried to do that by reminding her that life is about living and learning. No matter who you are, or how clean you live, or how many prayers you say, it's impossible not to experience moments of disappointment or disillusionment every once in a while. It's part of growing older and wiser. We reminded her that even though the disappointment of seeing yourself projected in the wrong way in a national magazine might taste very bitter today, in time it would pass. She would know to make a different choice the next time. And perhaps most importantly, even though we don't agree with her choice, we've still got her back.

## A HIP-HOP HOUSEHOLD

Since I just finished discussing drugs and sex, two topics that prove very challenging for most parents, now would probably be a good time to address another topic that proves challenging for many parents today: hip-hop.

Let me start by saying that hip-hop is always going to have a place in our house. I'm a rapper, my wife used to rap (that's right, she was "Jussy Jus" in Strong Island's The Fly Five—and if you saw her in the booth on *Run's House*, you know she can still spit!), my sons rap—basically everyone in my house loves the music and the culture. Of course, there are lyrics in some of the songs that I'm not comfortable with, but I try not to judge them too heavily. The truth is, I'm not even comfortable with all the lyrics *I've* said during my career. I feel that despite all the positive things Run DMC promoted, in retrospect many of my lyrics were too edgy. So while I don't censor the music my kids listen to, I do encourage them to look for songs that aren't so negative or degrading. I don't think negative or degrading songs are healthy for my kids or for the artists performing them.

At the same time, I'm not running around telling my kids (or my wife, for that matter) to turn off certain songs. Do I wish there wasn't so much talk about drugs, violence, and promiscuity in some of the music? Sure. I also know that if my daughters listen to songs about being a gangster, at the end of that day they're not going to emulate that lifestyle—instead they're going to emulate the type of lifestyle that their Uncle Russell or Aunt Kimora leads. Or if Diggy wants to run around the house talking about "My drink and my two step," that's fine, too. Because he's living in a home where we don't serve anything stronger than Kool-Aid.

If my family loves a song and has fun dancing around to it, I'm not going to get in the way. As a parent, you have to try to remember that hip-hop is mainly just teenage fun. Young people are always going to listen to music that their parents don't understand, or don't approve of. The blues were supposed to be a horrible influence on teenagers. Just like jazz and rock 'n' roll. So just as we can look back and laugh at the parents in the fifties who thought the world was about to end because their kids were listening to Elvis, in the future people will laugh at the parents who thought that hip-hop was going to ruin their children. Do you know what is really a great threat to your children? Setting a bad example for them as a parent. That is what will screw up their lives. Not the music that they're listening to.

Justine and I are the rappers who have the biggest impact on their lives, just like you are the rapper who has the biggest influence on your kid's life. Not someone they hear on the radio, or some rock 'n' roll singer, or some kid in their school, or some dude in a club. The bottom line is, if you lead by example properly, it doesn't matter what's in the songs. So as long as I'm not smoking weed anymore, I'm not worried about the kids listening to songs about rolling blunts. As long as I'm not being promiscuous, I'm not worried about the kids listening to songs where they talk about sleeping around. As long as I'm not acting like a gangster, I'm not worried about my kids listening to gangster rap. Because I know that *my* actions will speak louder to my children than anyone else's words.

## DROPPING OUT AND GOING HARD

I can relate to the awkwardness Joey sometimes feels talking to the kids about sex and drugs. That's because I've also struggled with finding the right balance between giving the kids freedom and making sure that they don't repeat the same mistakes I've made. The hardest area for me to do that in has definitely been in education. I go very hard on my kids when it comes to their schoolwork. I don't only want them to get good grades in high school, but to continue their education through college and beyond. And the reason I probably go so hard is because I am a high school dropout.

That's not something I'm proud of, or something that I even talk about much, but it's the truth. When I was in high school, I ran with an older crowd; most of my friends had already been to college, had jobs, and were starting to buy fancy clothes, nice cars, and even their own homes. And to my impressionable teenage eyes, they were on top of the world, and I wanted to join them. The problem was that I could never afford their lifestyle as long as I was a student. So in order to keep up with my friends, I started working several sales jobs and put all my energy into making money. And I did quite well, with a new car in my driveway before I was even old enough for my license! The problem was, I did *too* well. I was making so much money that school began to seem like a waste of time. During my junior year, I decided that I wanted to drop out and focus on my jobs full time. It seems like a crazy idea now, but I was set on it and my mother didn't try to stop me. Her attitude was, "Let her do what she wants." But since I couldn't just drop out of school on my own, my mother came in with me and we met with a guidance counselor. The counselor did her part, advising me not to rush into things, advising me to be patient and to stick around for my diploma. But I was adamant, and in the face of that stubbornness, my mom let me make my own decision. And my decision was to walk out of that school and never go back.

I don't totally regret dropping out, because I was focused on my career and I did manage to find the kind of work that I wanted. In fact, I'm very proud of my accomplishments. I did very well in sales and was even hired as a private detective, not because I had any experience in snooping around, but because the owner of the company saw what a strong work ethic I had. Even though I don't have that piece of paper, I have had a very interesting, enjoyable, and lucrative career.

At the same time, there's a part of me that's always been curious about what life in college would have been like. What sort of people would I have met? What sort of experiences would I have had? What great books would I have read? What else could I have learned about the world? Those are the questions I have asked myself over the years. And I don't want my kids to have to ask themselves the same questions one day. As I look back now from the perspective of a parent, I wish my mother had been firmer with me about staying in school. Instead of saying, "Do what you want to do," I wish she had sat me down and said, "Young lady, I don't care about what cars you want. You are going to college!" Even though I know I would have fought against it tooth and nail, I wish my mother would have forced me to get my diploma and to continue my education.

That lingering sense of regret is why I'm so determined to make sure my own kids get to experience everything I missed out on. For many years, my kids didn't know I had dropped out because I didn't want them to think that I was a hypocrite. Who was I to demand that they go to college when I couldn't even finish high school? But I've come to realize that I can't worry about my past actions or decisions. I should only worry about helping my kids avoid making the same mistakes that I did. So the same way that Joey can say, "I don't care if I was reckless at twenty-one years old. Angela, you're not going to live that way!" then I need to say, "Russy and Diggy, I don't care if I was a high school dropout. You two are going to college no matter what!" And the way I can ensure that they'll listen to me is to actually show them how much education means to me today. Instead of just talking about the importance of getting good grades, I'm going to go over their homework with them every night. I make sure that I'm a presence at their school and develop relationships with their teachers. I'm going to help them pick what classes they take. And when they're old enough, I'll take them on college visits. I'm going to put in the work to create an environment where it isn't a question of "Do I go to college?" but "What college do I want to go to?" Maybe Diggy will want to follow in Vanessa's footsteps and go to St. John's. Or maybe he'll want to follow Angela to the Fashion Institute of Technology. Or maybe Miley will want to go wherever Russy ends up. But they will all end up somewhere. That expectation was never there when I was growing up. And part of it was financial—paying for college tuition was probably a scary thought for my mother. But Joey and I are fortunate that we can handle that weight, so there's really no excuse not to create a different kind of environment for our children.

If there's anyone out there who's had an experience similar to my own, I want to encourage you not to let it stop you from going hard for your children's education. Don't think that just because you didn't get that degree, your kids are destined to follow the same path. Instead, work even harder to make sure that they get the richest education possible. Dedicate yourself to creating an environment in your home that demands educational excellence. Don't just preach to your kids about education—actually lead the way yourself. If they do poorly on a test, don't just take away one of their toys—actually take the time to go over the test with them and try to help them understand their mistakes. If they're not connecting with one of their teachers, set up a meeting with yourself and the principal to see if something can be worked out. If you don't feel comfortable with the vibe in their school (maybe it feels dangerous, or the kids don't seem to take their studies seriously), then try to find out about a better school for them to enroll in. I know what I'm promoting takes a lot of extra effort, and most of us mothers are already tired, but if you can create an environment that stresses education, your kids might complain a little now, but they'll always thank you later.

## KIDS MUST MENTOR ONE ANOTHER

I want to end this chapter by stressing that it's not only important for parents to set an outstanding example for their kids, but that it's equally important for your children to set a strong example for one another. Justine and I recently saw a great example of this take place between our two youngest sons. Russy was going through a little stage where he wanted to be like Diggy, since Diggy is so fly and all the young girls out there seem to love him. Russy started wearing extra nice clothes like Dig and walking with the same little swagger. But while it's natural for boys to want to be like their big brothers, in doing so, Russy was also losing a little bit of who he is. I noticed the change and was going to step in and say something to Russy about it, but Diggy beat me to it. He took his little brother aside and told him to be happy with who he is, because he's *already* cool. "You're the most popular person on the show, not me," Diggy told him. "Because you're the nicest person in this house. The person with the least ego. And people love that about you. So keep being yourself." Man, when I heard about that conversation, it made me so happy. I loved that Diggy was taking the time to make his younger brother feel good about himself and giving him the confidence to have his own swagger. A swagger rooted in kindness. It was such a great job of mentoring, and I'm sure it meant more to Russy coming from his big bro than from one of his parents.

Similarly, both Diggy and Russy have benefited from JoJo's

mentorship. One example that stands out is when the younger boys became jealous of the new car JoJo received as a graduation gift from high school. At first, I was worried that the car was going to create a jealous, greedy atmosphere in our house. It seemed like every time Diggy and Russy would walk by the driveway and see JoJo polishing that car, they would grow more and more envious. But just when I had become convinced I had made a mistake by giving JoJo the car, he flipped the script on me. On the morning of his actual graduation, a day on which most young people are only thinking about themselves, JoJo went out and bought some cool belt buckles for his brothers. It was his way of saying that not only was he sorry for showing off and making them jealous, but that he was also proud of *their* academic achievements. Of course Diggy and Russy were thrilled that their big brother was thinking of them on his graduation day, and the smile on JoJo's face was even bigger than the one he had on the day he got the car. Instead of antagonizing his younger brothers, JoJo actually became a great mentor for them. Not only did he remind them that academic achievement is always rewarded, but more importantly, that it feels even better to give than it does to receive.

I saw another great example of mentoring on JoJo's part during the "Simmons Family Olympics," a little competition I set up to teach the kids about the importance of being a good sport. One person who really needed to learn that lesson was Russy, who had developed a bad habit of breaking his Game Boys whenever he lost a game. Sure enough, when he couldn't throw a strike during the bowling competition, he did manage to throw a fit, punching Diggy, and then storming out of the bowling alley in tears. After that outburst, I had to sit Russy down from the game until he learned his lesson and wrote me an essay on being a good sport. But JoJo did me one better. After he won the $100 I had put up for leading his team to victory, he proved himself to be a good sport and, instead of keeping all the money for himself, split it with his younger brothers. He didn't have to do that, but by splitting the money when he didn't have to, he taught Russy about what it means to be classy and kind in victory.

We've also seen a lot of great mentoring between Vanessa and Angela on the subject of kindness. Not to say that Angela is mean-spirited, but like most young people, she's sometimes so caught up in her own head that she forgets about other people's feelings. That's why I was very happy the other day when I heard Vanessa tell Angela, "You know, you could have been nicer to the cab driver." It was a very small comment, and it wasn't said with any spite. But I loved that Vanessa was taking the time to remind Angela that it's never cool to be cold. That she wanted to remind her younger sister that kindness is the ultimate sign of sophistication. It's a message that I try to share with kids all the time, but I suspect it carried some extra weight for Angela coming from her sister.

We don't want our kids to only mentor one another—we want them to be mentors to all the kids they come into contact with. So when a young boy watches *Run's House* and sees Russy making it hip to be kind, he'll want to be kind, too. When a teenager watches Diggy taking the time to focus on his studies, maybe that kid will become more serious about his homework, too. Or when young girls watch the show and see that Angela and Vanessa manage to be cool without compromising their values, maybe they'll strive for a similar lifestyle. In fact, Angela and Vanessa take their roles as mentors so seriously that they recently signed on to be two of the new spokeswomen for the Girl Scouts. A lot of young women their ages wouldn't be interested in being associated with the Girl Scouts anymore, but my daughters were thrilled! They view the opportunity to mentor and influence a whole new generation of young women as a serious blessing.

Still, the girls know they won't reach any of those Girl Scouts if they only talk about leading a moral life—they understand that they have to actually lead that life themselves. That's a lot of pressure for two young women. That means they can't be photographed stumbling out of a club drunk. That means they can't be mean to a salesperson when they go shopping. That means that instead of the sexy, provocative outfits that their friends are wearing to the club, maybe they have to wear something a little more tasteful and understated. They accept that what some of the other young "celebrities" out there can do, they *can't* do, if they want to live up to our standards. It's a real burden to put on young people, but they accept it, because they know that walking the walk is the only way they can have a real impact on all those young girls.

When I see the girls embrace the pressure of being a positive role model, it makes me think that maybe we have been successful in teaching our kids the value of leading by example. And I consider that a major accomplishment, because providing a positive example is a very heavy weight to bear. So many of us stumble and take that drink, or smoke that joint, or cheat on our wives. It's easier to drop that weight than labor under it. But it's the weight you must carry if you want to help your children, your siblings, your friends, or even your fans stay on the right path.

## RUN'S TAKE BACK

If you want to take back your kids' attention from the world, the only way you're going to be able to reclaim it is through the strength of your own example. It won't happen overnight, but a great first step is to address one issue that is threatening your authority and then take a stand there.

In our home, we've done that with cursing. Personally, I used to curse a bit, and if you've ever watched my brother Russell on *Run's House*, then you know that almost every other word that comes out of his mouth needs to be bleeped. And as the kids began to grow older, we started to hear some of that salty language coming from them, as well. We realized that curse words weren't needed, that they weren't going to help our kids accomplish anything. All they were going to do was potentially hold them back.

So Justine and I agreed that if we didn't want the kids cursing, we would have to set an example by refraining from cursing ourselves. So since we made that decision, we've been very
careful about watching our language around the kids. Listen,
will a curse slip out of my mouth every now and then? Sure.
But for the most part, my children never hear me talking like
that, and as a result they've been able to keep their language
very clean, too. In fact, Russy's actually embarrassed now by
how his uncle talks and even asked me, "Why does Uncle Russell curse all the time on the show? Doesn't he know my friends
are watching?" Man, I knew we were winning when I heard
that. To most eleven-year-old boys, an uncle who curses a lot is
the coolest thing in the world. But our son is actually embarrassed by that sort of behavior. Why? Because he never hears
that kind of language in his own home.

Try picking a similar issue and then take a stance on it in
your home. It could be cursing for you, too. Certainly that's a
problem that many parents are grappling with. But maybe it
could be junk food, or violent TV shows. Whatever element
you think is gaining too much power in your home, sap it of its
strength by showing your family that if you can live without it,
then they can, too. So the next time someone brings home
some fast food, even if that hamburger smells delicious, be
sure to say "No, thank you. I don't eat that kind of food." Or
the next time you're all watching TV and one of the shows gets
too violent, even if it's your favorite detective show, be sure
you're the one who changes the channel. Let the family see
that you're not going to tolerate that sort of energy in your
home. And when your children see you set that sort of consistent example, you'll soon be able to take them back from whatever was taking on too much influence in their lives.

**CHAPTER 5**

# Run Your Family
# Like a Business

Another thing that people seem to appreciate about *Run's House* is how much fun we have as a family. And it's true—whether it's splashing around in the pool, playing basketball *inside* the house, bugging out in the recording studio, or just messing around with each other, we always want *Run's House* to be a fun place to live. But as pleased as I am that people can feel our good energy, I hope they are also able to see the incredible amount of planning and strategizing that Justine and I do in order to make all those fun moments possible. We want people to realize that the good times didn't just come by chance. We worked very hard to create that energy.

Too many people still make the mistake of "hoping" that things will turn out well for their families. They hope their family will have fun together. They hope their kids will be healthy. They hope that they'll get good grades in school. They hope they won't get hooked on drugs, or run the streets. They hope they'll go to college and then get a good job. They hope that they'll find someone special in their lives and then have children of their own. But simply "hoping" for those things is not enough. Hope alone is not a strategy. Instead of just crossing your fingers, you must take some action yourself. You must set up a structure that will give your hopes a chance to succeed.

We believe happy families are that way because of hard work

and planning. We believe that there is a real *science* behind taking back your family from drama and distractions and making it work. And in our family, I'm definitely the mad scientist, constantly in the laboratory (or in my case, the bubble bath), looking for the formulas and potions to keep my family successful and happy. And while there's always more experimenting to do, one strategy I've found that definitely works is structuring our family on a business model.

Suggesting that you run your family like a business might sound callous to some folks, but I think it's actually one of the most loving things you can do as a parent. Since happy families are always built on hard work instead of luck, running our family like a business is just a way of ensuring that all that hard work pays off. The only difference is that while a businessman like Donald Trump looks at the bottom line when it's time to gauge how successful one of his companies has been, in this business we gauge our success by how happy and loving our family is.

Just as every employee in a successful company has a specific duty, in *Run's House* every member of our family has a specific job to do. And just like The Donald, Justine and I still always expect results. That's why when it comes to the family business, our motto is "Everyone gets numbers." In other words, whether it's the parents bringing home paychecks or the kids bringing home good grades, everyone is expected to do their job to the best of their abilities and contribute to making *Run's House* a great place to live.

As effective as structuring your family on a business model can be, we also encourage you to take this approach one step further and start a real business venture together as a family. Nothing else has taught us so many lessons about not only how to survive, but how to to thrive in this world by working together as a team. From filming *Run's House*, to helping Bishop Jordan build his ministry, to working on Phat Farm and Pastry, my family has benefited so much from working on these tasks together. That's why if you can find a task or a project to take on collectively, I'm confident you will see the results in your family, as well.

## CHIEF EVERYTHING OFFICERS

When trying to structure your family on a business model, the first thing to remember is that just as all successful corporations have a clearly defined chain of command, everyone in a family has to know their roles. In our home, there is no question that Justine and I are the ones in charge. We are what I like to call the CEOs, or "Chief Everything Officers," with an emphasis on *evvvvverything*. Our job is to plan every aspect of our family's lives. We try to plan what our children eat, what sort of clothes they wear, what they study in school, what sorts of friends they have, what sorts of parties they can have, plus so much more. Because, as the old saying goes, when you fail to plan, you plan to fail.

Some of you might be asking, "OK, but how can a company have two CEOs? Don't most companies only have one person in charge?" Well, the answer is yes. And it's no different in *Run's House*. Because even though Justine and I are both CEOs, at the end of the day I have the final word. I understand that some of you might find that arrogant or chauvinistic, but for better or worse, it's a system that has worked fairly well for our family. Having said that, I'm not suggesting that I'm in any way smarter or more intelligent or a better parent than Justine. The truth is, I constantly look to her for guidance and insight. And I consider all the decisions that get made in *Run's House*, both small and large, to be collaborations. Yet we have found that the system runs best when one person has the final say. Just like the warden has the final say in the Big House or the president has the final say in the White House, Run has the final say in *Run's House*.

Again, I'm not trying to be cocky here. Sooo far from it. Running a family is the most difficult, frightening, demanding, and time consuming task I have *ever* undertaken in my life. But I also wouldn't have it any other way. Unfortunately, it seems that not enough fathers out there want to accept that same responsibility. To many men, the weight can feel too heavy. The responsibilities feel too confining. Too many fathers would rather leave it to someone else, or maybe just straight out leave. But my message to those men is, don't be afraid of the responsibility. Because when you run *from* responsibility, you always run *into* trouble. But when you run *to* responsibility, instead of hitting a wall, you're actually going to find freedom and happiness. I promise you nothing will make you feel freer when you go to bed at night than knowing you've done everything you possibly can for your family. Nothing will make you feel more alive than knowing that when you go to work, you're not just working for yourself, but for your children, too. And nothing will make you more happy than getting to see your children reap the harvest of your hard work.

This is an especially important message for African-American men, a lot of whom seem to want to pass the buck instead of saying "the buck stops here" when it comes to running their families. We've got to *stop* saying, "The white man's holding me down," or "A brother can't ever catch a break in this country," and *start* talking about the ways we can effectively run our families. We also need to stop blaming our women for our own failures at fatherhood. I hear too many men saying things like, "Well, I had to get out of that situation because she was always criticizing me and cutting me down." My response to that attitude is, "Man, if you were running your family the way you are supposed to be, you wouldn't be hearing all those complaints and second guesses in the first place!" When you're focused on your job and working your hardest, people can see your effort and respect it. I promise, when you're truly giving your all to your family, your wife will give you all the respect that you need. Your kids will sense it, too, and also give you that respect. And instead of feeling burdened by your duties as the head of the family, you'll start to experience the happiness and freedom that comes with accepting responsibility.

I'm really not trying to diss anyone here, but rather trying to help you understand that you *will* be a great father once you accept that job. Just because you didn't grow up with a father, or two good parents, does not mean that you have to follow the same life. You can change and lead your family out of hardship. You can end that family curse and start bringing home the blessings. Indeed, your family is a body that can change and grow just like your physical body—all you have to do is accept the challenge of being its head.

## BE A BEAST FOR YOUR FAMILY

I'll admit that there have been times when I've had trouble accepting that responsibility, when I've been afraid of the weight. When I was younger, I didn't realize that this family thing really is a business and I had to be a CEO; I thought things were just going to take care of themselves. But thankfully I've always had inspiring people in my ear encouraging me to do better and challenging me to accept the responsibility that's come with my life.

One of those people has been Will Smith, who's been an incredible inspiration to me since I first meet him more than twenty years ago. I've learned so much from Will, but I was recently amazed by a lesson he taught me about learning how to bear responsibility. Will said that back when he was filming I Am Legend in New York City, there was a point in the filming where he'd worked deep, deep into the night for several days in a row. He was also doing all his own stunts, so by the time he'd get back to his trailer, he'd be drop-dead exhausted. One night they ended up filming in the pouring rain until two or three in the morning. When Will finally got back to his trailer, he was shocked to see about twenty kids standing in the downpour waiting for his autograph. Will admitted to me that at first he walked right past those kids and went into his trailer so he could just go to sleep. He was sorry to disappoint the kids, but he was just so tired that there was no way he could wrap his mind around anything but sleeping. His body was aching from the stunts, he was cold from the rain—all he wanted to do was lie down. But just as he was about to get into his bed, he realized he couldn't go out like that. He had to do better. They weren't his kids, but they were his fans and he owed them more than a brush-off. So he looked inside of himself and tried to find the strength to go back out there and make those kids happy. And the way he found it was by telling himself, "I'm a beast. I know I'm tired. I know I'm sore. I know that I want to go to sleep. But I'm a beast. A beast with the strength to handle *anything*." And then he walked back out and stood there in the pouring rain, signing autographs and taking pictures with those kids. And he not only stayed awake, he also kept a smile on his face the entire time by just repeating to himself, "I am a beast. I am a beast."

To me, that example is very inspiring. Because when Will told himself "I am a beast," he wasn't saying that he was a monster or some wild dude. He was just reminding himself that he has the strength and the power to handle any situation. Like a bodybuilder trying to psych himself up before hitting the weights, or a runner trying to find that extra gear to get up a hill, Will realized that he if he dug deep enough inside himself, he would eventually find that strength he was looking for. So while another actor might have stayed inside his trailer and left those kids in the rain, Will turned into that beast and went back out there. And that's what I aspire to be every day for my family—the beast that shoulders the weight, that stands there in that proverbial rain and deals with situations that would be easier to avoid.

I can relate to Will's story, because in my own life there are days when the weight can seem too heavy. When instead of filming an episode, or picking up one of my sons from school, or helping the girls with their careers, I'd rather just shut my self off in a room and escape from all the expectations. But whenever the temptation to run away becomes too strong, I just think of Will's story and remind myself, "I am a beast, too!" A beast who is strong enough to film the scene, strong enough to drive to school and strong enough to sit down with the girls and help strategize their next career moves. And strong enough to be ready for whatever's around the corner. The incredible thing is, we *all* have that beast inside us. We all have the strength to dig in and take on whatever task is in front of us. It's just that sometimes we forget what we're capable of. So whenever you feel that urge to evade or sidestep what your family needs from you, just think of Will Smith standing out there in the dark rain and re-member, "I'm a beast, too."

## IT'S OK TO MICROMANAGE YOUR FAMILY

Whether I'm the "Beast" or the "CEO," the director of "Camp Run," or just plain old "Dad," running our family is always at the forefront of my mind. Just as someone running a Fortune 500 com-pany wants constant updates on the price of the company's stock and how its products are selling, I want to know what's happening every day in the various divisions of my family. First, I want to know where everyone is and what they're doing. I might not literally know where everyone is every second of the day, but I try to make sure I have a good idea. So if Vanessa is in L.A., she might be out of my sight, but she's not out of my mind. Even though she might be three thousand miles away, I want to have the same presence in her life as I do when she's sleeping down the hallway.

And I just don't want to know where they're physically at—I want to know where their heads are at, too. If Vanessa is trying out for a new acting role, I want to know, so I can give her a little pep talk before the audition. If Angela is having problems landing an in-terview for her magazine, I want to know about it. Maybe I can call in a favor and help her out. If JoJo is beefing with one of his friends, maybe I can talk him through the drama. If Russy has a big basket-ball game coming up, I want to know so I can be there in the stands cheering him on. If down the road Miley is having trouble in a class, I want to know about that, too. Maybe I'll be able to help her with her homework. And if I can't figure that math out myself, then I can find someone who can. And of course, I always want to know what's happening with my wife. Is she happy with how I'm treating her? Is she feeling neglected? Or maybe overwhelmed? As we said earlier, I can't get so caught up in worrying about the kids that I begin to ignore what she's going through. Because as hard I'm working on making *Run's House* run smoothly, Justine is working just as hard alongside me. So she needs to feel like her needs are being addressed and respected. In fact, now's a good time to get her take on running our family like a business.

Let me start by addressing what Joey said a while back about him being the head of this "company." That statement might have rubbed some people the wrong way, but it shouldn't have, because I'm not sweating any titles. Besides, as Uncle Russell always says, "Joey likes to tell people he's the boss, but he ain't really no boss. In that house, Justine's the boss." I always laugh when he says that, but ultimately it doesn't really matter who's got the title. I'm very secure in my role in this family, and I don't feel the need to make a big show of my power. I really don't have a problem with the concept of letting my husband be the head of the household.

In fact, I think giving men that responsibility actually helps them be better husbands and fathers. By just letting them have that dag-gone title, you're giving them confidence in themselves. You're letting them feel good about themselves, so that when the burdens of being a father start weighing them down, instead of feeling insecure, they actually feel like they can handle it. Or to put it more plainly, just because I'm a powerful, independent woman doesn't mean I want some sucker husband. I love having a husband who wants to be in charge, who wants to put all his energy and emotions into the welfare of our family. Growing up I definitely never thought I would feel that way, but now that I've experienced living with a strong husband, I wouldn't want it any other way.

In fact, growing up I was one of those women who enjoyed telling off men in public. I wanted to let everyone know, "He ain't the boss of me." It sucks to say this now, but looking back I can see that my whole attitude was, "I'm going to play you before you play me." I was so intent on asserting my independence that I never really gave the men in my life a chance to prove themselves. Instead of trying to big them up, I would belittle them. And in doing so, I really just ended up playing myself.

Now that I'm more mature and have a better understanding of what makes a family tick, I want to promote a different way of dealing with your man. Not only to the women out there who watch the show or are reading this book, but to my own children, as well. I certainly don't want my kids to feel like they have to cut down their spouse in order to assert themselves. I wouldn't want Vanessa, Angela, or Miley to ever try to cut down their husbands, just as I wouldn't want JoJo, Diggy, or Russy to be married to someone who tried to beat them up emotionally or constantly tried to make them look dumb. To think that my children were in that sort of relationship would be very painful to me. Instead, my hope is that all of our kids can be blessed with the kind of relationship that Joey and I enjoy—one based on mutual respect, support, and love.

Of course, those last qualities are really the key. I'll be the first to admit that there's no point in supporting your man if he's not doing the same for you. But Joey has always gone out of his way to be there for me. He's always been in tune with what I like, what I don't like, what I'm feeling, and what I need. I think a lot of men might do that when they first meet you, but then they stop once they think they have you. I've seen it—they literally stop. And after you have kids, then they really stop paying attention to you. They stop worrying about your needs and emotions and start looking at you as a combination of a nanny and a maid. In their minds, anything related to the kids or the house is women's work. Which is a terrible attitude to have. Just like I wouldn't want my kids to grow up around a woman who's constantly undercutting her husband, I wouldn't want them around a father who disrespects his wife by treating her like a maid. Thankfully, Joey has never acted like that. In fact, he does as much for the kids, and as much around the house, as I do. This is truly a joint business.

However, I do sense that some people still might think that my husband is "getting over" on me. I could understand why someone who watches a little piece of our lives for eighteen minutes a week might have that impression. Heck, even my mother and sisters have wondered about that before. But even if they don't totally understand how we structure our family, they do understand that Joey has made my life so wonderful. That's why I've told them, "If some guy was guiding me the wrong way, then there would be an issue. But if my husband is guiding me the right way, and my life is great, what's there to argue about? Who are you to say that it's wrong?"

The bottom line here is that we're both the boss, even if my husband makes the final decisions. And I really do love working alongside him and being his partner in this business. I believe that titles are nice, but what's really important is finding someone you not only love but can work well with, too. I think once you have that, you'll love your role in the family business.

## EVERYONE GETS NUMBERS

If Justine and I are the CEOs of this business, then it's only logical that our kids are the workers. And like most workers, their job is to bring in numbers. And by numbers, I'm not talking about having them go out and sell things. The numbers I'm talking about are 100s and 95s—the grades that we expect them to get at school. In this business, our kids' main responsibility is to do well in school. When they get older, as we're starting to see with Vanessa and Angela, that emphasis begins to change a bit. But while they're still living under my roof, the first thing Justine and I are going to be looking for are those numbers on their report cards.

For instance, you might have seen an episode on the show when

JoJo started slacking off a bit in school. In JoJo's mind, it wasn't the end of the world if he got a C here or there. I decided I had to nip that attitude in the bud, because not only would it mess up his grades and his chances of furthering his education, but it could easily carry over to how he approaches things later in life. So I sat him down and reminded him that while *he* might not be sweating his test scores, in this family we *all* get numbers. I wanted to remind him that his numbers are just as important as mine. Suppose I started slacking the same way he had been? Suppose I started bringing back bad reports from my companies? Suppose Run Athletics stopped selling sneakers? Suppose Justine started slipping and her deal with Simmons Jewelry wasn't renewed? Suppose I started slacking with MTV and they decided to drop the show? There would be real consequences if we stopped bringing in those numbers.

When I put his numbers in that perspective, it got his attention. He was able to accept that just like I gotta bring back paper with presidents on them, he's got to bring back papers with As or Bs on them. From JoJo to Diggy to Vanessa, no one in this family can slack off (OK, Miley can get a pass for now). We're all in this business together. And everyone's got to pull their weight. Because I want my kids to understand that life will tax you when you don't handle your responsibilities.

Some of you might think that we're putting too much pressure on these kids by talking so much about numbers and responsibility. But we don't promote getting good numbers because we're competitive or greedy. We believe that learning how to excel under the pressures and demands of an academic institution is how kids will learn how to excel under the pressures and demands of whatever profession they end up choosing later on in life. So while I push for the numbers, I also tell the kids, "Don't feel like I'm putting this pressure on you guys just to hurt you. The pressure is only meant to help you grow." And most of the time, hearing that little speech helps them handle it better. If after that speech I feel like they're not getting it and I'm giving them more weight than they can bear, then hey, I'll back off a bit. Instead of telling them to hit the books, I'll free them up and encourage them to run out and get ice cream, or go play some ball, or get into any activity that is going to help them recharge. Then after they blow off some steam, they can refocus on their numbers without feeling like they're under such intense pressure.

Ultimately this numbers thing isn't only about getting material rewards for your efforts. I want my kids to understand that the beautiful thing about making your numbers is that life is always going to give you so much more than just a new Game Boy, or even a new car, when you do well. More importantly, when you handle your business in life, the best reward you're going to get is a strong sense of self-esteem and accomplishment. When I send out a new *Words of Wisdom* e-mail or finish taping a season of *Run's House*, or even rip a stadium with Kid Rock, afterward I feel great about what I've accomplished and my place in the world. Yes, it's great to get a check for those jobs. But it's even greater to know that after spending countless hours working on those projects, I was able to not only finish them, but finish them *well*. Don't tell the concert promoters I said this, but when I walk off stage after making seventy thousand people get up out of their seats and rap along with me, they could hand me a check for a dollar and I'd still feel like I was on top of the world.

So while we definitely want our kids to get good grades, we don't want their only motivation to be the material reward they'll occasional recieve for those grades. We want them to begin to understand that the greatest reward they're going to get is actually the satisfaction that comes from successfully completing the process.

## GETTING HOUSEHOLD NUMBERS

Since getting good grades is so important in this family, the number-one job that our children have around the house (although right now this mainly applies to Diggy and Russy) is to make sure their homework is the *first* thing they do when they get home from school every day. As I mentioned earlier, that means no video games, no text messaging, no playing basketball, no watching TV, and no running around in the backyard or skateboarding until they've shown me that they've finished their homework. That's a daily job that's non-negotiable. Sometimes Russy will even get a jump by starting on his homework on the car ride back from school, but he's still got to prove to me that he's finished before he can get into the other stuff. And there's no TV show that they "just have to see," or game that they have to play "really quick" that can get them out of that job. Doing their homework is their number-one priority in this house.

But while it's true that we put a very heavy emphasis on getting good grades at school, it's also important that they get good numbers around the house. That's why we also give our children household chores to do each week. Frankly, there's really not that much to do, since we've been blessed with a housekeeper who helps around the house and landscaping crews that rake the leaves and cut the grass. But while we appreciate those blessings, we also don't want our kids to grow up expecting other people to be cleaning up for them and after them. And since they're growing up in this sort of privileged environment, Joey and I feel like it's even more important that the kids have chores, to help teach them about responsibility and hard work.

Having said that, the only kids who actually have assigned chores right now are Russy and Diggy. Since the older kids were always splitting time between here and their mother's house, we never really assigned them specific chores around the house. While the three of them definitely helped out a great deal when they were home, we really didn't have set jobs for them. But since the younger boys are here all the time, we've decided to handle things a little differently with them.

The way it works for Diggy and Russy is that they are both

assigned a set of chores for a week or two. For Diggy, it might be emptying the garbage on the first floor, cleaning up the bathroom he and Russy share, and sweeping out the garage. For Russy, it might be feeding the dog (and cleaning up after him if he poops in the house), taking out the garbage on the second floor, and cleaning the fish tank. If they finish all those chores and do them well, then we'll give them an allowance on Friday. And after a few weeks, we'll rotate the chores to keep things fair and balanced.

What's a little different about our house is that we'll also give the kids extra money for doing jobs outside of their assigned chores. Their allowance is enough to cover little things like a snack after school, a new CD, or a trip to the movies, but not enough to pay for all the clothes or gadgets they're always asking for. The idea is that by doing extra stuff, they'll be able to start to develop a sense of financial independence. So far, though, the only one who's really taken advantage of that option is Russy. While JoJo and Diggy seem content to just ask us for stuff, Russy really hustles to build up his savings. He'll unload the dishwasher, rub my feet, help shovel the driveway, clean out the pool—anything to get a few extra dollars in his pocket.

At first Diggy and JoJo thought he was a little crazy for doing all that extra work around the house, but they've started to notice how much it's paying off for Russy. When we go to the mall and they're asking for a $20 loan, Russy's pulling out his Rush Card (a banking card his Uncle Russell helped create for people who have trouble getting a credit card) and buying whatever he wants to with his own money. In fact, Russy's got so much money saved up that sometimes he'll loan my husband and me a few bucks when we're short on cash (provided we pay him back with interest, of course!).

I'm hoping that JoJo and Diggy will follow their little brother's lead and become more focused on earning extra money for themselves and less dependent on asking my husband and me for things. When kids can start paying for things they want themselves, it gives them a much greater appreciation for the value of a dollar. When it's just a matter of Mommy saying yes or no, kids don't put too much thought into whether that sweatshirt they want costs thirty or three hundred dollars. It's just a swipe of Mommy's credit card to them. But when they pay for that sweatshirt themselves, they'll start to think about just how badly they "have to have it." For instance, the little boy across the street from us has one of those four-wheel all-terrain vehicles that they make for kids. Whenever Russy would see him riding around on it, he'd come running inside and ask us to buy one for him. Finally one day I looked them up online and saw that they cost around $600. So I told Russy that while that was more than his daddy and I wanted to spend, since he had that much in the bank, he could use his Rush Card to buy one if really wanted it. Well, when Russy was faced with spending his *own* money on that ATV, he suddenly didn't need it so bad! He realized that when you're buying things for yourself, rather than asking for them from your parents, the cost actually does matter.

That's a very important lesson for kids to learn. Granted, I think Russy's a bit of a special case—not every ten-year-old is going to save up enough money to be able to buy his own ATV. But if you can encourage your kids to save up enough of their allowance to buy even the little things in their lives, it can make a big difference in how much they ask for things. If they can even just pay for the candy bar they want when you're in the checkout line at the supermarket, or the popcorn they're begging for at the movies, it will give them a better sense of what things cost in life, and just how hard you have to work to get them.

I do want to add one more thing about Russy—even though he really is focused on getting paid, the ultimate motivation for his hard work is love, not greed. That's really become clear to me through the amazing job he's done helping me with Miley. He's always offering to help feed her, or to rock her, or to watch her if I have to run out of the room for a minute. Just the other night Miley woke up crying at around 3:00 A.M., so I went into her room to give her a bottle. While I was getting it ready, Russy came in, picked her up and started trying to rock her back to sleep. "Sweetheart, you can't be up right now," I told him. "You've got to be ready to go to school in the morning." "But I heard her crying," he said. "And I wanted to help you." "That's very sweet," I replied. "But you've really got to go back to bed." So he put her back down, but as he was walking out of the room he stopped and told me, "If she won't go back to sleep and you need me, just call. I'll come back and help." And I could tell he really meant it. He wasn't looking to earn a few extra bucks for some clothes or a new Game Boy. It was three o'clock in the morning, and he really just wanted to help out. That's because he gets a genuine sense of satisfaction from being helpful and a good worker.

That sense of satisfaction you get from working hard and helping out is something that I hope JoJo and Diggy will also start to develop. I'm not saying that they don't help out with Miley, because they do. All the kids, including Angela and Vanessa when they're home, have helped whenever they've been asked. The difference is that Russy doesn't have to be asked— the good feeling he gets from working hard has him *asking* us for ways he can help. And I believe the satisfaction he derives from working hard is going to pay off for him down the road. It's why he's got more money than his brothers combined right now. And if he does end up following in the footsteps of his Uncle Russell, that love of helping out and pitching in will probably have a lot to do with it.

The amazing job Russy has done with Miley leads me to the last point I want to make in this section, which is the importance of teaching your children not to "typecast" certain responsibilities. In other words, we don't want them to think that some jobs around the house are only for girls, while others are only for boys. We want them to understand that if there's a job to be done and they're capable of doing it, then that's the job for them. There's no job that Diggy and Russy can get out of just because they're boys, just like there's no job that Vanessa and Angela should think they can get into just because they're girls. Starting at a very young age, we want our kids to understand that there are no restrictions on what you can or should do because of your gender.

That belief is another reason that I really love the job Russy's doing helping out with Miley. He doesn't look at giving a baby a bottle as something only a girl should do. He sees it as a way to help his mother, and that's all that really matters to him. And my hope is that he'll carry that attitude with him throughout his life, so that when he's married and has kids of his own, he won't look at changing diapers or feeding a baby as "women's work" but will be right there helping his wife the same way he's been helping me.

## MAKE TIME FOR MEETINGS

Demanding that everyone get numbers is just one of the ways we copy a business model in *Run's House*. Another way we try to operate like a business is by holding family meetings. But instead of in an office or a boardroom, our meetings usually take place with all of us sitting around the couch in our living room. Despite the informal setting, I've found that holding meetings is one of the most effective ways of making sure that *Run's House* is running smoothly.

My strategy on when to call a meeting is pretty simple: If I feel like stupidity or negativity or laziness has infiltrated our house, I call a little church session in our living room and preach on the problem. Anytime I see stupidity invading our home, my meetings are like roach spray: I pull it out and kill whatever's not supposed to be there.

Meetings are particularly helpful because it allows us to collectively address what's troubling the family. By airing out our issues in
a group setting, we can avoid the kind of one-on-one confrontations
that can become tense and uncomfortable. That is why if I have a
problem with how Angela is handling her money, I won't call a
meeting and only come down hard on her. Instead, I might start off
by addressing a similar situation, but one that's not as serious, that
JoJo or Russy recently went through themselves with money. And by
handling it that way, I can send subliminal messages to Angela without having to put her out on an island in front of the family and
make her feel uncomfortable. Or sometimes I'll call a meeting that's
not aimed at anyone in particular, but that still allows me to speak
on a subject that I think needs to be addressed. For instance, I might
talk about sharing as a concept, rather than bringing up something
selfish I saw one of the kids do. And I believe the lack of direct confrontation in our meetings is what has made them so effective. We
want to confront issues, not necessarily people. The result is that
while a lot of kids would rebel against the idea of constantly having
to sit down and discuss sensitive topics with their parents and their
siblings, our kids are comfortable with it. Not only don't they seem
to resent having meetings, they've even suggested holding a few on
their own. They trust that the meetings won't become a screaming match, or a blame game, or an excuse for me to start handing
out punishments. They know the meetings are a genuine attempt to
clear up issues without making anyone feel bad about themselves.

We've had a lot of family meetings in *Run's House,* on all sorts of
different subjects. Probably the most powerful one we ever had was
also the first one we ever called. It was around the time Justine and
I were about to get married and we were worried about how Vanessa, Angela, and JoJo were going to react to Justine becoming their
stepmother. We sat them down and tried to explain that there was
nothing bad or weird about getting a "new mommy." Instead, we
told them that they were actually incredibly lucky because now
they had two sets of parents when most kids only had one! Instead of

feeling bad about the situation, we tried to help them see it as a positive. It was a very difficult meeting to have, but I'm very glad that we went through with it. Because not long after the talk, I heard Vanessa, with obvious pride, repeat the "double parent" thing. That made me feel so great. I knew then that even though it had been an uncomfortable subject to bring up, by doing so we had helped our children not only address, but embrace, a potentially distressing period in their lives. And as Justine can tell you, when big changes in a family *aren't* addressed, it can create a lot of bad feelings.

## TALK BEFORE IT'S TOO LATE

It's true, holding meetings is one of the most important things we do as parents. We've found that the more we confront the problems in our family, the easier it is to get past them. I've also lived in a home where issues were rarely confronted, and in retrospect I can see how that avoidance created some painful times.

My parents split up when I was a teenager, and after living with my father for a minute (a situation I'll talk about in more detail later in the book), my mother took my sister and me to live with her new husband and his daughter. Her new husband always treated my sister and me well, but I always sensed tension between my mother and our stepsister, Tiny. Over time I became convinced that my mother was being unfair to Tiny, and as a strong-willed teenager, I decided that it was my job to do something about that injustice. Using my twisted teenage logic, I decided that I would be mean to my younger sister Michele in order to even things out! I never talked to anyone about how I was feeling—I just made it my business to be mean to my sister! It all came to a boil one night at dinner when my mother asked me out of the blue, "Justine, why are you always treating your sister so mean?" And with more than a little attitude in my voice, I replied, "Because you're so mean to Tiny!"

Well, I had barely gotten the words out of my mouth when my mother came flying across the table, grabbed me by the hair, and threw me up against the fridge in a headlock! Lord, I had never seen her that mad before! I was literally scared for my life, so I started yelling, "Mommy, stop! Mommy, I love you!" hoping that she would calm down and let me go. And of course after a moment she did regain control of herself.

And similarly to my blow up with JoJo, once my mother and I let all that emotion out of the box, things did get better. My mother probably became more aware of how she was acting toward her stepdaughter, and as a result, the dynamic in the house improved a lot. It just took someone to say something about it. I can laugh about that incident now, because my mother and my stepsisters are so close now that it's ridiculous. And my baby sister, Michele—the one I was so mean to—we're that close, too. It feels like we talk ninety times a day, we stay on the phone so much.

But looking back, I still feel bad about the whole situation, because Michele was innocent and didn't deserve to be treated badly by me any more than Tiny deserved to be treated badly by my mother. I know that we didn't all treat each other that way out of spite—we did it because we didn't know how to communicate the pain and confusion we were all feeling after the divorce. I truly believe if we had called a family meeting when the families had first blended, that scene would have never taken place. We would have been more honest about how we felt and worked our way through our issues. But instead we all kept what we felt inside, and like all combustible things that get bottled up for too long, it was only a matter of time before it exploded.

That's why I want to encourage all of you to make meetings a big part of your family life. None of us look forward to sitting down and discussing the pain we're feeling, or the bad times we're going through, but if you can't talk about those things with the people you love, then who can you talk about them with? My kids know that there's nothing under the sun that they can't talk to me about. The same thing with my husband. Whatever is troubling anyone in my family, I want to talk it out. The same way I know they would want to talk about whatever is troubling me. So the next time a situation starts bubbling in your family, sit everyone down on the couch or at the kitchen table or wherever and just talk your way through it. Meetings only take a few minutes, but they can save you from years of hurt and resentment. I promise you'll feel much better sharing what you're feeling with the people you love instead of keeping it inside.

## THE SIMMONS CYCLE OF SUCCESS

While meetings are definitely a great way to get everybody on the same page in our family, we've also found that another effective way to teach unity, discipline, and hard work is for the family to work on an *actual* business together. Not just to run the family like a business, but to actually roll up our sleeves and take on a project together. We've been fortunate to do that on *Run's House*, although I realize that hosting a reality show isn't possible for most families. Similarly, most fathers aren't lucky enough to be able to help their daughters sell sneakers, or their sons to sign record deals. Still, I don't want our situation to discourage you from trying this in your own family. As many times as we've been blessed with high-profile projects, the truth is, we've taken on just as many jobs that weren't as glamorous or lucrative. And even though that work was done outside of the limelight, I believe it was absolutely crucial in bringing this family together and teaching it about the importance of hard work and trusting each other.

One such situation was when our family decided to help Bishop Jordan build a new retreat on Holy Ground—an old hotel on a hundred-acre plot of land he had purchased in upstate New York. Bishop Jordan is a rich dude—he lives in a mansion, drives a beautiful car—but the situation we found on our first day at Holy Ground looked pretty poor. The buildings were broken down, there was no running water, no heat, no this, no that. But Bishop Jordan asked for our help, so there was no turning back. For the rest of that summer, we'd leave New Jersey by around 6:00 A.M. just to get to Holy Ground by nine. And once got there, we'd work all day fixing up rooms, throwing out old junk, and cleaning up the grounds until the bishop would finally say, "You are now dismissed!" sometime after dusk. And then we'd just pile into the car and drive three hours back to our home. It was serious work!

We didn't just work together out on Holy Ground, either. On the weekends, we would help tape the bishop's sermons at his church in Manhattan. Every Sunday morning, Vanessa would be upstairs assisting the director, while Russy and Diggy would each be working a camera. JoJo would get there early to help set up the audio for the broadcast, while Angela would wait around to do whatever she could to help out. And once we had finished taping the broadcast, we'd head to the back of the church and fold mail for the rest of the afternoon. Whatever the bishop asked, that's what we would do.

I'll admit that there were times that I worried we were asking the kids to carry too heavy a load. That maybe it was too much to ask an eight-year-old boy to hold a camera for a four-hour church service. That maybe it was too much to ask our daughters to help out at church on Sunday mornings, when many girls their age were just getting in from the clubs. That maybe it was too much to ask a teenage boy who wanted to produce rap records to instead spend hours setting up the audio for a gospel church service.

But over time, I began to see that they *could* handle the load. That instead of weighing my family down, the hard work was actually lifting it up. I first began to see the change during the days at Holy Ground, but one moment stands out in particular. On the way home, we'd always stop for a sandwich at this roadside diner. After we'd been working at the Holy Ground for a while, I noticed that after we were finished, all the kids would talk about how good the sandwiches tasted. Now trust me, there was nothing special about those sandwiches (no disrespect to the restaurant—they really just weren't that good). It's just that my kids were learning that *all* food tastes better after a long day of hard work. And it wasn't just food— soon my kids were starting to have more appreciation for *everything* in their lives after putting in that kind of hard work.

What really cemented their new attitude of gratitude for me was one day when we returned home from a particularly long day working upstate. As we walked in the front door, Russy suddenly turned to me and said, "Daddy, we have the perfect life!" Now most kids aren't talking about perfection unless they're talking about a gift or a party. But walking into a big, comfortable, air-conditioned house after working all those hours felt so good that Russy couldn't help but think it was perfection! Mind you, I'm not talking about the big crib you see on MTV—at the time we were living in a little house around the corner. The house was nothing fancy, but after Russy spent all day working alongside his parents and his siblings, it felt like a castle to him! Most kids would have been sulking after getting their butts kicked the way Russy's had been that day, but all the hard work had taught him a lesson instead. It had taught him to appreciate his life.

That's why I can't do anything but laugh when I hear people say that my kids are spoiled. I'm not trying to brag, but my kids are actually some of the most hardworking, responsible, disciplined kids out there. And not just because of the work they've done for Bishop Jordan—they've also exhibited those qualities in filming *Run's House.* I know some people might say, "It's a reality show. How hard could that be?" But trust me, filming that show *is* hard work for those kids. As I'm writing this, they've given up their whole summer to tape the fifth season. And as a result, they are not getting to do what other kids are doing this summer—namely, running around without a care in the world. Instead, they're getting up early in the morning to meet with producers, then strapping on mics for hours at a time, never knowing when the work is going to end. That's not an easy job for kids. In fact, when we were recently planning a birthday party for Diggy, his main request was, "Please, please don't make me film it for the show." Because to Diggy, filming isn't glamorous—it's work. And when we said, "Fine, it won't go on the show," that was the best birthday present we could have given him.

I don't want anyone to get the wrong idea here and think that I'm complaining about filming *Run's House*. Just the opposite—the show has been an incredible blessing for this family and we're all so thankful for it. I'm just trying to demonstrate that whether it's working for the bishop, or working for MTV, or whoever, this family accepts that the world will only pay us as much as we work.

And to be perfectly honest, things aren't always peaches and cream when you're in business with your family. You don't have the luxury of leaving your arguments and frustrations behind at the office the way someone working a traditional nine-to-five job does. When you work with your family, those issues don't disappear when you clock out and head home. They're still present when you're eating dinner or getting ready for bed or driving the kids to basketball practice. It's not easy to put those issues in your back pocket and forget about them until the next day.

I'll admit that the constant connection to our professional lives has been an issue for Justine and me at times, the main issue being that we have decidedly different approaches to how we do business. Personally, I like every move I make to be very well thought out. When it comes to our careers, I spend a lot of time thinking about the implications of every phone call I make, every meeting I take, or every e-mail I send. I'm a very hands-on manager.

While Justine takes our family business just as seriously as I do, she is probably a little more impulsive than I am. Because she's such a good-hearted, trusting person, she is more likely to just pick up the phone and ask a producer on *Run's House* for a favor, or make a promise to a stylist, or approve a photo shot because she is trying to make someone happy, without giving as much thought to the long-term implications. Her heart will always be in the right place, but her actions can sometimes drive me a little crazy when I don't think they necessarily fit into whatever game plan we've been working with.

They way we get around those issues in our professional life is the same way we get through them in our marriage: communication. When you and your spouse are working on raising a family *and* running a business together, it's absolutely critical that you two always be on the same page. Which is why I have to remind Justine sometimes, "I know you just want to make these people happy, and that's beautiful, but you also have to let me know what you're doing. We don't want to step on each other's toes. Let's stop making decisions on the fly and stick to the script."

And if you can keep that line of communication open, I think you'll find running a business with your family is one of the most beautiful things you can do. Yes, some of the drama that comes with running a business might occasionally leak into your family life, but ultimately we've found that the positives far outweigh the negatives. Whether it's a reality TV show, a restaurant, or a clothing boutique, there's nothing like seeing your family build a project from the ground up and turn it into a success. That's why I love walking into the Chinese restaurant near my house and seeing the daughter up front taking the orders, the cousin making the deliveries, and the mother and father in the back making the food. Sure, there are probably moments when they get frustrated as all heck with each other, but I also know that in their hearts they are thankful for being able to work every day at that restaurant with the people they love. And when, because of their hard work, that restaurant becomes a success and they open up a new one with more seats, and then maybe a chain of restaurants after that, I know that their success will taste much sweeter than if they had been working with strangers. I really believe that God wants us to operate in that manner: working, sharing, and succeeding side by side with our loved ones.

## NO FAMILY FREEBIES

One of the reasons we're committed to teaching our kids to work hard today is so that they'll be prepared to step into the various Simmons family businesses down the road. I don't know how much I'll be able to hand over to them, but hopefully it will be substantial. And I don't want to be one of these wealthy people that pass on their wealth on to kids who don't understand the hard work and dedication that's needed to maintain it. It's a story as old as business itself: Kids are given free passes and allowed to run amok in the family business, and eventually they ruin the business, themselves—or both. I don't want my kids hanging around waiting on an inheritance. I want them to remember that God gives every bird its food, but he does not throw it into the nest. God gives us the nuts, but he does not crack them. So rather than waiting for their ship to come in, I want my kids to swim out to it! In other words, I want my kids to be ready to work their hardest and take advantage of any opportunity that's presented to them.

That's why one of the mottoes in the Simmons world has always been, "No Family Freebies." In other words, just because I run a business, or Uncle Russell or Aunt Kimora has a company, doesn't mean that our kids get a free pass when it comes to doing the work. If they want to work at Run Athletic, or Phat Farm, or Baby Phat, that will be arranged. But they have to pay their dues once they get there just like everyone else. To paraphrase what I said in the last chapter, we don't operate under the concept of "I'm rich, so you're rich, too." In fact, that attitude is the opposite to how we think. This isn't a family that's going to produce heirs and heiresses who think that they can get over on the strength of their last name. I don't think that's fair to them, and I don't think it's fair to our family.

In fact, as I'm writing this we're taping an episode that follows JoJo as he interns for Uncle Russell, who is making sure that JoJo is getting anything but a free ride. On the first day, Russell let JoJo sit down at the desk from which Russell runs his empire. The seat where I know JoJo wants to sit one day himself. Russell let JoJo chill there for a few moments and then asked him, "Do you like how that feels?" When JoJo said, "Yes," then Russell yelled, "So what? Get up!" and threw him out of his office. Not because Russell doesn't like JoJo, but because he wanted him to know that just because he was his nephew didn't mean he was going to be able to sit in that proverbial seat without putting in the work. JoJo was going to have to earn that spot. The first step was interning for Kevin Leong, Russell's top clothing designer. That means JoJo's job is getting coffee, running errands, picking up clothing samples, taking food orders — even cleaning up after Kevin's dog when it poops! And it's proven difficult for JoJo, because like most other eighteen-year-olds, his main objective in life is to be cool and accepted. Not to be running errands and getting laughed at for picking up dog doo-doo. But Uncle Russell isn't trying to let JoJo play it cool — he's trying to make a man out of him. He's going to show him how hard he has to work, how many sacrifices he'll have to make, how he has to humble himself and learn how to tap into his inner discipline. And if he can do those things, then hopefully he'll be able to write the next successful chapter in the Simmons family story.

If you look at our family's history, we've been able to achieve so much by working together. I can remember working for Russell in the late 1970s, taking subways all over New York City and taping up flyers for the disco parties he used to throw. It wasn't glamorous work, but it certainly paid off. Because working with Russell helped expose me to the business side of hip-hop, an experience that ultimately turned into Run DMC. And the success we enjoyed with Run DMC in turn helped provide Russell with the opportunity to start Def Jam. In turn, the success of Def Jam helped pave the way for Phat Farm. The success of Phat Farm helped pave the way for Kimora's success with Baby Phat, and my own success with Run Athletics. And the success of all those ventures helped pave the way for the important charity work our brother Danny is doing with Rush Philanthropic. And now we're seeing that cycle happen all over again. Russell's success with television shows like *Def Comedy Jam* and *Def Poetry* helped make *Run's House* possible. And the success of *Run's House* has paved the way for Justine's Brown Sugar

Jewelry, for the girls' Pastry, for Angela's *Run Down* magazine, and for whatever moves JoJo, Diggy, and Russy end up making too. But despite having all these individual projects on the table, we still always operate as a unit. Everyone in our family knows they must support each other and look out for one another if we're going to lay the groundwork for even more family success.

## RUN'S TAKE BACK

Meetings are an incredibly effective way of taking back your family from whatever forces are pushing it out of your control. So if you aren't holding them already, try to make meetings a regular part of your family's life. Since the idea of sitting everyone down in a formal setting might seem a little intimidating or awkward to your kids at first, it's OK to ease your way into it. Maybe you want to start by holding a brief family conversation at the start of every dinner. It could be as simple as asking your kids, "So, how was your day today?" Or you might want to get a little more specific. For instance, a friend of mine's father used to start dinner every night by asking each of his kids, "So tell me, what have you done today in our family's pursuit of excellence?" And then each child would have to talk about a test they did well on that day, or a game they scored a lot of points in, or even just a chore that they completed around the house. Anything that could prove that they had improved their lives a little bit that day. And while their father's question was always posed in a friendly, not-too-serious manner, it got my friend and his siblings comfortable with talking about their lives in a family setting. And of course, that nightly questioning also served to reinforce his parents' expectations for their children. So see if you can integrate a regular question, or a short report from each of the kids, into your dinner routine.

(One quick aside about meals: Try to make sure the TV

isn't on when the family sits down to eat together. That's something that we admittedly struggle with ourselves, since we have two TVs in the kitchen. But we've found that if we can have everyone sitting around the same table and actually talking to each other instead of zoning out to whatever's on the screen, lots of important information can be shared during dinner. So remember, as soon as you serve the meal, turn off the TV.)

And when that short dinner discussion starts to feel natural to your kids, then maybe move on to scheduling a more formal family meeting once a month. It doesn't have to be too intense, maybe just half an hour after dinner on the last Sunday of every month. But you should try to establish some sort of set time when your kids know they're going to have to sit down with you and discuss whatever the main issues in your home are. You should even post a sign-up sheet in the kitchen where the children can write down their suggestions for what they'd like to see discussed at the meetings. So rather than viewing family meetings as a time when you're going to address all the issues that are bothering you as a parent, the children can see it as a time when they can get some things off their chests, too.

And once you've made those monthly meetings a normal part of your family's rhythm, you can start to hold them the way we do in *Run's House*: impromptu sessions that quickly address whatever sort of drama seems to be threatening the status quo in your home. For my money, those are the most effective kinds of family meetings—quick strikes that can nip arguments or insecurities or bad behavior in the bud. But ultimately, whether you want to schedule them in advance, or only hold them as situations arise, as long as your family feels comfortable sitting down together and tackling the issues that face you as a team, you've really scored a touchdown as a parent!

## CHAPTER 6

# Make Your Children
# Feel Large

I can still remember when word first spread that I was now calling myself Reverend Run. Listening to the radio in New York City, it seemed like every caller had something negative to say about me becoming a reverend. It was a dumb idea. I wasn't a "real" reverend. I looked like a fool wearing a collar. I must be trying to run some sort of con on people. But even though those comments stung, I can't say they really surprised me that much. After all, hip-hop at that time was more focused on celebrating gangsters than God. The idea of Run trading in his godfather hat and Adidas for a collar and a cape was laughable to most people. Yet despite all the ridicule I knew I would encounter, despite how silly I knew I might look to some, I never for a second lost confidence in my vision for Reverend Run. The laughter didn't depress me and the doubters didn't dissuade me. Despite all the hating, I still felt very large about myself.

I've always been blessed with a strong sense of confidence. For most of my life, even during my times of struggle, I've still felt tremendous self-esteem. That confident outlook is what allowed me to believe I could find fame and fortune as a rapper at a time when hip-hop was considered to be a passing fad. It's what later gave me the strength to put on that preacher's collar when most people thought I looked like a fool. It's what gave me the swagger to pitch MTV a reality show about a functional family when the rest of their reality shows celebrated dysfunction. Without that innate sense of confidence fueling me, I would have never been able to make it this far in my journey.

That's why I'm very, very focused on instilling a similar feeling of confidence in my children. In the Simmons house, we describe that sense of steady confidence as "feeling large." In other words, instead of looking to shrink into the background, we want our children to feel comfortable standing out. No matter what room they step into, we want our kids to feel so comfortable that they look like a piece of furniture. We want our children to feel like they can always take a chance, or go against the grain instead of being worried about what other people think. Instead of feeling insecure about who they are, or how they look, we always want them to feel beautiful and proud. Instead of feeling small and deflated when they walk out these doors and into the world, we want them to always shine brightly and feel large.

I realize some people aren't as comfortable encouraging their children to walk around with that much swagger. They don't want their children to appear arrogant or to look too haughty. While I can appreciate that mind-set, I've always been inspired by a quote I've heard attributed to Nelson Mandela: "As we let our own light shine, we unconsciously give other people permission to do the same." I relate very strongly to that sentiment, because I absolutely love people who shine hard. While others might be put off by the swagger of a Puffy or a Donald Trump, I'm actually drawn to the light that they emit. Instead of making me feel small, I find their self-confidence contagious, a reminder that we're all capable of big things. If you have a bright light shinning inside you, I don't think it ever helps the world to cover it up. Personally, I'd be hurt if Donald Trump dulled down his shine, or if Puffy suddenly stopped flossing so hard. To me, it would be a tragedy for those things to happen. Because the world would have fewer sources of inspiration.

My belief that emanating confidence elevates the people around you instead of alienating them is why I encourage my kids to shine as brightly as they possibly can. Just the other day I told Diggy, "Man, stop being embarrassed to be number one in your class. People aren't going to resent you for that; they'll just be inspired to work even harder." Just like I encourage him to be the best basketball player on his team, or the flyest dresser in his school, or the smoothest dancer at the party. Justine and I don't want anyone in our home to *ever* feel weird about being number one at *anything* they do.

Of course, we also don't want our kids to feel so large that their heads swell up. So while we encourage our kids to feel like royalty, we don't want them looking at everyone else as peasants, either. We want our kids' confidence to radiate from within, not to come at the expense of someone else's sense of worth. So while we encourage Russy to feel great about his fresh new pair of Phat Farm Classics, we never want him to tease another kid for having scuffed-up sneakers. Or while we want Diggy to be the first guy out on the floor at his school dances, we don't ever want him teasing the insecure kid who's holding up the wall. Instead, we want him to reach out to that kid, to pull him off the wall and make him feel part of the party, too. So yes, while we want our kids to be cool, it's with the understanding that nothing is cooler than kindness. That's the balance that we seek every day.

And as we'll detail in this chapter, there are still moments when our children lose that balance. When Angela might not feel as beautiful on the inside as the world perceives her to be on the outside. When Russy might feel intimidated by Diggy's success, instead of being inspired by it. When JoJo might feel overwhelmed by matching my success as a rapper. But as our kids grow and evolve, as parents we just try to stay on top of the changes. So that we can be ready with a hug if a kid's feeling down, or a pinprick if their heads are looking too swollen. We want to let them know that no matter what the world says, or how they feel about themselves, they'll always be large to us.

## ARE YOU INTERESTED IN EVERYTHING THEY DO?

The first step in helping your kids to feel large is also the simplest: Let them know you're interested in evvvvvverything they do. That you're listening to everything they say. That no matter what's happening in your adult life, nothing is as important to you as what they're doing that very moment. It might seem like a lot to ask, but you have to remember that as a parent, your approval means everything to your child. At times they might try to act like they don't care what you think, but don't let them fool you. Even as adults, we still care about what our parents think about us. Keep it funky—consciously or subconsciously, don't we all *still* seek our parents' love and approval? Of course we do. So just imagine what an eleven-year-old is thinking. That's why you can never forget that in your child's eyes, you're the coolest kid on the block. You're the most popular girl in school. You're the upperclassman they want to impress. You're the president of the club they want to belong to. They can talk about the other kids all they want, but ultimately only *you* possess the approval that will build real confidence in their hearts. That's why if your kids don't feel like you're interested in what they're doing, or listening to what they're saying, they're going to feel small. But when they sense that you're always paying attention, cheering them on and listening to what they say, they're going to feel large, like they're capable of anything.

For example, on a recent Friday night I saw Diggy out in the driveway practicing a skateboarding move that was giving him trouble. To be honest, I was in the mood to just chill out and watch a good movie, but I sensed that Diggy was getting frustrated and needed some encouragement. So instead of heading downstairs to our movie room, I said, "Hey Dig, want to take a ride over to the skate park?" I wasn't really offering him anything other than a ride and my time (I certainly can't help him with a skateboarding move), but when he saw that I was interested in what he was doing, his eyes lit up. We went over the skate park and I stood there for an hour watching Diggy try to get that move down. (I think it was called "grinding," where he jumps up on a rail and slides across it on the bottom of his board instead of the wheels). Anyway, I must have watched him try that move a hundred times in a row until he finally got it right. And when he finally did nail it, he skated right over to me and said, "Daddy, did you see that? I did it!" Man, when I reached out and gave him a pound, it was a magical moment for both of us. I could tell Diggy felt large, not only because he had mastered something that had been a struggle for him, but because his daddy had witnessed him do it. And this is the key: It wouldn't have felt as special to him if I had stayed home and watched a movie and only heard about it from him after the fact. It wouldn't have felt the same if I'd just paused my movie for a second, said, "Uh-huh. That's great, son," and then pushed "Play" again. What made that moment so inspiring for Diggy was knowing that his daddy cared enough to stand there for an hour on his movie night, watching all the struggle and then sharing in the triumph. That's the kind of moment that makes a child feel very large.

To build up your child's self-esteem, you have to try to be there for all those small, seemingly insignificant moments. If Russy has just learned how to do the "Superman" dance, I have to come over at watch him do it. Because he'll feel small if he learns a new dance and I don't seem excited. Or if he's standing on the diving board screaming "Dad, look! I'm going to dive in backward!" then I have to watch him do it. If he screams "Daddy, look!" nine times, then I have to watch at least eight times and clap each time he dives in. Otherwise, he's going to think that Daddy doesn't care. And that's going to leave him feeling small.

It's also very important to get involved in whatever your child's passion is. If they're like Diggy and love skateboarding, then you need to get used to spending a lot of time at that skate park. Or, for example, let's say that like millions of kids out there, your kid likes hip-hop. It all might sound like noise to you, but if that's what your kid is passionate about, then go to a rap concert anyway. Or if that feels like too much of a stretch to you, find out which rappers your kids like and then go buy their albums. Listen to the music yourself, get into what's inspiring your kid, and then try to build some common ground. Even though it may feel unnatural at first, it can be a very effective way of staying close to your child. For instance, Jam Master Jay's mother Connie Mizzel was always close with Jay and all his friends. So when she heard us talking about "cham" shirts (that's what all the cool kids in Queens wore back in the day), she would go out and buy some for us. She didn't particularly like the shirts herself, but she knew that's what we liked and she wanted to be part of her son's life. We used to wonder, "How does she know that we're rocking cham shirts?," but we also loved her for trying to be such a supportive presence in our world. Or take the mother of JoJo's friend Zach. She doesn't want him out in the streets and up in the clubs, but she also knows how much Zach loves hip-hop. So she takes him to the concerts and the clubs herself. That way he can be around the scene and see his favorite artists, but she can also keep an eye on him. Instead of taking an extreme approach like, "No, I don't want you going to concerts," or "I don't care, do whatever you want to do," she takes the middle path and actually goes with him. And the result is that with his mother's unwavering support, he's become very confident about being successful as a rapper.

I love seeing that sort of relationship, because my father supported me in a similar way. When I first told him that I was going to drop out of school and go on tour with Kurtis Blow, he was very concerned about that decision. He believed very strongly in education and wanted me to focus on school. Yet despite his reservations, he also wanted to support my passion. So when I was about sixteen, he wrote me a poem to try to express the pride he felt watching me follow my dreams. He told me how much he liked my energy, my confidence, and the people I was surrounding myself with. He told me he could see me going very far one day.

Man, hearing those words from my father made me feel so large. Even though I knew it was his dream to see me become a doctor or a lawyer or a professor, the poem let me know that he respected *my* dreams, too. And knowing that he had my back fueled me through a lot of tough times, even to this day. I'm so thankful that my father took the time to share those thoughts with me, and I always want to make sure that I show similar love and support to my own kids so that they can feel the sense of confidence and self-esteem that I enjoyed.

One thing that Jay's mother, Zach's mother, my father, and all great parents have in common is that they didn't try to judge their children's dreams. They might not have understood the music their kids listened to, or the clothes they wanted to wear, or even their choice in careers, but ultimately all of that wasn't important to them. Rather, they were willing to step out of their own ideas and into the dreams of their children. That's a tremendous lesson to remember, because too often as parents we want to focus on the things we're into, instead of what's going to capture our children's interest.

I've certainly been guilty of making that mistake myself, most recently in my relationship with JoJo. It was addressed in an episode of *Run's House* that focused on my concern that JoJo didn't seem interested in hanging out with me anymore. In fact, I was so concerned that we were drifting apart that I bet him $800 that he would still have fun if he spent the day chillin' with his old man. So in this quest for fun with my son, I organized a basketball game, a trip to a batting cage, and a visit to a bookstore. But while my intentions were honorable, I made the mistake of picking activities that might have been fun for a younger kid (basketball and baseball) or me (the bookstore), but not necessarily things that JoJo would be into. Not surprisingly, JoJo viewed our day together as more of a chore than as a chance to reconnect with his dad. In retrospect, instead of forcing things on him that *I* thought would be fun, I probably should have taken him to a custom car shop, or a fresh clothing store in the city, the types of places that an eighteen-year-old boy would more likely get excited about.

So even though my heart (and my wallet) was open to having

fun with my son, my *mind* was still closed. And as the saying goes, "Having a closed mind is like having a closed parachute: You'll crash." That's why as parents, we can't lose sight of the fact that as our kids get older, their interests shift. The activities that helped us bond with an eight-year-old might not work anymore for an eighteen-year-old. We can't get settled in our ways and our comforts. We have to evolve with our kids, because forcing them to remain close on *our* terms can actually drive them further away. Try to remember that when you accept the change, you won't become estranged.

## LISTEN TO THE WHISPERS

Another crucial component in helping your kids feel large is to support them all the time, not just when it's fun or convenient. It's not enough to be a cheerleader when they're doing well or making you proud. You have to be there to soothe their wounds when the world beats them up a bit, too. While it's great to be able to give Diggy a pound when he's grinding on his skateboard, it's probably more important that I be there to support him all the times he falls on his butt. Just like it's great to be able to celebrate with Vanessa when she gets a role on *The Guiding Light*, but more important that I be there to give her a hug every time she comes home from an audition disappointed. It doesn't take much effort or insightfulness to help a kid feel large when they're doing well. They're going to rush over and tell you that they landed a big role, or scored the winning basket. However, they're probably not going to make as much noise about the fact that they didn't get off the bench in the game, or weren't picked for the school play. But those are precisely the moments that you have to hear their disappointment, to be in tune with how small they're feeling.

I was reminded of that truth during JoJo's internship at Phat Farm. As I mentioned, I loved the fact that Russell and Kevin Leong were challenging JoJo, giving him difficult assignments and even testing his humility by making him clean up dog doo-doo. But while

I loved their intention, I also began to notice that those methods were taking a toll on JoJo's confidence. Instead of making him feel like he was proving his worth, I sensed that the internship was starting to sap some of his swagger. I didn't want him to get too down on himself, so I decided to let him know just how much respect I had for how he was handling the situation. "Dear JoJo, you're a fine young man," I e-mailed him. "I don't know if I told you this, but how you've been dealing with working for Uncle Russell shows so much maturity and humility on your part. I couldn't be prouder. If you had the number-one record on the radio right now, it could not compete with how great I feel about your growth as a young man. I love you, and never forget that your father is so proud of how you're handling the situation." Of course JoJo tried to play it cool and only hit me back with a "Thanks, Pop," but I still believe he absorbed my message. After that e-mail, I noticed that a little bit of his swagger came back. Instead of looking withdrawn and unsure of himself every time he headed off to Uncle Russell's office, he seemed more upbeat about going to work. He seemed like he was looking forward to getting in the mix and rubbing shoulders with the big boys, instead of worrying about what was around the next corner. And I think a lot of that confidence came from my e-mail. Those words let him know that he wasn't playing himself when he picked up that dog doo-doo. Instead, he was just paying his dues, and in the process making his daddy proud.

It's particularly important that I always help JoJo feel large because he's following in my footsteps as a rapper. It can be a tremendous challenge to a child's confidence when they choose the same career as a successful parent, whether it's as a rapper, a football player, a politician, a writer, or whatever. When I think of JoJo trying to emulate my success as a rapper, I'm reminded of the words of the British philosopher Ben Jonson, who wrote: "Greatness of name in the father oft-times helps not . . . but overwhelms the son; they stand too near one another, the shadow kills the growth." I think the phenomenon that Jonson described was as real four hundred years ago in London as it is in New Jersey today. It's always very hard for a child to live up to the legacy of a parent. And let me say this—that would be true even if I had never sold a record in my life.

Every father, no matter what their profession or position in life, is a legend to their son. My father was a legend to me. I'm a legend to JoJo, and God willing, JoJo's son will feel the same way about him one day, too. I just feel that my professional success has given that truth a little extra weight in our relationship. I therefore need to go out of my way to make sure my stature never overshadows JoJo. I need him to understand that whether he sells ten records or ten million records, he's still going to be large in my mind. Whether it's through an e-mail or just a hug, I need him to know that I'm soooo happy with who he is right now. In my eyes, he's a star. By showing me that he's filled with humility and a strong work ethic, there's nothing else he could do to impress me. That's all I need.

Almost every parent has that same sense of pride in their own children. Unfortunately, not every parent knows how to express it. The key is to remember that you always have to sense your child's insecurities and then soothe them with love. Remember, JoJo had never come to me and said, "Dad, I want to be a rapper, but I'm worried that maybe you set the bar too high for me." Kids aren't going to articulate when they're feeling small. As a parent, it's up to *you* to read the weather patterns in your home, to know when things are getting chilly or it looks like it's going to rain. It's up to you to recognize the little signs of depression that your kids leave scattered around the house. It's up to you to not only interpret that there was a little something extra in that sigh, or that the bedroom door was slammed shut a little bit harder than normal, but to then step in and address the situation head-on. I believe it was the Navajo who used to say, "Listen to the whispers so you don't have to hear the screams," and that's at the heart of what I'm suggesting here. If your daughter feels small and insecure, make sure you hear it when she whispers that pain. Because when she's forced to let that pain out in a scream, it's going to blow out every window in your house. Or if you don't hear your child whispering that they're feeling the pressure of living up to the family name, the next sound you might hear is the police cruiser pulling up your driveway. Trust me, the papers are filled with stories of famous families that don't heed those warning signs. And since I never want to hear those kinds of screams, or any kind of screams for that matter, in *Run's House* I always try to listen to the whispers.

## WORRYING ABOUT THE WORLD

When it comes to making my children feel large, one of my concerns has always been that they are going to feel too large in relation to the world. While I want my kids to feel like they're capable of anything, I also don't want them to be too casual about the dangers that are out there. My family jokes that I worry too much, but it seems to me that there are so many dangers out there nowadays that you can't be too careful. For instance, a few months ago Diggy asked me to drop him off at a carnival with some of his friends. But instead of having me wait for him, he wanted me to leave him there, then come back and pick him up four hours later. Well, when I heard that, I told him he must be crazy, because I didn't think any parent in their right mind would let a thirteen-year-old wander around a carnival without any supervision. But Diggy told me that I was the one who was tripping, that his friends' parents didn't have a problem with them being at the carnival alone. At first I thought he was just lying about the other parents, but when I called around, his story checked out. Hearing those other parents say they weren't worried about leaving their kids at the carnival unsupervised really made me wonder, "Am I smothering my kids while these other parents are letting their kids feel large and in charge of their own lives?" For a moment I thought about changing my mind and letting Diggy go alone. But I decided that as a parent, you can't go by what other parents think is OK. You have to trust your gut and go with what you think is going to be

OK for your kids. And my gut told me that carnivals are a place where predators might be looking for kids, and I didn't want Diggy to be vulnerable, no matter how unlikely it was that something would happen.

I think finding the proper balance between letting your kids feel independent and being overprotective is one of the biggest challenges for parents today. Especially with the Internet becoming such a big part of children's lives. Of course I want my kids to be able to go online and take advantage of all the incredible information that's available to them. But I get scared by sites like MySpace because I'm very uncomfortable with the idea of my kids communicating with random strangers. While they're under the impression that they're chatting with other kids their age, they could really be talking to one of these sickos out there. And a kid like Russy is so innocent that when one of his online "friends" asks him, "Hey, where do you live?" he's liable to tell them, "Oh, I live on such and such road, in such and such town." Next thing you know, we'll have some guy in a car cruising outside of our house, looking for our kids.

My way of dealing with this dilemma has been to be very open about my fears with my kids. I tell them that while I know they'd like to go on sites like MySpace and Facebook, I just don't think they're safe. I don't mind Diggy watching skateboarding videos on YouTube, but I don't want him and Russy on these networking sites. They complained a little bit when I declared those sites off-limits, but they calmed down a bit after I told them, "Go to MySpace and Facebook. Type in your names and see how there are people out there pretending to be you. After you see that, there's no way you can tell me everyone is who they say they are on these sites!" And it's true—someone's got a fake Diggy page up, a fake JoJo page, a fake Vanessa page, a fake Angela page—someone even wasted their time making a fake MySpace page for me! And since it's set to "private," I don't even know what's on there. It's insane.

In my eyes, if you haven't met someone and spent time

with them, then they're not really your "friend." I don't feel like my kids need any "friends" that they've never met. I'd rather they make friends from school, from their sports teams, or from our church. Real live human beings with parents that I can call, not people who hide behind a fake name or picture. Maybe I'm a little old-fashioned, but that's how I feel.

And I'll keep it real—I don't only worry about online predators. I'm worry about them in day-to-day life, too. That's why I sometimes ask Diggy and Russy, "Has anyone tried to touch your pee-pee?" Again, maybe I'm being overprotective, but I've read about too many kids being taken advantage of by people they trust. I'm especially worried about Diggy, since he thinks he's thirteen going on twenty-three. He thinks he's grown and can handle himself, but in reality he's very naive and sweet— just like a thirteen-year-old boy should be. So rather than be embarrassed about it, I'm going to keep asking until they're grown.

I think the reason that I'm so paranoid is that a few years ago I learned that someone very close to me had been molested by their father. By a father that I would have *never* suspected of doing something like that in a million years. So when I learned that this man, a man that I trusted absolutely, was capable of such a thing, it turned my whole world upside down. The result is that now I feel like I have to ask my kids about everyone they're left alone with: babysitters, teachers, family friends, relatives—I don't care, I'm asking. So even though my kids might roll their eyes or my husband might tell me to stop being so paranoid, I'm going to keep asking. That's what really worries me—that if someone close to our family ever did do something, my kids wouldn't tell me because they'd want to protect that person. I'm trying to create an environment where there's no one they would feel bad about turning in.

However, I am concerned that my questioning is starting to get a little out of control. Not too long ago Russy was looking very sad after he came home from a basketball game, and when

I started to ask him what was wrong, he just looked at me with a really annoyed expression and said, "No, Mom! No one touched my pee-pee. Okay?" I had to laugh at that one, but it made me think that I'm going overboard with this. I do feel stupid after I ask them, and I don't want my kids growing up thinking that every man that they meet is a potential child molester. Because living in constant fear of that kind of situation would almost be as bad as going through the actual situation itself.

That's why I'm trying to find a balance between protecting my kids and spending too much time worrying about them. I know some parents who I feel are raising their children in an environment of fear, and I know that those children do not feel large about themselves. That's why my goal is to be a smart parent, not a scared one. So while I might err on the side of caution when it comes to the Internet, or where I let my kids go by themselves, or who I let them go with, I'm trying to make sure that they're still going to feel large, not fearful.

## SPREAD YOUR SHINE

I want to take a moment and talk now about the importance of parents spreading their pride and affection equally among their children, so that no child feels like they're being left out or overlooked. I take that challenge very seriously, because one of the worst things I can do as a father is misappropriate my praise. I can't tell Diggy how cool he is without being sure to tell Russy that he's "that dude," too. I can't say, "Great job, Vanessa!" when she lands a role unless I compliment Angela for one of her accomplishments, too. I'm not being insincere, because I'm genuinely proud of all of them. I just know that since I have a lot of kids, I have to make sure each one gets quality time in Daddy's sun. My eyesight has to be their sun and if I don't share that shine equally, someone's going to end up half-baked.

It's also important to remember that even though you are the biggest influence on your child's life, the influence of their siblings isn't far behind. Diggy might look up to me first and foremost, but JoJo is probably the next person he seeks approval from. That's why I have to stay very aware of any potential sibling rivalries. For instance, I've noticed that there is a little competitive thing that goes on between Diggy and Russy, though I sense that it's mostly a friendly rivalry. In fact, it reminds me of the relationship I had with my brother Russell. We'd talk smack, scream, and go hard at each other, but at the end of the day, we always had each other's back. And we still do.

So while overall I feel good about their relationship, there still have been instances where Russy has tried too hard to be cool like Diggy. I can certainly understand where Russy is coming from—when I was young, I wanted to have the same white rabbit coat that Russell did, just like I wanted my hat and my sneakers to match the way Russell's always did. But while I certainly admired Russell's style, I never felt small compared to him. I was inspired by his flavor, instead of envious or intimidated by it. However, we have started to see a little bit of that envy from Russy. Which is why I want to reiterate how important it was that Diggy was one the one who told him to stop being envious of his style. I loved that instead of teasing Russy for copying him, Diggy told his younger brother to never forget that "people like you for you." What's even better is that when Diggy told him that, Russy asked all of us, "Did Mom tell him to say that?" And when we told him no, Russy thought about it for a moment, then in his little squeaky voice said, "That's deep." And he was right, it was deep. Because if Diggy had teased Russy for copying him, or started playing on his insecurities, Russy might have grown up feeling very small next to his big brother. But by encouraging Russy to have confidence in himself, Diggy played a major role in helping his little brother grow up feeling large.

Another relationship that I try to monitor closely is the one between Vanessa and Angela. Even though Angela is a beautiful, intelligent, and dynamic young lady, she sometimes still has a tough time stepping out of her older sister's shadow. For example, not too long ago, both Justine and I noticed that Angela was looking very skinny—too skinny, in our opinion. Sure enough, when I asked Angela what she wanted for lunch that day, she told me, "Thanks, Dad, but I can't eat anything. I'm on a special diet." When I pressed her about this "diet," it came out that she hadn't been eating any food at all—instead, she'd just been drinking a mixture of cayenne pepper, maple syrup, and lemon juice. Apparently she heard that's what Beyoncé drinks to lose weight. Justine and I couldn't believe she felt so badly about herself, so when we asked why on earth a beautiful, healthy girl would think she had to starve herself, it came out that she wanted to be as skinny as Vanessa. Thankfully, I've learned that when Angela starts to feel a little small compared to Vanessa, it's very important that I step in and help her start to feel large again. So I told her, "Angie, yeah, you got a little different shape than Vanessa, but please stop acting that you're anything less than perfect. First off, it's absolutely insane for you to feel badly about your body! You look incredible! And second, no matter how *you* feel about your look, so many other people are just in love with you. When they see you on the show, they see someone who's smart, grounded, ambitious, *and* definitely beautiful. So see yourself the same way." And after that pep talk, she started to feel better about herself and even let me fix her a hamburger—with cheese!

## THE GORILLA SUIT

Another irony we're learning about making our kids feel large is that while Justine and I have worked very hard to make sure our kids are always surrounded by plenty, there have been times when my kids have felt insecure about possessing too much! In other words, the abundance we've been blessed with as a family, which I always assumed would make them feel large, has actually made them feel smaller. And as someone who didn't grow up rich, it took me a long time to realize that affluence could make a child feel insecure.

My kids have probably been searching for ways to handle their affluence for a while, but it didn't become a big issue in my house until recently, when I started picking up Diggy at the bus stop in my Rolls-Royce. I figured Diggy would love having his daddy waiting for him every afternoon in a Rolls—after all, he was the one who pushed me to buy the car in the first place! But Diggy responded much differently than I had assumed he would. While I thought he would be excited that all his schoolmates were going to see his father's fancy car, instead he was embarrassed. In his mind, it was too showy, too much flash. He was more comfortable blending in with his friends than standing out.

At first, I took exception to his embarrassment. Instead of seeing a kid who was feeling awkward, I saw a kid who wasn't proud of where he came from. I worked very hard to be able to afford that car, and I didn't appreciate him saying it wasn't appropriate. "If he's going to act like I'm embarrassing him with that car," I decided one day, "let me give him something to really be embarrassed about!" So when Diggy's bus came to drop him off the next day, there I was waiting for him in front of my Rolls—in a gorilla suit! While the other kids on the bus thought it was the funniest thing they'd ever seen in their lives, Diggy was completely mortified. He refused to get in the car with me and insisted on walking home instead.

When we got back, I felt like I had taught him an important lesson. But when I talked to my brother Russell about it later that evening, I realized that maybe *I* was the one who had some things to learn. "We wouldn't have been mad if Daddy had picked us up from school in a fancy car," I said to Russell, thinking he would back me up. "We would have thought it was the most incredible thing in the entire world, right?" "Maybe," Russell replied, "but we were in a different situation than Diggy. He's seeing all *your* flash as weight that *he* has to carry. He's a very perceptive kid, and if he thinks that car is going to make him stand out too much, maybe he's right." And when Russell told me that, I realized that while my basic message was on point, I had failed to look at the situation through my son's eyes.

After my talk with my brother, I pulled Diggy aside and tried to explain where I had gone wrong. "I made a mistake in embarrassing you the way I did," I told him. "My intention wasn't to hurt your feelings. I just wanted to teach you to be proud of what your father has worked hard for, not to be embarrassed by it. But now I can see how a half-million-dollar car could make you feel uncomfortable. Just try to understand that I'm not trying to show off, it's just that since a Rolls-Royce makes me feel good, I assumed that it makes everyone else feel the same way. Now I realize that's not necessarily the case. At the same time, try to understand that I'm not going to change—I loved beautiful cars when I was living in Queens, I love them in New Jersey, and I'm going to love them wherever we end up next, too. It's just who I am, and you should be comfortable with that. And I'm always going to act how I want, because nobody's going to make me live under a microscope. So whether I'm picking you up in a gorilla suit, or ordering food with a funny voice in a restaurant, or running down the street backward for no reason, try not to let me embarrass you so much. My uniqueness, my eccentricities, are actually what make me cool. They're just my way of shining, and you shouldn't be afraid of them. Just like you should never be afraid to shine in your own way."

And while I'm glad Diggy and I had that little chat, I'm the one who learned the biggest lesson about self-esteem. What I learned was that we can't try to tell our kids what they should and should not be comfortable with. All kids, whether their parents drive a fancy car or take the bus, whether they're black or white, rich or poor, are trying to find their way through this confusing world. It's tough enough without us telling them what they should or shouldn't be embarrassed by. Instead, all we can do is love them. That's it. We can't always make our children see things the way we do. Instead, we have to try to see things through their eyes and be sensitive to what they're feeling. That's what ultimately is going to giving them the pride and self-esteem that they need to feel large.

## DON'T CHASE COOL

When we talk about making our children feel large, we have to make a very important distinction: "large" does not equal "cool." So while we always want our kids to be confident, we never want them to be obsessed with being cool. We want to remind them that trying to be cool is a waste of time and talent. No matter how many diets Angela goes on, and no matter how many fancy purses she buys, she'll never feel as skinny as the girls on the magazine covers. Just as no teenage boy is ever going to feel as "cool" as their favorite rapper. Styles change, fads come and go, and what's hot today is cold tomorrow. Kids need to understand that as long as you worry more about what appears on the outside than how you feel on the inside, "cool" will always just be out of your reach.

Now some of you may be thinking, "That's easy for you to say, Rev, because you were on MTV and sold a million records. You've always been cool." But if you really look back at my history, if I was ever considered cool, it was only because I didn't chase it. When Run DMC first started performing, we shocked a lot of people by wearing sweatshirts and pressed Lee jeans—the same outfits we were wearing on the streets of Queens. It was shocking because all the "cool" rappers back then were into performing in very theatrical outfits—tight leather pants, crazy blouses, and studded wrist bands—almost like heavy-metal rock stars. We weren't into that kind of over-the-top style. We just wanted to dress like we always did, rocking jeans on our legs and Adidas on our feet. And ultimately, because our style was true to who were, people decided that look was cool. But we certainly didn't chase cool in that instance. Instead, we created it.

And as I alluded to earlier in the chapter, no one thought it was very cool when I first decided to become a reverend. Back then, I might have been considered cool for a brief minute if I had tied a bandanna around my head like Tupac, but certainly no one was giving me cool points for putting a collar around my neck. If I had tied a bandanna around my head, it would have felt fake. But the collar, as absurd as it might have seemed to some people, at least honestly reflected who I had become. So I stuck with it, because I've learned that following my own vision, even if that vision doesn't seem "cool" at first, is how I've usually made a name for myself in this world. People might say, "I love this dude," when they see me on TV, but it's only because I've always loved myself first. Do you know how much self-esteem you have to have to be a middle-aged rapper who goes on MTV and sends out e-mails about God from a pink bubble bath? Man, you have to have real confidence to do that. And I cherish that confidence, because I've learned that having self-esteem, no matter how silly it looks, no matter how wacky your idea sounds, is what's fly to the world. Chasing cool isn't.

That's a lesson that I try to share with my family all the time. I had to bring it up the other day when Russy got a box full of new shirts form a clothing company that wanted him to wear them on the show. While Russy was dying to put them on, he was also afraid to take them out of the box, because he noticed that JoJo doesn't wear his new clothes right away. So when I heard that foolishness, I had to school him. "Russy, you do what *you* want to do, not what you think the cool thing to do is," I told him. "If you like putting on those new shirts, then put them on! Don't think that only JoJo's way is cool. I remember that Jam Master Jay used to walk out of the store wearing the sneakers he just bought. He wasn't letting them sit in a box for a week. And you can't tell me that Jay wasn't fly! So be like Jay and just do whatever feels right for you."

I see similar things happening with Diggy. Since he's super cool and as fly as can be, he thinks he should be hanging out with the older kids in his school. However, when he does run with those older kids, they wear him out. A year or two makes a very big difference at his age, and trying to keep up with those older kids is really too much for Diggy. So whenever I see him trying a little too hard, I have to step in and tell him, "Diggy, stop trying to be like those big kids. You might not even realize it, but you're happier when you're around kids your own age. You don't feel as much pressure to be cool and you can just be yourself, which is why they all like you in the first place. So stop fishing for cool—you ain't going to catch nothing good anyways!"

In fact, I sat all my kids down for a self-esteem speech when we started filming *Run's House* because I knew they were about to be exposed to a level of scrutiny and criticism that they hadn't experienced before. As someone who had been under that sort of microscope before, I had to tell them that you can never let the outside world change how you feel about yourself. "In this house, your power is your self-esteem. Don't give away your power to the TV critics, or to the fashion critics, or to the gossip folks on the radio," I told them. "Don't give away your power because our ratings go down one week. Don't give away your power because you hear someone in the lunchroom diss our show. Don't let any voice except your parents' or God's get inside your head. Remember, low self-esteem comes from neediness. As soon as we get a few good reviews, you're going to start to feel like you need to hear 'you're great' or 'you're beautiful' every day. Don't give the industry that power. I'm telling you right now that you're great and that you're beautiful, and that endorsement is the only one you need." I'm telling you, I'm stuffing self-esteem down those kids' throats! And for the most part I think they've absorbed the message and have resisted letting the show affect their self-esteem, in either direction.

Still, I feel like I have to pay attention to Vanessa and Angela on this issue a little more closely. Maybe it's because they're older, but they're the ones who I feel are the most tempted by the lure of cool. For instance, not too long ago, Vanessa and Angela came to me and asked if was OK for them to appear on the cover of *Vibe Vixen* magazine. I could tell from the way they asked me that they would feel very cool if I let them be on that cover. And Vanessa went out of her way to make it clear that unlike the earlier situation with *Maxim*, the photos were going to be very tasteful. But before I could give them my blessing, I said to Vanessa, "I know you want me to say yes, but before I do, let's just look up the word 'vixen.' Because as much as I'd like to make you girls happy, I'm pretty sure that you two ain't no vixens!" Before I could even break out the dictionary, Vanessa said, "Come on, Daddy, the title's not that big a deal. Let us do it—a cover would be really nice while we're hot." She wasn't really barking, more like chirping, but I could still tell that this cover held a certain allure for them. So I tried to break it down for them one more time. "Dudes," I told them. "First of all, please understand that you're *already* hot. Having the best clothes, or appearing in the trendiest magazines, or being photographed at the most exclusive parties is not what made you hot. What made you—and all of this family—hot were episodes like when we were all playing basketball in the pool together. People love watching that kind of stuff. They didn't care if you were wearing a designer bathing suit. They just loved that you were having so much fun with your family. It was hot because it warmed their hearts. People respond to you because you're God-fearing, humble, family-oriented young women. Not because you're on this or that magazine cover. I know you're afraid to walk away from a cover, but what you walk *away* from in life is actually what determines what you walk *into*. So it might hurt this moment to walk away from *Vibe Vixen*, but by doing that you might walk into something the fits you better. You might walk into the cover of *Forbes*, or *Black Enterprise*, which will profile you as young entrepreneurs on the move, instead of 'vixens.' And in the long run, that would be so much hotter." And even though I could tell that they were a little disappointed that I didn't approve of the cover, I could also tell that they appreciated hearing their daddy remind them of just how great they already are. Whether you're four, fourteen, or twenty-four, it always helps to hear your daddy say how much he loves you, and how proud of you he is. I've learned that these self-esteem speeches aren't one-time deals, because as much as you tell your kids they're hot, the world is just going to try to cool them back off again. That's why I've got to keep shoving it down their throats. I don't want them to ever forget how much they're really worth.

And let me say that while the example of turning down magazine covers is not one that most families can relate to, my core message here still applies to everyone: What you *walk away* from in life determines what you *walk into*. Let your kids know that by walking away from something that might seem very cool to them, they might actually be walking into something that is so much greater. By walking away from those cool kids who like to drink 40's during lunch period, they might be walking into a college scholarship. By walking away from a guy who might be very fly, but who doesn't treat her right, your daughter might be walking into the arms of a guy who's a little less hip but who'll show her a lot more respect. By walking away from the way everyone else wears their clothes, your son might be walking into a whole new fashion trend. And the only way they can take those steps is by having confidence in themselves.

## THE FAMILY THAT PRAYS TOGETHER

I hope that so far this chapter has demonstrated that I try to do everything possible to help my children feel confident about themselves. I try to let them know that I'm always excited by what they're doing with their lives. I try to soothe them when the world is making them feel insecure, or step in when they're making each other feel small. I encourage them to stop chasing cool and instead find strength in their own uniqueness. I try to encourage them to appreciate other people's quirks, instead of being embarrassed by them. And while I feel that all those techniques have helped the process, I've also come to realize that if I really want my kids to feel large, the most important thing I can do is encourage them to have a more personal relationship with God through prayer.

Before I go any deeper into my thoughts about prayer, I still want to make it very clear that even though I am a reverend, I'm not trying to push a Christian agenda here. Not because I have any misgivings about my own faith, but rather because I know some people tune out when they hear a reverend start talking about prayer. I want to be careful that my particular brand of faith doesn't stop someone who doesn't share that faith from hearing this message. I truly believe that whatever religion you subscribe to (or even if you don't subscribe to one at all), we can all hear the voice of God inside us. And it's a voice that we should probably all converse with more often than we do. All I'm really encouraging in this section is for people to increase their conversation with God. Whether your God goes by the name of Jesus Christ, Allah, Buddha, or Krishna doesn't really matter to me. What matters is that you are having that conversation.

The irony is that even though prayer plays such a major role in my own life, for quite a while I didn't push my own kids too heavily toward prayer. Maybe it was because prayer was never a big part of my own life growing up, or maybe it was because I felt like being asked to establish a relationship with God would feel like too much of a burden to a young kid. Instead, I simply tried to show them how prayer has brought so many blessings to my life, and then hoped that they'd be inspired by my example. I've let them know that prayer is the source of all my confidence and self-esteem. That prayer is how I arrive at most, if not all, of my important decisions. That prayer is how I plan for the future, just as it is how I come to grips with the past. And that prayer is what helps me find peace when it seems like my world is spiraling out of control. But while I hoped (and yes, prayed) that my children would come to view prayer in a similar light, I was willing to let it happen at its own pace.

Thankfully, that pace picked up recently after I took a copy of Norman Vincent Peale's *The Power of Positive Thinking* with me on a family vacation. Since I had found the book in the self-help section, I wasn't expecting to learn any spiritual lessons from it. However, it turned out that the book had a chapter about the power of positive prayer which touched me very deeply. Essentially, Dr. Peale's belief was that when praying on life's hardest problems, it's very important to talk to God as if he's your buddy. Rather than praying to God in a formalized manner like, "Our father, who art in heaven . . . ," Peale suggested it's more effective to keep your prayers much more conversational. In my mind, that meant praying to God like, "Hey, what's up, God? It's your man Run again. I'm dealing with a lot of drama these days, and I need you to hit me off with some of your wisdom before I really bug out."

I know that prayer might sound a little more informal than Peale had intended, but the approach has really worked in my house. When I started to think of prayer in terms of a friendly, conversational activity, it suddenly felt much more accessible for my kids. Instead of a chore, I thought I could pitch prayer to them as a relaxed way to develop a healthy relationship with God. I was so inspired that as soon as we came back home, I made every kid read about positive prayer and then even write a little book report on that chapter. I wanted to be extra confident that they really absorbed Dr. Peale's teachings. And it seemed to work, because I noticed that after that exercise, the kids were definitely more comfortable talking about prayer.

In fact, they got so comfortable with the concept that now they even write letters to God on their own, little notes in which they explain what they're struggling with and what sort of help they need. Russy even keeps his letters and then comes back later on and checks off each one of his prayers that God has answered. I really love that, because I want all my kids to feel comfortable communicating with God, even if it's in an unconventional way. So if Diggy's going through something, I want him to hit up God on that Milo (I knew we'd eventually find a good use for it) and say, "Yo God, it's your man Diggy. There's an emergency going on in New Jersey and I need your help for a minute." Or he could send God a text message. Whatever he's comfortable with, it's all good, as long as he stays in constant communication with God.

When JoJo was feeling insecure about his place in the world, I encouraged him to pray about it. When Angela was trying to decide whether to get a tattoo or not, I told her to pray about it. When Vanessa was wondering about the *Maxim* spread, I told her to pray on it. Some might think those kinds of issues are too trivial for prayer,

MAKE YOUR CHILDREN FEEL LARGE

but I don't see it that way. Don't we always tell our friends about the little things we're going through in life? Of course we do. Well, our relationship with God should be the same way, since he's the best friend we have. God doesn't care how you get at him, as long as you get at him. If you ask, he's going to be there for you. Christian, Jew, Rastafarian—it doesn't matter. All you have to do is start the conversation.

And "conversation" is really the key word here. I don't think God likes to be asked for things in a dry, boring manner anymore than we humans do. For instance, the other day I got a call from my old friend Runny Ray, who can always be counted on to hit me up for some help every now and then. When I initially saw that it was Ray calling, I almost didn't pick up the phone because at the time I was worrying about money a bit myself and the last thing I felt like doing was giving Ray a handout. But since Ray is my man, I picked up anyway. Sure enough, Ray launched right into his pitch. "Man, Run, I'm down here in Georgia and they're really hating on me. I got a new job, but my mother won't let me use her car to drive to work," he told me. "Rev, this situation is making me so depressed that I'm about to jump out my window. And I live in a ranch house!" Well, when Ray told me that joke, plus plenty of other funny anecdotes about his Southern relatives, I suddenly found myself in a much more giving mood. When I picked up the phone, I had promised myself that wouldn't give Ray any money. But by the end of the conversation, I was taking down his info so I could wire him some cash for a car. The key is that if Ray had just called me and said without much fanfare, "Rev, I need some money for a car. Please send me some cash," I probably would have made up a quick excuse and then hung up the phone. But by making me laugh and making me reminisce, Ray brought our old friendship to the surface, and that put me in a very giving mood. He made me want to help him. And I suspect that God feels the exact same way when we pray. If you never talk to God and treat him like a friend, but then try to suddenly call on him when you find out you have cancer, or when you get stuck in the middle of a bank robbery, then I believe there's a good chance God won't give those prayers any special consideration. But I think that if day in and day out you talk to God like a friend, make him laugh a little, maybe even make him cry, then he's going to be more likely to answer your prayers. Especially your important ones. Friends like to help friends. So if you develop a real, lasting friendship with God, you're always going to get the help that you need.

Just as importantly, prayer teaches our children to feel comfortable asking for things. Well, maybe they're usually comfortable asking their parents for new clothes, or gas money, or to have their curfew extended. But they aren't as quick to ask for emotional and spiritual help. They're not going to ask you for help finding direction in their lives. They're not going to ask you about how to find clarity when they're confused. And even though they probably need to more than most of us, they probably won't even ask for forgiveness when they've done something wrong. But when they make prayer part of their lives, they will feel comfortable asking God those things. And when kids start really asking for spiritual help, instead of material or social things, that's the proof that they've conquered their teenage pride. That they're confident, but not cocky. Because by learning how to ask, to admit that they don't have all the answers, they've become a little bit more humble.

Those are such powerful lessons for young people to learn. That's why we plan to start teaching Miley to pray as soon as she's old enough to talk. We believe that if she's old enough to talk to us, then she can start having conversations with God, too. Obviously that relationship will become deeper and more meaningful to her as she grows older, but by starting so early, those conversations will feel like second nature to her. And if she can grow up believing that God is listening and will always have her back, she can't help but feel large when she's older. I can try to instill self-confidence in Miley, and in all my children, but the sense that God believes in them is stronger than any sense of confidence that I can share with them.

## KINDNESS IS KING FOR KIDS, TOO

Before we end this chapter, I want to take a moment and add something on the topic of self-esteem and feeling large. Like my husband, I feel that God has blessed me with a lot of self-esteem, and I also want to share that confidence with my children. But what I don't want to do is build my children up with so much self-esteem that they start to think, "Oh, I'm better then everyone else." And that's very, very important, because not only will that attitude make their peers feel bad, but as a parent, you need to remember that "everyone else" also includes you. As soon as your kid starts to think that they're better than you, your house will not be a happy place to be.

Instead of allowing our children to get too self-centered, we push them to be friendly and kind to everyone they come into contact with. I know we mentioned this earlier in the book, but it really bears repeating: In our house, confidence is cool, but kindness is king. And when I push our kids to be kind, I'm not expecting them to be Mother Teresa or some sort of saint. I'm simply pushing them to be considerate and treat other people with respect. I know that sounds very basic, but I think we can all also admit that those are traits that many kids don't seem to have anymore. Especially some of the kids from the well-to-do families we come into contact with. I'm always shocked at how these wealthy families can have all these maids, servants, and gardeners working in their homes, yet the parents and the kids barely even seem to acknowledge them. The lawn guy can be at their house every week, but when these kids walk outside, they go right past him without saying a word. When I see that, I want to say, "Boy, are you crazy? That man is making your lawn look amazing. You better go over there and say thank you, for making your life better!" I don't care how much money we have or don't have—I'll never feel comfortable seeing anyone in my family act that way.

While I can't control what sort of behavior people tolerate

from their kids, I can control how my kids are going to act in my house. That's why I make sure that they go out of their way to make all the people who work for us feel large, too. So if Barbara, who does an amazing job helping me around the house, is working when my kids get home from school, I make sure I hear each of our kids say "Hi, Barbara" as soon as they walk into the house. I want each of them to go out of their way to show her some respect, because she's the person who's helping this family have clean clothes. Let's keep it funky here: I'm not the person who's washing the boys' bathroom, or matching up Jo-Jo's socks anymore. Barbara's the one who's doing that, the one who is really keeping this house in order. I won't even front: With six kids and everything we have going on here, if it was still left up to me, the dirty clothes would probably be over-flowing from the boys' daggone hamper right now. These kids would constantly be looking for clean drawers. So they better acknowledge how good they have it and thank the person who's keeping it good.

I hate if it sounds like I'm bragging about the fact that my kids say hi to their housekeeper—that sort of behavior should be a given, not something that's exceptional. But it seems like kids today are losing even the most basic sense of manners. For instance, every time we take a flight, when we're getting off the plane the attendants always tell us, "Your kids were so polite." So while I thank God that people feel that way, I'm also thinking, "They didn't do anything other than say 'Thank you' and 'Yes, ma'am.' What must these other kids be like on these planes?"

If I don't manage to teach my kids anything else, at least I've taught them to say thank you. I just pray they never forget it. And even though JoJo, Vanessa, and Angela are older, if we're at an event and see someone we know, if I don't hear them say hi, I'll go over to them and say, "Please make sure you say hi to such and such." Or if we're in a restaurant and I don't hear them say "Thank you" to the waiter when they get their food, nobody's eating until they say it. I know they're grown, but it would break my heart if they ever started making other people feel small. I really go very hard on this issue. It's almost like my husband with keeping the house clutter-free. I feel that if my kids aren't polite and kind, our house is going to fall apart.

## FILL YOUR KIDS UP WITH LOVE

I want to end this chapter by discussing an added bonus of always making your kids feel large: When they're already filled up with love and confidence, it won't sting as hard when you correct their mistakes. As I always like to say, you can't correct a relationship that you haven't already first filled up to the brim with love.

I'll give you an example. The other day, I called my friend Mike Kyser, who's a big-deal executive in the music business. When I got put through to his office, I heard Mike say, "Hold on, Missy, I've got Rev Run on the other line . . . Run, I've got to call you back in five minutes, OK?" So I hung up and waited for his call. And waited. And waited. And when it became clear that Mike wasn't going to call me back, I started to get upset. Not only wasn't he returning my call, but he had named-dropped on me too, letting me know he wasn't taking my call because he was already on with Missy Elliott. But it was impossible for me to get too upset, because Mike Kyser is one of the nicest guys I know. Every time I speak with him, he fills me up with so much love. Every time we meet, he's always making me feel good by saying something like, "Joe, you're the best that ever did it," or, "Joey, you're a living legend. You know that, right?" So while I would normally get upset with someone who never called me back, I couldn't stir up those feelings for Mike. And when he did eventually call me back a few days later, the first thing he said to me was, "Joe, I'm so sorry I jerked you the other day. . . ." But before he could continue, I cut him off and said, "Mike, how could I get mad at you for jerking me when you always fill me up with so much love? Because we're talking about you, I can handle it, man." And it's true. It's impossible to get mad at someone who fills you up with so much juice. So if Mike takes three sips of that juice by not calling me back, I'll hardly even notice. Even if he takes a gulp, or drinks a gallon of that juice, I can never get too upset because I've got plenty of good vibes still left inside me.

On a similar note, I want to make sure every one in my house feels filled up with my love and affection. That's why when it's time to make a correction, my touch won't hurt too much. I know the only way I can successfully correct Angela when she gets too concerned with her weight is if I've *already* filled her up to the brim with love. If she feels like our relationship is on empty, then she's not going to be receptive to my message. Similarly, I have to make sure that JoJo is always so filled with love and confidence that when I say, "Pull up your pants, boy. They're sagging too low," he'll be comfortable with that correction. If I notice that Russy's breath is smelling funky, before I tell him to go brush his teeth, I have to ask myself, "Have I ever told Russy that his breath smells great?" And if the answer is no then I can't make that correction. If I haven't put anything in his love account, then I can't make any withdrawals. The only way you're going to be able to successfully discipline and correct your children is when they're *already* feeling large from all your love.

## RUN'S TAKE BACK

It's very important to take your children back from the insecurities that plague them. Childhood and the teenage years have always been times when young people question themselves and their role in the world, but I believe that's even more of an issue today. There's so much media out there—Web sites, commercials, television, etc.—constantly trying to get in their heads and tell them that there's always something else that they'll need to be cool. That's why Justine and I try to use all that new technology to our advantage. If JoJo needs to have some special kind of Sidekick, or Russy has to have the cool new phone, then that's fine. But we're going to use those phones and BlackBerrys and other gadgets to help our kids feel large. Every day I'm going to send JoJo a text message telling him how proud I am of him, how much I respect him for being a leader and not a follower. And Justine is going to try to send Diggy an e-mail saying that she just knows he's going to do well on that big science test. Nothing too deep, maybe a few sentences here or an inspirational quote there. But since our kids live in an age when they are constantly being bombarded with messages and images that can make them feel small, Mommy and Daddy are going to be working overtime to make sure we send them just as many messages of love and support. Think of those little messages as being like a virtual hug. And then try to give your kids a virtual hug every day (in addition to the real thing, of course).

I also like to employ a slightly less high-tech approach to taking my kids back from self-doubt and insecurity. In this particular strategy, I like to wait until my kids and I are around a group of people—maybe it's at a party, or after church—and then set it up so that my kids overhear me bragging about them. So if I'm standing with a group of people outside of church and somebody asks me about Vanessa, I'll say, just loudly enough so that she'll have to hear it, "Vanessa? Oh, she's doing incredibly well. She doing all these great things with her Pastry sneakers, plus she's acting on *The Guiding Light*, not to mention she's doing a lot of modeling. We're really so proud of how hard she's working." Or if I see Angela talking to some people in the corner of a room, I'll barge in, grab the first person I see, and, loud enough for Angela to hear,

I'll tell them, "You know, we're really so blessed with our children. They all have their heads screwed on so straight. Like I was just saying to my wife, 'Look at Angela. She runs a sneaker company. She has her own magazine. And she's in school. Yet she never lets her head get too big. Isn't that remarkable for someone her age?'" And then you have to keep sprinkling those little moments in throughout the year. For each kid. Maybe even for your wife, too. Really, you need to do it for everybody in your family that might need it.

Of course, your friends will probably find this tactic a little annoying—no one really likes to listen to someone loudly brag about their children. But annoying your friends is the price you might have to pay to help your children feel secure about themselves. Remember, the voices that are going to make your children feel small are constantly in their ear. So you have to be just as aggressive in taking them back from that negativity. Your reassuring and loving and confident voice needs to be the loudest one they hear.

# CHAPTER 7

# Surviving the Hard Times

*Hard times are coming to your town*
*So stay alert, don't let them get you down*
*They tell you times are tough, you hear that times are hard*
*But when you work for that ace you know you pulled the right card*

"Hard Times"—RUN DMC

When I rapped those lyrics back in 1983, I thought I had a pretty good idea about what sort of hard times I would face in life and how I was going to handle them. But in retrospect I can see that I still had a lot to learn about life's struggles and what is required to overcome them. While it's true that you're going to need to pull a strong card to make it through life's tougher times, I can now see that the ace isn't any of the things I probably thought it was back then, like holding a fat bankroll or spitting a hardcore rap or even rolling up a dime bag of weed. The only ace that is going to consistently get you through life's hard times is a strong and united family.

That's why when hard times hit, it's imperative that instead of fracturing or falling apart, your family must pull even *closer* together. You can't get so caught up dealing with the hard times that you let up your grip on your family. Because hard times are *exactly* when you're more likely to "lose" a child. When Mommy and Daddy are preoccupied with a relationship drama, the loss of a job, an illness, or even a death, that's exactly when a child is going to be more likely to slip away with the wrong crowd, to start using drugs, to stop working hard in school, or to start having sex. So while it's very natural to lose some of your focus as a parent when dealing with a crisis, that's exactly when you must become even more focused, even more aware, and even more determined to keep your family together.

And please understand that this truth applies to *all* families. No matter how it might look from the outside, no family truly leads a "charmed" life that's protected from hard times. No matter how much money a family might have, no matter how big their house is, no matter how good-looking their kids are, no matter how much money they give to charity, or even how religious they are: Sooner or later, hard times are going to come knocking at their door. Just like those hard times are going to come knocking at yours and mine. And when that knock comes, what will matter isn't all the material things, but rather how well your family can look out for each other.

Of course, pulling together during hard times is easier said than done. When the pain of hard times hits, it's very difficult to keep your own head above water, let alone help your kids or spouse stay afloat. But the truth is that in hard times you're often faced with two choices: pull closer together, or risk someone getting pulled away with the current. I'm not trying to be too dramatic here, but the dangers are very real. When a parent moves out of the house, there is a real chance that a child will react by acting by having behavioral issues (remember, that's what happened to me when my father moved out). When a parent is faced with a serious illness, a child will often turn to drinking or drugs to deal with the frustration and fear that they're feeling. And unfortunately, when a couple loses a child, too often they can't fill that void in their lives and end up losing their own relationship.

Thankfully, while this family has dealt with its share of hard times, we've never let them get the best of us. As we'll discuss in this chapter, when my children from my first marriage felt real pain over their mother Valerie's lack of a role on *Run's House*, Justine and I were able address and correct the situation before that pain began to eat away at the core of our family. Or when I stumbled a bit following the death of my own mother, my brothers never held my missteps against me, or allowed them to create any rifts between us. And even the most severe pain my wife and I have ever experienced—the death our daughter Victoria—still wasn't able to pull our family apart. If anything, looking back I can see that those hard times actually brought our family closer together and only strengthened the bonds between us as husband and wife, parent and child, and siblings. But we were only able to keep things together when the hard times hit because we didn't turn against one another or retreat into our own pain. Instead, we worked very hard to let our love for one another shine through whatever dark clouds had gathered around us.

## TEARS FOR THEIR MOTHER

One of the hardest periods we've faced as a family ironically came during a time that in many ways should have been one of our happiest. The problem first came to the attention of my husband and me after the first season of *Run's House* had aired. One thing people really seemed to like about the show was how well we operated as a "blended family" (a situation we'll discuss in much greater detail in the next chapter). In particular, people seemed to really respect my relationship with Vanessa, Angela, and JoJo. I'd always hear comments like, "It's so great, I can't even tell they're not really your kids." But while those comments made *me* feel good, it turned out that they were having the opposite affect on Vanessa, Angela, and JoJo. From their perspective, it was painful that the public was assuming that I was their mother. Not because they didn't love me, but because their actual birth mother, Valerie, was getting left out of the equation. They were very conflicted about the world celebrating their relationship with me if it meant that this would completely overshadow their relationship with their mother.

At first, they didn't share their hurt with Joey or me. Maybe they didn't want to seem ungrateful for the success of the show. After all, what kind of kid complains about starring in a reality show that's getting so much love? Or maybe they simply didn't want to hurt my feelings. Whatever the reason, they kept the fact that they were going through some hard times to themselves. Thankfully, Bishop Jordan's son Manessah must have sensed what they were feeling, because he mentioned it to Joey and me when we were meeting with him one Sunday following church. "I think there might be some feelings out there that need to be talked out regarding the older kids," he advised us, "specifically about their mom and the TV show."

Like we do for his father's, we have a lot of respect for Manessah's intuition, so we decided not to waste any time in addressing the issue. We arranged for some friends to watch Diggy and Russy at the church and then immediately took Vanessa, Angela, and JoJo on a drive to a nearby park, where we pulled over so that we could talk.

From the moment we asked them, "Is anything bothering you about your mother and the show?" the tears just started flowing. Everyone was crying, but as the oldest, it seemed Vanessa was taking it the toughest. "It's very hard," she explained to us. "We're on TV, but people don't know about our mother, that whole other half of our lives. They only know the *Run's House* half. So it looks like our mom's not doing anything, like she doesn't play any role in who we are, or why we've turned out the way that we have. It makes us wonder, 'What are her friends thinking? How does it make her look to her family?' Having the country think she's not a part of our lives hurts her, and that hurts us."

Now, I have to admit I wasn't completely surprised to hear

them say that. We had just started shooting the second season of *Run's House* at that time, and there had been several moments where I felt a strange energy coming from the three of them while we were filming. I felt like they were behaving a little differently with me when the cameras came on, and interactions that had always felt so natural were suddenly feeling strained. I hadn't said anything about it because I thought maybe I was imagining things. Or if something was going on, I didn't feel like I had a good enough read on it to talk to them about it yet.

But now that everything was bubbling up to the surface, I told them how I had been feeling during the tapings. And with more tears, they admitted that they had been acting a little differently with me. They explained that they weren't trying to be malicious or hurtful to me, but they were feeling uncomfortable because they weren't sure how to act anymore. As crazy as it might sound, when they filmed the first season, it hadn't really occurred to them that people, especially their mother, would be watching the show. Or rather, while they knew people would be watching, they just weren't thinking about the ramifications of all that attention.

So while it saddened me that they had been hurting so much without me having addressed it, it was also a bit of a relief to understand where all that awkwardness was coming from. I wasn't mad at them for acting that way on camera; instead, I sympathized with the tough position they had unwittingly been put in. We weren't intentionally trying to shut their mother out. It was just that the show was called *Run's House*, and that's where all the focus had been. The truth is, we would never have agreed to do the show if we had thought it would cause them any pain whatsoever. But now that we had become aware of their unhappiness, we wanted to correct the situation immediately.

That's why right there in the car, we said, "OK, let's get Valerie on the show as soon as we can. Let's talk about her more.

Let's show her spending time with you guys, so that people will be aware of that part of your life." And as a result of that conversation, we shot a scene that showed the kids hanging out at Valerie's house in Queens, so that people could see where they lived, what their life was like there, and what the rest of their family looked like. Then we taped another scene with the girls getting a pedicure with Valerie while they debated the pros and cons of moving to L.A., so that people could see how involved Valerie is in their lives. Once those steps were taken, the kids definitely felt better. Before they had felt like something was being taken away from their mother, but afterward they felt like she had gotten some of the respect and credit that she deserved. Before they had felt like something very big was broken in their lives, but after Valerie became part of the show, they felt like that fracture had been healed.

In retrospect, we were very fortunate to emerge from that situation without our family suffering any real damage. If the kids hadn't opened up about how they were feeling, their guilt would have festered and eventually made our entire family ill. Instead of sharing in the excitement of filming a hot reality show, they would have probably begun to resent it. And resented Joey and me for making them a part of it. It could have become very toxic.

And I'll be real—as much as I hope I wouldn't have, there's also a chance that I might have begun to feel resentful of how they were acting with me on camera. Even worse, that awkwardness could have spread to how they interacted with Joey, or even Diggy and Russy. While the world was celebrating us for being a strong, united family, we could have had a situation where behind the scenes the members of that family were actually drifting away from each other.

We learned a very important lesson from that experience, which is that even when everything seems to be good, sometimes the hard times are hiding just beneath the surface. You can't ever assume that just because you're happy about how things are going that everyone in your family necessarily feels the same way. As a parent, you always have to be vigilant in checking to see that during the laughter and celebration, someone isn't feeling left out or hurt. Because before that talk in the car, there's no way Joey or I would have said that those kids were going through hard times over the show. Shoot, it seemed like everywhere they turned, someone was telling them how much they liked watching them on TV, how it was inspiring to see kids who stayed in school and out of trouble. Not to mention that the show was beginning to open up all sorts of professional opportunities for them, like Pastry sneakers, or JoJo's rap career with Team Blackout. It was really a huge, incredible time for our kids. But the fact is, even in the midst of all those praises and opportunities, they were also hurting very bad.

Hopefully you'll have plenty of good times to celebrate with your family, but try to remember that those times can also be hard for your kids. For instance, let's say you get a lucrative promotion at work and decide to buy a big new house in a better neighborhood. While you'd probably be proud and excited about the move, your kids might not see it the same way. Instead of seeing an opportunity to live in a bigger house and go to a better school, they might only be thinking about having to leave their friends in the old neighborhood behind. Instead of being excited that all your hard work has paid off and that the family is finally moving up in the world, they might be feeling a lot of resentment and anger over having to leave their comfort zone.

Or let's say your son got accepted to Harvard. When he opened that letter and it said, "You're accepted!" it probably felt like one of your greatest moments as a parent. And of course you wanted to celebrate and tell all your friends the good news. But you might also have a daughter who doesn't do as well in school as your son. While he got straight As, she's struggled in most of her subjects. So every time she hears you talking about your son the "Harvard Man," she's feeling worse and worse about her own situation. She's proud of her brother, but she also probably feels a lot of resentment toward him. His good times have made her feel small by comparison and have created expectations that she feels she can never meet. If that resentment isn't recognized and addressed, what started as an incredible moment for you and your son could also be the beginning of some very hard times for your daughter.

I don't want to rain on anyone's parade by implying that every time something good happens to your family, you need to start looking over your shoulder for the bad thing that's going to follow. You should always celebrate the good times that you have been blessed with and savor the moments that bring joy to you and your family.

Instead, I'm suggesting that you should always remember to make sure that everyone in your family feels completely invested in and connected to those good times. If you sense that someone's feeling a little left out, or a little bit conflicted about the celebration, do everything within your power to pull them in even closer to the rest of you. Instead of letting them drift away, take them back by letting them know that there can never be truly good times unless everyone in the family can feel them.

## MY MOMMA'S HOUSE

The pain that Vanessa, Angela, and JoJo felt after the first season of *Run's House* really taught us that the hard times can sneak up on your family when you least expect it. However, we've also learned that even if you can see the hard times coming from a mile away, it still doesn't make them any easier to deal with. That's something I experienced personally when my mother passed after her long battle with cancer.

While it was hardly unexpected, my mother's death still had a very strong effect on my brothers and me. When we learned of her death, Danny and Russell immediately decided to retreat to Russell's house in the Hamptons so that they could mourn and reminisce together in some solitude. They wanted me to be there too and kept calling, saying, "Come on out here with us, Joey. Let's do this together." While part of me definitely wanted to go, a larger part of me thought that I could better serve the family by staying in Queens. If all three of us were out in the Hamptons, who would plan our mother's funeral? My father and his second wife had already moved out of the area, and most of my mother's people were in D.C. or Baltimore. Since I had just become a reverend, I decided it would be best if I stayed back and tried to organize things. After all, that's what reverends do, right?

But while I was determined to step up for the family, I was also in a lot of pain. My mother and I were very close, and even though she had been sick for a long time, it didn't make losing her any easier to deal with. I was making plans like I had everything together, but the truth was that I was still hurting very badly. Russell and Danny might have been right—I probably could have used a few days out in the country to get my head together. Instead, by trying to organize and mourn at the same time, I ended up pushing too fast. While I wanted my mother's funeral to reflect her elegance and sophistication, instead it ended up feeling very haphazard and slapdash.

To be fair, with Justine's help I did manage to organize the basics. I picked out a funeral home, a cemetery, and a tombstone for my mother. But I didn't manage to do much more than that, especially when it came to the service the day of the funeral. My brothers and I each said a few brief words, and that was it. The whole thing couldn't have taken more than forty-five minutes. When it was over, people were expecting something else to happen, but I had nothing for them. I was basically like, "Peace—I'm hurting and I want to go home." Probably my biggest mistake was failing to plan a reception after the funeral. The family and friends who had traveled to pay their respects were rightfully expecting some sort of get-together afterward where they could sit around and eat and reminisce. Apparently I'm the only African-American in the country who didn't know you *have* to have a fried chicken dinner after a funeral.

In fact, I had actually left the cemetery and was headed home when I got a call from a couple of my uncles who were pretty upset by the fact that there didn't seem to be a reception. "Joey, this doesn't feel good," they told me. "Before we head home, we felt that we had to tell you that it's just not right for us to come all the way up here and not even sit down and break bread as a family." I couldn't argue with that, so I agreed to meet them and some other aunts and uncles that were particularly close to my mother at a restaurant in Manhattan. And while it was good that I partially corrected my initial mistake, I also ended up offending a lot of other aunts and uncles by not inviting them to the restaurant, too. In short, there were some hard feelings created that day.

Believe it or not, it seemed like things only went downhill after the funeral. Since I had assumed the role of family organizer, I also took on the job of handling my mother's estate. The biggest asset was her house in Queens, the same one that Justine had shared with her before our wedding. The plan was for me to sell the house and then split the money with my brothers. However, with my mother's death still so raw to me, I found dealing with her house to be very stressful. As a result, I let the house just sit there. The lack of maintenance wasn't a problem at first, but then the winter came. I forgot to have the hot-water heater turned on and so it wasn't long before the pipes froze and then burst. I was hurting so bad that when I went to check on the house one weekend, I actually saw a leak, but my attitude was, "It's not a big deal." I didn't know how to fix it myself, and since I wasn't focused enough to fix it, I just let the water sit there. However, that was a terrible idea, because soon the whole basement was flooded and the house began to rot and grow all sorts of mold.

By that spring I was finally able to pull myself together and properly address the situation. I found someone who specialized in buying beat-up old houses and was able to sell it to him. But if the house had been worth around $200,000 when my mother passed, but the time I was done with it we could only get around $140,000 for it. That made me feel like I had not only failed to respect my mother's legacy, but I had also cost my brothers some money in the process. I had tried to be the caretaker of the family, but things had only fallen apart under my watch. I felt very hurt inside, like I had let my mother and my brothers down.

Thankfully, nobody else in my family tried to put that weight on me. While I was worried that my actions, or lack of actions, might drive a wedge between me and my brothers, in the end they really didn't care at all. I don't mean to make them sound apathetic about my mother's funeral or the house, because that wouldn't be accurate at all. Rather, they understood that I had tried to do my best, but since I was hurting just like they were hurting, I had fallen a little short. As we used to say in our house growing up, "I'm not OK, you're not OK, and that's OK."

I'm proud of the kindness and empathy that my brothers showed toward me, because there are too many stories out there about family members who begin fighting after the death of a loved one and end up never speaking to each other again, often ripping the entire family apart in the process. Maybe two brothers get drunk after their father's funeral and then starting beefing over an old insult. Maybe two sisters end up fighting over their mother's possessions, even though it's really just an extension of their childhood fights for their mother's attention. An uncle brings up an old debt. Or an aunt brings up an old misunderstanding. And then family members who should be supporting each other are instead at each other's throats.

So while almost every family might experience those kinds of moments, the strong ones are the ones that won't allow them to tear them apart. Those families realize that when people are in pain, mistakes might be made and harsh words might be said, but it's important not to hold on to those hard moments. In our family, we have a saying: "An argument don't mean it's over." In other words, just because Russell and I scream at each other today doesn't mean we can't laugh with each other tomorrow. In fact, three minutes after we hang up the phone, it feels like the argument never even happened. We might have our share of arguments and disappointments, but we don't focus on them. We focus on the love instead. And that's really one of best ways to take your family back from the dangers of hard times: to let go of the hurt and hold onto the love instead.

The fact my brothers never lost sight of the love they had for me truly helped me weather the storm of my mother's death. And though I made my share of mistakes during that period, I also learned a great deal about what it truly takes to navigate your family through the pain and sorrow of a loss. And that was a lesson I would have to draw on very heavily during the greatest crisis that's hit my family, which was the passing of our daughter Victoria.

## LOSING VICTORIA

After we had Russy, I was convinced that I wasn't going to have any more children. When people would ask me if we were going to try for one more, I'd always say, "No, thank you. I'm definitely more than good with five!" And that was really my story until Vanessa and Angela moved out of the house. Once they were gone, I started to suffer from a little bit of empty-nest (or at least partially empty-nest) syndrome and became very focused on adding another child to the family. Since Vanessa was nine and Angela was seven when I first met them, I still wanted to experience raising a real little baby girl. I wanted to be able to put ribbons in her hair, dress her up in cute little outfits, throw tea parties for her, and all that sort of stuff. And in my mind, I figured the most sensible way to get that little girl at that point in our life was adoption. But when I told Joey what I was thinking, he felt that instead of adopting a baby, we should try to have one more baby ourselves. So after a lot of prayer and discussion, we decided to try to go that route. And not long afterward, not only did I find out that I was pregnant, but that I was pregnant with the little girl that I had wanted so badly. We felt incredibly blessed.

## THE WORST NEWS

My husband and I first learned that Victoria might be sick about halfway through my pregnancy. Until then, I had been throwing myself into the joyous jobs that come with preparing for a new child—painting the baby's room, picking out new furniture, looking at strollers and car seats, buying cute little onesies, and of course, eating for two.

But after one of our routine sonograms, our doctor sat Joey and me down and told us that he had some troubling news. The sonograms had revealed that Victoria was likely suffering from a birth defect called omphalocele, in which a child's abdominal organs begin to grow outside of their body. The doctor also added that because of my age and the baby's condition, I might want to consider terminating the pregnancy. There was a chance that not only might the baby not make it, but that I could be in danger, as well.

When I first heard that diagnosis, I could hardly breathe. As an expecting mother, you don't even want to hear that your baby has a problem with its little toe, let alone something as serious as what the doctor was describing. It was literally the worst news I had ever heard in my life.

In fact, we were so freaked out by what the doctor was telling us that we decided to go see another obstetrician for a second opinion. We hoped that there was something wrong with the first doctor's sonogram machine, or that maybe he had misdiagnosed the situation. Frankly, we were looking for any kind of miracle, any kind of news that wouldn't be so terrible. But the second doctor said the same thing that the first doctor had: Victoria had omphalocele, and we might want to seriously consider having an abortion.

After getting that second opinion, my husband and I tried to pull ourselves together and address the situation we were facing. On one hand, what the doctors were describing sounded so terrible, and so disturbing, that it seemed like maybe this pregnancy just wasn't meant to be. But on the other hand, we knew that a friend of mine, Alicia, had also been counseled to terminate her pregnancy after sonograms showed a dangerous growth on her baby's head. But she went ahead with her pregnancy anyway and is now the mother of a completely healthy, beautiful baby girl. In our minds, we thought there might be a chance that Victoria could beat the odds just like that little girl had. And without making a judgment on anyone else's decisions or beliefs, we also knew that when we looked into our hearts, an abortion simply wasn't something we could go through with, especially this late in the pregnancy. We were scared, even terrified, of what lay ahead, but we also knew we weren't ready to give up on this baby.

Despite our fears, we also had a very strong faith that God would protect Victoria. We believed that as terrible as her condition sounded, in the end, God was going to fix her. "I've heard the doctor's reports in my ears and I'm hearing God's report in my heart," Joey told me after our trip to the doctors. "And God's telling me that he might give us a miracle." After he said that, together we made the decision to go ahead with the pregnancy. We stopped worrying about what the sonograms were showing (when the doctor would look at them, I would just turn my head) and instead tried to walk straight ahead in faith.

But while we were confident in God's ability to grant us a miracle, we didn't share Victoria's condition with anyone except Bishop Jordan. It was very difficult for me not to speak about the situation, especially with our children. I felt guilty for not telling them what was happening, but I also knew that the news would scare them out of their minds. My husband and I knew we would have to carry that weight ourselves and have faith that Victoria would be born without any issues.

## GOD, GIVE US STRENGTH

Victoria wasn't due until late October 2006, but she ended up being born several weeks early, on September 26. She was delivered via cesarean section and weighed four pounds, five ounces at birth. But despite our prayers, there were problems right from the start. As the doctors had predicted, Victoria was born with her liver and intestines in a sac outside of her body. And even though the doctors worked very hard to help her, ultimately the stress created by her condition was too much for her little body to bear. Less than two hours after she entered the world, God took Victoria away from us.

Bishop Jordan was with us in the hospital and right after Victoria passed, he suggested that I take a few minutes to be alone with her. So despite physical and emotional pain that felt like it might overwhelm me, I gathered myself together and shared a few moments with the daughter I had been waiting for. And strangely, as I held Victoria and looked down at her, I felt a sense of peace. She looked so beautiful to me, especially her eyes. Even that clear little sac, which I had imagined would look so scary, was actually amazing to witness. Even though I had prayed so hard that it wouldn't be there, it still reminded me of God's perfection.

And as I held Victoria, I felt tremendous pride in my daughter, pride that she had fought for so hard and for so long. Pride that she had even made it to that moment. I still cry whenever I think about our short time together on this earth, but I'm thankful that at least we had those few minutes together. Because even though it might have left her body, I could still feel Victoria's soul in that room very deeply.

After I had a few minutes with Victoria, Joey and I decided to hold a funeral service for her right there in the hospital. The nurses dressed Victoria up in a beautiful pink outfit and Bishop Jordan prayed over her body, asking God to grant strength to our family. It was incredibly difficult to say goodbye to Victoria after only having her with us for such a short time, but there was really nothing else to be done. God had made it clear that he had other plans for her, and it was time to let that plan take effect. We tried to focus on Victoria being in God's hands now, and that he must have had a reason for wanting her there with him.

Before my husband shares some of his thoughts on Victoria's death, I want to say a few words to anyone reading this who might have a child or know of a child that's been diagnosed with omphalocele. As terrible as it is to think about your baby in that condition, it's important to understand that omphalocele is *not* a death sentence. Victoria suffered from a very severe case, but many babies born with this condition go on to lead healthy lives. In fact, a woman drove four hours to one of my book signings last year just so I could meet her two-year-old daughter, who had also been born with omphalocele. She wanted me to see that even though her daughter still had a long road ahead of her, she was going to lead a normal life. At the time, I was surprised that she had driven so long with her little girl just to tell me that, but now I think I understand why. I believe she drove all those hours so that I could share that message of hope with you now. Because while it's important that I talk about our loss, I also don't want to unnecessarily frighten any mothers out there who are dealing with a similar situation.

## WHY WE TAPED

As many of you know, we allowed the cameras from *Run's House* into Justine's hospital room shortly after Victoria passed. And since that decision seemed to surprise some people, I'd like to take a moment and explain why we were willing to share such an intensely painful and private moment with the world. Essentially, I felt we had an obligation to let the cameras roll. I didn't believe it would be fair to give MTV access to all the good and joyful parts of our life, but then shut the door when things turned bad. I couldn't invite people to laugh with us when we're having fun at the bowling alley or throwing a pool party, but then tell them they couldn't cry with us when we felt pain. It would have felt hypocritical to preach loudly about comparatively trivial issues like cleaning out your clutter or helping your kids do better in school, but to then have nothing to say about a devastating issue like losing a child. So for better or for worse, we decided to share what we were experiencing, just like we always had. When we decided to tape *Run's House,* we made a commitment to inviting people into our lives. And I intended to honor that invitation in the hard times as well as in the good ones.

Like most people going through such intense pain, I also wanted to make some sense of our loss. While I'll never claim to have any true insight into God's plans, I believed then, and I still believe now, that one of his reasons for taking Victoria was from us was so that we could use our show to help others dealing with a similar tragedy. I truly believe that by letting the cameras into that hospital room, and by exposing our grief and pain to the world, we were doing God's bidding. That while it might have been easier to suffer in private, perhaps by sharing our grief, we could teach our audience an important lesson about the powers of family and faith. And in doing so we could heal ourselves a little faster as well.

## DEALING WITH LOSS

If you've watched the episode of *Run's House* that dealt with Victoria's passing, then you probably noticed that while Justine and I were certainly emotional, we also tried to maintain our composure after we told our children what had happened. That's not to suggest that our pain wasn't intense. It was *soooo* intense. It was as intense as any pain or sorrow either of us had ever felt. But we knew if we let all the pain, confusion, and disappointment that we were feeling fill up that room, it would only magnify the pain and confusion and disappointment that our surviving children were feeling. We had to remember that no matter what we were going through, as parents our first job is always to ease our children's pain, not to make it even worse.

Suffering a loss is devastating for any family. But because we are a particularly close-knit group, in which everyone knew just how badly Justine wanted a little girl, I was concerned that the kids were going to take Victoria's death especially hard. I was worried about JoJo in particular. When we first held a family meeting about having another child, JoJo was very much against the idea. "It's too many kids," he kept saying. "I don't want any more brothers or sisters." So when Victoria passed, her loss hit him with a extra force. He felt like he was responsible for her loss, as if by saying he didn't want another sibling, he had somehow wished for her death. Of course the moment he started expressing those emotions, Justine and I went right to work and let him know that he shouldn't blame himself for a single second. We assured him that we knew he loved Victoria just as deeply as the rest of us. And we also reminded him that he didn't even possess the ability to wish Victoria into or out of existence. Only God has that sort of power.

Receiving that reassurance and understanding from his parents made JoJo feel much, much better. But if Justine and I had been falling over ourselves in grief, there's a chance we would have been blind to JoJo's pain. Then we would have not only lost Victoria, but we would have lost a little bit of JoJo, too. That's why you must always remember that in the hardest of times, your children are going to act like you do. If you start to go crazy with grief, your kids are going to go crazy too. If you retreat into a dark place, they're going head into their own dark places. But if you can stay strong, they can tap into that strength when they need it. After Victoria's passing, Justine and I felt that what our children needed the most—and not just JoJo, but all our children—was strength. That's why right after she passed, I stood up in front of my children in the hospital room and told them, "If you feel lost right now or in the days ahead, look to your father. And if you see any strength, try to grab some of that strength from me. Then use that strength to help us pull together as a family."

I was also worried about our kids having to grieve in public. Because Justine's pregnancy had played such a large role in the third season of *Run's House*, there was a lot of anticipation for Victoria's arrival. And when Victoria didn't make it, I knew there would be a lot people looking to express their sympathies to our family. But while I knew those people had only the best intentions, I was also concerned about how all that attention would affect the kids. I knew that when Diggy and Russy went to school, or when Angela was on the street, someone would probably come over and say, "Hey, I'm very sorry to hear about your sister." Those people would just be trying to help, but in the long run they would just be building more obstacles in my kids' roads toward recovery. Because every time someone reminded them of Victoria's death, it would just reopen their wounds.

Since I knew the world was going to constantly remind the kids of what had happened, it was very important that Justine and I promote the healing process at home. Just as I would enforce kindness or fun in another situation, after Victoria passed, I went to work to enforce healing. And to me, that meant allowing my family to get back to their regular lives. It meant Diggy getting back on the skateboard. It meant Russy getting back to hoarding his money. JoJo getting back in the studio. Angela getting back to running her magazine. And Vanessa getting back to acting and designing. It meant that without forgetting about Victoria, the kids could heal by getting back to the things that created joy and happiness in their lives.

I do want to be very clear on one point here: I am not suggesting that our approach is the "right" way to deal with the loss of a child. This is a very sensitive subject, and I don't want to appear critical of any family that's dealt with their loss differently. The truth is, there isn't any right or wrong way when it comes to dealing with a loss. Every family is going to approach it differently, depending on their particular situation. So while it was helpful for my family to try to return to normalcy as quickly as possible, another family might feel healthier going a little slower.

By sharing how we dealt with our loss, we're only trying to inspire other families who might want to take a similar approach but are having trouble moving forward. We only want them to know that if it feels like despair and depression are enveloping their house, it's OK to try to move those clouds away. We only want to serve as an example that it is possible to return your home to the happiness and joy that was present before your loss. That despite all the pain and heartbreak, it can be done.

## THANKFULNESS IN PAIN

In addition to enforcing healing, I also tried to enforce thankfulness after Victoria passed. As I said earlier, one of the first things I said to my wife after Victoria passed was, "I know this hurts, but you still have to be thankful." And while she couldn't help but look at me like I had lost my mind, she also understood the truth in what I was saying. Our loss was a test of our faith. The most severe test we'd ever faced, but one we were determined to pass as a family.

You can't claim to have faith by only thanking God when things are going your way. I'd be a hypocrite if I got down on my knees and said, "Thanks for this big house," or "Thanks for this hit TV show," but then started screaming, "I can't believe you're doing this to me, God!" when he took away my daughter. Who am I to be resentful, as good as God has been to Reverend Run? I have to be thankful no matter *what* the situation. And even though it might seem impossible to think of anything to be thankful for when your child dies, I had to remind myself that even in that pain, I still was surrounded by so many blessings. I was incredibly thankful that Justine wasn't seriously hurt in the delivery. I was extremely thankful that even though I lost Victoria, I still had Vanessa, Angela, JoJo, Diggy, and Russy gathered around me. For that day, and for a long time to come. And that mantra, of being thankful for family, is what I kept repeating to my kids in the wake of Victoria's death, and it's what I still tell them to this day: No matter what kind of hard times hit, we're still a family. No matter what I lost, I still have all of you. I know in my heart that Victoria came here to drop off a message, which was "be thankful for each other."

So if you were to ask me, "How do you rebound from an extraordinary loss?" my answer would be, "By saying 'thank you' over and over again." The only way you'll ever find any peace in that kind of pain is by being thankful for the loved ones who are around you. By hugging them, by loving them, by laughing with them, and even by crying with them. You must remember that by appreciating the joys your family can bring you, you can always make the sorrow a little easier to swallow.

## MOVING FORWARD WITHOUT GUILT

I'd like to end this section with a single message to all the other mothers out there who have suffered a loss of their child: Please do not feel guilty about moving forward.

After such a terrible tragedy, it becomes very easy to start asking yourself, "How can I go forward when my baby isn't here?" I can understand that mentality, because it began to grip me after Victoria died. But as much as I felt like I needed to mourn my dead baby, I felt a stronger urge to live for my children who are still here. While I wanted to lay in bed all day crying about Victoria with the covers pulled up over my head, I also knew that I need to help Russy with his homework when he got home from school. I knew that no matter how depressed I might feel, Diggy still needed someone to tell him to clean up his bathroom. That JoJo still needed someone to tell him to stop letting his pants sag beneath his butt. Because even though

Joey was helping me out as much as he could, my children needed their mother. They need me to be there for them every day. Physically and emotionally.

Please understand that I'm not trying to tell anyone to forget their loss. The truth is, you couldn't forget losing a child even if you tried. But I am encouraging you to try to stop constantly looking back. Because when you lay in that bed all day long, you're looking back. When you don't want to eat, you're looking back. When you stop taking care of yourself, you're looking back. But looking back isn't going to reverse your loss; all it's going to do is return you to a moment of debilitating pain.

I know some women were concerned with how I dealt with Victoria's death. I remember reading a letter a woman wrote to *Essence* in which she said, "I don't think Justine's husband let her mourn enough. She needs to mourn more for that child." And while I really do appreciate her concern, I want her and everyone else to know that I *did* mourn. I actually mourned very hard—it just might not have always come across that way on the show. As I said, for the sake of my children, I tried not to let my pain pervade the entire house.

But I did have my own way of addressing my loss, which for me came through writing letters to God. After Victoria passed, I would sit down every day and share how I was feeling with God. Sometimes I would only share basic sentiments. "Dear God," I might write. "I saw a young baby today at the mall and it made me sad." I know it sounds very simple, but even sharing those kinds of thoughts truly eased my pain. At other times, I would get a little deeper and talk to God about how thankful I was. How even though I was in pain, I was still so thankful to be given the strength to get through the day and be there for my family.

I also thanked God for revealing the true meaning of faith to me. Prior to losing Victoria, I *thought* I had faith. If I had a friend who was going through something, I'd be quick to tell them, "Girl, just have faith. You'll be OK." Or I'd tell people, "I'll pray that God gives you his strength to help you through this." But in retrospect, I can see that while I meant to help those people, all I really was doing was saying words. Faith was just a word to me. But after Victoria passed, it became something very real. Something I could hold on to and touch. Something that I could count on to hold me together when everything seemed to be falling apart. I realized that faith is something firm, something that I could lean on so hard that if it suddenly disappeared, I'd crash to the ground. I wish that I could have learned about real faith in another way, without needing it. But having truly felt it, now I feel like I can move forward in life without fear. I know that whatever sort of hard times hit my family, I'll have the faith to get through them. So when I wrote to God, I thanked him for revealing that faith to me.

And finally, I thanked God for giving my husband the strength to keep pushing our family forward. For giving him the wisdom to understand that the worst thing we could do after Victoria passed was to become stagnant. That's why when MTV came to us and said they would understand if we needed a break from taping, my husband said, "Nope, we gotta keep it moving. We gotta stick to our schedule and continue on with our lives." My husband knew that the worst thing I could do, and really the worst thing the family could do as a whole, was to sit around and slowly drown in our pain.

I knew that was a real possibility, because when I was still recovering from my cesarean section, I would stay at home and rest when everyone went off to church. And even just those few hours alone, without the sound of my children in the house or my husband acting silly, were too much for me. In my mind I would return to Victoria and spend the rest of the morning laid up in my bed crying. And the truth is, I would have spent every day like that if my husband hadn't encouraged me to come downstairs and tape segments for the show. If he hadn't pushed me to interact with the world and to get back to what makes me happy, which is spending time with my family, I might still be laid up in that bed right now. But by keeping things moving, I never became completely bogged down in that pain. I can laugh. I can enjoy my life and my wonderful family. And though it still makes my eyes well up, I can even talk and write a little bit about what we went through.

Like Joey said ultimately we all have to mourn our own way. What worked for me—pushing myself back into the world and sharing my pain with God in a more private manner—might not feel right for you. But I do believe that no matter how we mourn, we all must move forward. I've gone to Web sites for parents who've lost their children and I've seen some women write that they don't think they can go on. That essentially they've given up. They'll keep on breathing, eating, walking, and talking, but they're resigned to not living anymore. I can sympathize with that emotion, but I don't think there are any parents out there who can truly afford to do that. No matter how much you've lost, there's still always someone in your life who needs you. You might not even be aware of it, but they probably need you very badly. That's why we all have to keep on walking straight ahead. Some of us might need a push, and others might be able to do it on their own. Some might want to do it right away, while others might have to do it slowly over time. Some might want to scream their pain out into the world as loudly as possible, and others might want to keep that pain very private. And all of those ways of coping are fine. But no matter who you are, you must move forward.

A few months after I lost Victoria, a mutual friend told me that Tameka "Tiny" Cottle, the girlfriend of the rapper T.I., had just lost her baby during her pregnancy. Even though I didn't know Tiny that well, I picked up the phone and gave her a call, because I knew what she was going through. I wanted to let her know that while she probably felt as lonely as she had ever felt before, she wasn't alone. "Tiny, as hard as this is right now, you can't let it break you," I told her. "I was there not too long ago, and I know how you feel. But you have to keep pushing forward. Just like I gotta keep pushing forward. Because we really don't have any other choice. You've got a beautiful family that loves and depends on you. Even if you feel very weak inside, you have to stay strong for them."

While I didn't keep her on the phone for long, Tiny told me that she appreciated my call and promised to try to stay focused on moving forward. So I felt really great when I picked up the paper the other day and saw that Tiny and T.I. are pregnant again! Despite what she went through, she'll soon be blessed with another beautiful child, just like we've been blessed with Miley. And while neither of us will ever forget the child we lost, we'll also both be here 100 percent for the children we still have.

And whether it's by calling up Tiny, or talking to a woman at a book signing, or even just reaching some of you right now through this book, I really believe that all the pain I suffered was for a reason—to help other women heal. (I should actually say to help women and men heal. Because I know my husband was hurting just as much as I was.) I think Victoria's stay was so brief because God wanted me to be able to share this message with you: When you have a strong belief in faith and family, you can make it through any hard time. Even losing your child.

## RUN'S TAKE BACK

Taking back your family from a loss is one of the most difficult, delicate, and demanding tasks a parent can ever face. And as Justine and I have tried to stress, there simply is no right way to do it. Yet no matter what speed you move at, no matter what angle you approach it from, or no matter what sort of tools you employ, I believe the first step you must take is trying to talk about what has happened with your children.

My children were pretty quiet after they first learned that Victoria had passed. It's not that they didn't have anything to say, but rather that they didn't really know how to say it. That's why in the wake of Victoria's death, I tried to provide my children with as many ways to express themselves as possible. Of course I held a family meeting, where Justine and I tried to share what we were feeling and encouraged all of them to do the same. But I also went to each of them individually and tried to talk to them about how they were feeling in a more private setting, maybe in their rooms or during a walk or even a ride to the store. And it was through those conversations that I learned how Russy was worried if it was OK that he cried at the hospital ("You were perfect," I reassured him). I learned how Diggy had been looking forward to having a little sister more than he had let on when Justine was pregnant. I learned how Angela wanted to talk about what she was feeling, while Vanessa found that discussing Victoria was too draining. And the first time I spoke to JoJo and asked if he was OK, he tried to be cool and told me, "Yeah, of course I'm fine." But when I went back again a few days later and asked him how he was feeling, he opened up and admitted that he felt terrible about having said that he didn't want any more siblings. Those conversations weren't always easy, and it took a while for some of the kids to open up, but I believe discussing what they were feeling with me helped ease their pain considerably.

So if your children are dealing with a similar loss, or maybe the loss of a parent, a grandparent, a friend, or even a pet, make sure they know that they can always come and talk to you about it. You can tell them that you might not even have an answer for all their questions, but there's nothing they can't ask you. It might take one conversation, it might take three or four, or it might take a year's worth of talk, but you'll try to work it out together.

After you've done your best to address the pain, I would then encourage you to focus on bringing back some of the happiness that was in your home prior to your loss. And again, I have to stress that this is a process that every family must undergo at their own pace. For some, the idea of returning to life's routines might seem overwhelming after a loss. For others, the danger is by not returning to those routines fast enough, they run the risk of becoming permanently trapped in their pain. That's why as a parent (and a spouse) your job is to take the pulse of your family and, despite your own pain, try to make the necessary adjustments.

Personally, I sensed that it would become dangerous for our family if Justine drank too deeply from what I call the "sour soup of sorrow." That's why once she had physically healed from her ordeal, I tried every day to make that soup a little less sour. One day I sprinkled in a little sugar in the form of having Diggy and Russy watch a movie in bed with her. A few days later, I sprinkled in a little more sugar in the form of her coming downstairs to eat dinner with the entire family. A few days after that, I added even a little bit more by having her sister and her niece over. And so on and so forth until the soup didn't taste as sour anymore. Then I really tried to pour it on by encouraging her to get back to the things she loves, like working on new designs for the house, messing around with the kids, and even filming scenes for *Run's House*. And in time, the joy she felt from being around so much positive energy helped turn that sour soup into something that tasted less bitter and more like lobster bisque (her favorite kind). Which is not to say that she *forgot* about Victoria, but rather that it was important to help Justine *remember* all the things she loved about the life she still had. She needed to be reminded that there was a reason that she wanted to bring Victoria into this family—because she wanted her to be a part of all this love and happiness and laughter.

That's why the first day Justine came home from the hospital, I had the entire family sit on our bed with her and hold hands. And then I led the family in a short prayer. "Father, we are thankful that we are here together as a family," I said. "We ask your blessing for Victoria Anne Simmons, and we miss her very much. And we ask that you know that we're thankful for the children that we have here. We are thankful that Mommy made it through this ordeal. We thank you for letting us know that by having our family together in this room, that everything is OK and in due time you'll heal our hearts so that we may be able to go forward." And while a lot of tears were shed that morning, I'm thankful to say that our family has been able to move forward. We have been able to take back our hearts from the pain we felt and now have an even greater appreciation for each other and the love that we share. And I truly believe that if you can, you need to talk with your family and help them understand that the pain they're feeling today is only going to help make them stronger and more loving as a family tomorrow.

## CHAPTER 8

# Blending Is Beautiful

W hen I was about thirteen years old, one day my mother started kicking my father out of our house. It was a shocking thing for me to see, because while they had had their share of disagreements, none were ever big enough to make me think their marriage was on the rocks.

As I watched my father load his stuff into his van, I couldn't understood how my mother could be so mean and just throw him out onto the street like that. To my impressionable teenage eyes, it seemed the most unfair thing I'd ever seen. I was definitely a "Daddy's little girl," and I hated the thought of him having to be alone out in the world. So right then and there, I decided that if he had to leave, then I was going with him.

As we got into the van, I didn't have a clue as to where we were going or how long we'd be gone. I was just excited to hit the road with my pops. I figured we'd drive around the country, live out of the van, and make a grand adventure out of it. Just me and my dad on the road together, like some sort of buddy movie.

Well, after we pulled away from our home, my father made a few lefts, took a couple of rights, and not even ten minutes later, pulled up in front of another house. My father just looked at me and then started unpacking his stuff at some woman's home! So much for our big adventure! We never even made it off Long Island!

I wanted to share that little story because it turned out that the house we pulled up to belonged to a woman named Daisy. I guess my father had been seeing her all along and she was why my mother threw him out of the house. Frankly, I've never gotten the full story about what happened, and by this point, it doesn't really even matter to me anymore. Because even though we met under such crazy circumstances, Daisy ended up having a tremendous impact on me as a mother. As my stepmother, Daisy never showed me anything but total love during the years I lived with her. She never made me feel uncomfortable or unwelcome in her home, or treated me any differently than she treated her own son. In fact, if you could have seen us back then, you would have thought that Daisy was my biological mother and my father was the stepparent. Her love for me really felt that deep and our relationship was that strong.

It's very important that I acknowledge the influence that Daisy's example had on me because a lot of people seem to have a similar respect for the relationship I enjoy with my stepchildren. "You treat them like they're your own flesh and blood," is one of the comments I'll often hear. And while I'm very thankful that our family is perceived in such a positive light, I owe my approach to how Daisy treated me back then. I wasn't with her that long—shorter than the time Vanessa, Angela, and JoJo have been with me—but she taught me how important it is to treat all your children, whether they're your blood or not, as part of your heart.

That's an approach I want to share with all the other parents out there who have what I like to call "blended" families. I'm very proud that *Run's House* seems to be providing people with an example of how a blended family can work. I'm often stopped by people (I know we keep saying that, but it's true! People must find us very approachable!) who tell me, "We're a blended family, and you guys are helping us so much." But while I'm proud that *Run's House* has inspired other blended families out there, I want to stress that that our success hasn't always come easy. A lot of work and consideration has to go into making our situation work.

I believe the most important key to making a blended family work is for the parents not to take out their frustrations on the kids involved. For instance, if you're marrying a guy who already has kids, never forget that those kids didn't ask to come into your life. They didn't ask to live under the same roof as you, to take up space, to cost you money, and, perhaps most importantly, to take away your man's attention and affection. They didn't ask for any of that. They're just along for the ride. So try to treat them the same way you would want to be treated if you were a young kid who was being forced to leave your comfort zone and go live with a new mommy or a new daddy for the first time.

Or let's say you're thinking about marrying a woman who already has children of her own. If you're serious about that lady, then go out of your way to show her kids love. Please don't be one of these dudes who goes around talking about how he doesn't want to be bothered with someone else's "baggage." What a terrible way to think of young children! Imagine if I had looked at Vanessa, Angela, and JoJo as "baggage" when I first met Joey. Those kids are such a huge part of my life that I can't even picture my world without them. But if I had been worrying about "baggage" back when I first met Joey, I wouldn't be surrounded by all the love that I have today. Never look at someone else's kids as something that has to be tolerated. Look at them as an opportunity to increase the love in your life.

Similarly, I want to say something to all of the single parents out there who are getting into a new relationship. If you feel like the person you are seeing is not accepting of your children, then you need to check that situation right away. Sit down with that person and have a very serious talk about their attitude toward your kids. Most importantly, do not let them move in with you unless you feel that they have an honest and deep love toward your children! And while this applies to both men and women, I see so many women in particular make this mistake. They let men who are at best ambivalent about their children, or at worst a potential danger to them, move into their homes! Please understand that you can never give someone access to your children unless they have real love for them. And no matter what some of these guys might try to tell you, it's impossible to love you without loving your kids, too. If a man is disrespecting your kids, then he's disrespecting you. Period. And he's not someone that you, or your children, should be spending serious time with.

## THE BLENDING BLUES

My husband and I work very hard to shower all our kids with love and make sure no one in our family feels left out or different. And while I think we've been successful for the most part, I can't lie: There will be times when your kids struggle with living in a blended family.

In our home, it's probably been the toughest for JoJo, who went from being the youngest in his family—the baby, so to speak—to being a big brother. Like most "babies," he was used to getting a lot of attention. But after Russy and Diggy were born, JoJo saw his role in the family change. Instead of getting all the attention himself, he had two little brothers who wanted attention from him. And that's been a hard transition for him.

Diggy and Russy have also gone through their little blending issues. In particular, they're convinced that I'm harder on them than I am on my stepkids. Since most moms are usually harder on their stepkids, Russy and Diggy complain that I overcompensate by yelling at them more than I do at Vanessa, Angela, and JoJo. But as much as they like to say they're getting a raw deal, in their hearts they know that I'm a mother that believes in justice. Biological child or not, in my book, when you're wrong, you're wrong. I'm not taking sides or playing favorites. Which is why I say, especially to Russy and Diggy, that the reason I don't yell at Vanessa and Angela as much is because they usually don't act as stupidly as you two do.

It's also hard on Diggy and Russy because they don't get to see their older siblings as much as they'd like. As we've mentioned, it might seem on TV like this family is together all the time, but the truth is that as Vanessa, Angela, and JoJo grow older and start to have more of their own lives, they have less time for Diggy and Russy. It's painful for the boys, especially when it comes to their relationship with JoJo, who they really look up to. That's why every time JoJo goes off to Queens, I try to remind him, "Please call your little brothers and check in on them. They miss you." And even though sometimes he likes to act like he won't, he always ends up calling.

## VALERIE'S CONTRIBUTION

We talked about her in the last chapter, and now I want to say again that we can't really discuss the success that we've had as a blended family without acknowledging the crucial role that Valerie has played in raising Vanessa, Angela, and JoJo. And while we tried to make her more of a part of the show after the kids opened up about the pain they were feeling over her role, I still have to imagine that it's very hard for her to hear people talking all the time about what a great job Joey and I are doing with the kids.

So while I'm grateful for all the positive press we've received, I hope this book can generate a little more recognition for the great job that Valerie, her husband, Fonzi, and her father, Danny, aka Grand Pa, have done. It's funny, but it seems like when people in the media ask us about Valerie, our answers never make the final story. Maybe it's because we say, "Oh, their mother is a very big part of their lives and does a great job with them." I almost feel like if instead of praising her, we said, "Oh, their mother's on crack, she's crazy," the reporters would put that in their stories. Maybe saying that she's a teacher, that she sees them all the time and that she's happily married doesn't seem interesting enough to people in the media. But no matter what the media thinks, I believe that two families getting along and working together like this is a great story. We need to celebrate and encourage this kind of relationship, not just take it for granted or gloss it over.

One of the reasons we've enjoyed such success is because Valerie has been very supportive of my relationship with her children. Without that support, I don't think things would have worked out as well as they have. As important as it is to show love toward your stepchildren, it's equally important that their biological parent doesn't throw hate toward you. If Valerie had spoken negatively about me with her kids, or questioned my role in their lives, they would have looked at me differently. No matter how much love I gave them, our relationship wouldn't be as strong as it is today. That negativity would have always kept some distance between us. But instead, she has always been thankful that when her kids weren't with her, at least they were in a loving environment. Her attitude has been, "This is great. Or at least as great as things can be under the circumstances." Instead of trying to impede my relationship with her children, she's supported it and helped it flourish.

I believe Valerie's been that way because she's a trusting person with a big heart. But if you look at her situation in a more practical light, it's also a very smart approach to take. If you were in a similar situation, what would you prefer? To have your kids living with someone they feel negativity toward? Or living with someone that they feel genuine love and respect

for? Obviously, you always want your kids to be surrounded by
as much love as possible. Unfortunately, too many parents feel
threatened by someone else loving their kids, and as a result try
to poison that relationship before it gets too deep. Thankfully
Valerie has never gone that route, and in doing so has made a
difficult situation not only much more manageable, but also
more rewarding.

## WORRYING ABOUT THE WEDDINGS

Even though our journey as a blended family has been a relatively smooth one, there are still times when I catch myself
worrying about potential bumps in the road. For no particular
reason, just the other day I started thinking, "What's going to
happen when Vanessa meets someone and gets married? Who's
she going to have walk her down the aisle?" It's crazy, but that
thought really did pop into my mind. Then I started thinking
about everything else that would go into a wedding: picking out
a gown, getting the bride's hair ready, and even sharing the first
dance. All things that I'd want to be a part of, but things that I
realize I might to miss out on because Vanessa has a biological
mother who's a major part of her life. I know it sounds dramatic, but just thinking about having to miss out on some of
those moments made me start to cry. By the way I was bawling,
you would have thought that Vanessa, who doesn't even have a
serious boyfriend right now, was getting married tomorrow!

While I know my reaction was pretty dramatic, these are
the kinds of issues you have to be ready to deal with in a
blended family. I try to prepare myself now, so when those days
come, I can step back a bit and let the girls do what feels right
to them. As a stepmother, I feel it's very important that I don't
insert myself into situations and force the kids to make difficult
choices. Whether it's a wedding or a graduation or a school play,
it's important to remember that it's the kid's day, and if I make

a fuss about my role, it would only ruin their happiness. I have to have faith that they'll come to me and say, "Can you help me with the dress?" or "Can you help with my hair?" rather than make an issue out of it. I won't lie, it can be tough. No matter how good your relationships are, you'll still need some thick, thick skin to get through some of these situations.

But as awkward or as painful as some situations might feel, we've also experienced plenty of moments where everything seems to come together beautifully. Probably the best example came during a little party we once had for JoJo. We were really thrilled that at the height of the party, JoJo pulled Valerie and me out on the dance floor and started swinging both of us around, yelling, "Look, everyone, I got two moms!" Because as my husband mentioned earlier, one message we've always tried to share with the kids is that having a blended family is a blessing. That instead of feeling bad about having a stepmother, they should actually feel blessed about having two moms and two dads.

So when JoJo had both of his mothers out on the dance floor, it felt like all the positive reinforcement we tried to give the kids had finally paid off. While the children might have felt pain after their parents divorced, now they were feeling some of the joy that comes from doubling the love around them. At that moment, I felt like we (and when I say "we," I mean both families) had finally made it.

## GROWING CLOSER

Has being the father of a blended family been easy? No. Does it take a lot of sacrifice and patience? Yes. But as Justine just said, I really do feel like we're finally pulling this thing together. And I believe one of the keys to that progress has been identifying whatever pain my children might be feeling about their situation and then addressing it before it gets a chance to fester. Whenever I sense my children might be hurting, instead of letting that hurt drive us all farther apart, I always want to try to find a way to bring us all closer together.

For example, in the last chapter we discussed how Valerie's role, or lack thereof, on *Run's House* had created tremendous issues for Vanessa, Angela, and JoJo. And in that chapter, we discussed the public ways that we tried to rectify the situation. But I think it's also important to note that we made a real effort to bring our two families closer together in private, too. It happened because when the kids became so emotional about the show, Justine and I had the same reaction. "This isn't only about *Run's House*. This is really about the kids being at a stage of their lives where they need to feel that sense of connection between the families. Whether the cameras are on or off."

The first step we took was to go out to dinner with Valerie, Fonzi, and their daughters Darien and Tiffany. And while there was probably some hesitation on everyone's part before that night, we all ended up having a very lovely evening. Everyone put their fears, their insecurities, and whatever old grudges they were carrying in their back pockets and instead gave the children a night that they had been waiting a long time for.

In fact, that dinner worked out so well that a few months later, the kids asked if Valerie and her family could come to our home for Thanksgiving. Of course we said yes, and again we were able to enjoy a very special night. Diggy and Russy had a great time running around with Valerie's kids, Darien and Tiffany, who they hardly ever get to see. Fonzi and I got to shoot some hoops and kick it a bit about old school hip-hop. And most importantly, it warmed Vanessa, Angela, and JoJo's hearts to see their two worlds coming together in such a happy and loving setting.

I have to stress, however, that it wasn't by accident that Thanksgiving went off so well. It had a lot to do with the fact that everyone made a concerted effort to be on their best behavior that day. Which is not to say that people were acting fake or insincere, but rather that they were aware that since there might be weird or intimidating moments, we had to go extra hard to make everyone feel comfortable. For instance, we made a point of inviting Valerie's best friend, La Rose, so that if Valerie felt any awkwardness, there would be someone there for her to lean on a bit. Also, we didn't serve any alcohol that day. You already know my feelings about booze, so in a sense it was an easy decision. But it's also one you might want to consider if you're planning a similar sort of blended family function. I've been around long enough to know that family plus raw emotions plus alcohol often equals too much drama. So do yourself a favor—until the families that are blending get really comfortable together, try to leave alcohol out of the equation.

Having said all that, I don't want to make it sound like you have to go crazy planning every time you bring blended families together. Instead, always just try to approach these events like calm, mature adults. If you're polite and mind your p's and q's, there's a good chance everything will work out in the end. So that in the midst of all these relationships that used to represent hurt and distrust in your life, you can actually create something that will feel peaceful and positive.

## EMBRACING YOUR BLENDED FAMILY

Another reason to embrace your extended blended family is that it will not only make your children feel better, it will make *you* a better parent as well. As much as we might like to think we can do it by ourselves, the truth is that you can't really have a firm grip on your children if half their lives take place outside of your influence and knowledge. You really have to know what's going on that other half of the time. That's why it's very important to keep an open line of communication with your ex-spouse, or baby momma, or whoever you share the responsibility of your children with. No matter what sort of personal issues you guys have gone through in the past, if the two of you truly have your child's best interest at heart, then you're going to have to communicate with each other.

We recently witnessed how powerful that sort of communication can be during a difficult period we recently went through with JoJo. Right before Vanessa and Angela were scheduled to move to Los Angeles, we noted that JoJo was becoming increasingly mean-spirited toward them. Every time he saw them he'd diss them by saying something like, "I can't wait for you two to be gone," or "Would you two please just leave already?" Justine and I weren't really sure why he was acting that way, but one night Valerie called and helped solve the mystery for us. She explained that they had all just gone out to dinner together and that JoJo had been acting particularly moody around the girls. When she asked him if he was acting that way because he was actually scared that he was going to miss them, he broke down and admitted that that was the case. He actually started crying and explained that since they'd been through so much together, he was having a hard time imagining living so far away from them. He confessed that the meanness was just a cover for his pain! And since we have open communication, Valerie was able to call me up and tell me what was really bugging JoJo (and even better, she got it on tape so we could use it for the show!). But if that line of communication had been closed, Justine and I might have stayed in the dark about the true cause of JoJo's behavior.

I'll give you another great example with JoJo. Remember that beautiful scene Justine was telling you about, where she was dancing with JoJo and Valerie and he was yelling, "Hey, look! I've got two moms!"? Well, as beautiful as that scene was, JoJo almost ruined it a few seconds later by trying to play Justine and Valerie off against each other for a new phone. Basically, while they were dancing, JoJo told Valerie, "You know, if you don't get me that cell phone I've been asking for, then my other mother here is going to get it for me." But rather than going for that bait, Justine and Valerie both just looked at him and rolled their eyes. "Don't try to play us against each other. Because it isn't going to work," Valerie told him. And Justine added, "Right, and now you aren't getting that phone from either of us." Even though it was a silly game for JoJo to play, the end result was great to see. It let JoJo know that he can't hide behind the shields of "Oh, Justine said she would get that for me," or "Oh, my mom in Queens said it was OK for me to go away with my friends this weekend." Their united reaction let him know that both of his mothers are on the same page and communicating when it comes to his life.

It's very important that not only JoJo, but all our kids understand that there's an open-door policy between Valerie, Fonzi, Justine, and me. If I suspect that Angela is going to try to run some game when she's out in Queens, I'm not going hesitate to call up Valerie and give her a heads-up. Just as if Valerie senses that JoJo is trying to lie about some rule that I laid down for him, she's going to tell him, "I'm going to call your father and see if that's real." It's very important for them to know that they're accountable in Queens for what happens in New Jersey, and accountable in New Jersey for what happens in Queens.

But again, I have to stress that that line of communication is only open because the four of us have been able to put our egos aside and focus on what's best for the children. If I call Valerie and ask whether JoJo's been breaking the rules out in Queens, she's not going to start complaining, "Who does Joey think he is? Trying to act like I don't have control over these children!" Similarly, if Valerie calls me about something that JoJo is doing over here, I'm not going to think, "Why is she so worried about what's happening in my home? She needs to worry about her own backyard." No, I'm going to listen to what she has to say and then try to work out a solution that is the best for our children.

It hasn't always been easy, and it's required a lot of humility, patience, confidence, and commitment. But those are the traits you're going to need in order to make a blended family work. They're not optional. They're necessary. Yet if you can find the strength and faith to tap into those qualities, I promise that you'll be able to take a situation that ruins many families and use it to actually make your family stronger.

## BE RESPECTFUL TO YOUR SPOUSE

Before I wrap up this section, I want to share one very small but practical piece of advice on this subject. As important as it is to have an open line of communication with your ex-spouse, it's just as important to remember that that sort of communication can be very uncomfortable for your current partner. It's crucial that when you do have these conversations with your ex, you do so in a way that's very transparent and respectful to the feelings of the person you're with now.

For example, whenever Valerie calls, I always make sure Justine is in the room and that the call is on speakerphone. Always! That's not a diss to Valerie, or to suggest in any way that's she calling about anything other than the children. It's just a way of respecting Justine. The fact is, people are always going to feel weird listening to their husbands or wives talk to an ex. Especially when it's about something as personal as the children they've had together.

It's not even a major issue for me, because I'm lucky to be married to someone as open-minded and secure in themselves as Justine. She's never questioned me once about being on the phone with Valerie. But even so, put those calls on speakerphone anyway! And since most people aren't as trusting as Justine, be sure to make your spouse feel very secure and comfortable in how you handle these types of relationships. In other words, don't get in the habit of taking a lot of calls from your ex without your spouse knowing about them. Because even if your intentions are pure and every one of those calls sticks to the parenting script, it's only a matter of time before your spouse will start to feel suspicious. Don't even go there in the first place. When you're dealing with something as potentially touchy as an ex and their kids, you simply want to avoid anything that could cause extra drama in your life.

## MEETING MILEY

While I like to think that we've done a good job raising a healthy, happy blended family, Miley has only been with us for a few months as I'm writing this, so I don't want to make it seem like I'm any sort of expert on adoption. But despite my inexperience, I can already sense what a beautiful thing adoption can be and what an incredible addition Miley is going to be to our blended family.

Before I talk about the adoption process, I should start by saying that the decision to add another child to our family was not made overnight. As I mentioned in the last chapter, I had actually wanted to adopt before I became pregnant with Victoria. And after Victoria passed, I was still determined to have a little girl. Perhaps even more determined than before. But since it seemed too risky and painful to attempt another pregnancy, our thoughts returned to adoption. Not so much in order to replace Victoria, but because I still had this yearning, a real need to experience all the different stages of raising a baby girl. Remember, I missed Vanessa's first-time crawling, or Angela's first words. I still wanted to experience all of that very badly.

Joey wanted to support me, but he was concerned that adding an infant child to the family would be too much for me to handle in the aftermath of losing Victoria. In his mind, it made much more sense to adopt a baby that was at least two or three years old. But I was determined to have my baby. So one day I sat down and wrote a letter to God, explaining just why I had my heart set on an infant and asking him to help Joey feel the same way. And not long after I wrote that letter, Joey came to me and said, "You know, I've been thinking about it and you're right—the newborn thing is great!" I'll let him explain what changed his mind.

## RUN'S RELUCTANCE

It's true, I had a lot of issues when Justine first said that she wanted to adopt an infant. To me, an infant meant a ton of work and the loss of our freedom. And in my selfish mind, my desire to have freedom and independence superceded Justine's desire to have that baby girl.

One day I was sharing those feelings with a friend of mine over lunch. I was giving him the same pitch I'd been giving Justine, breaking down all the reasons why adopting an older child would be much more practical. Why an older child would take up less of our time, require less extra help around the house, and in general be a lot easier to blend into a family that was already pretty chaotic with five kids to look after. My friend heard me out, then just looked at me and said, "Do you really have a choice?" And when he said that, the truth of the situation hit me like a ton of bricks. Of course I didn't have a choice! There were no pros and cons to debate, no options to weigh. My wife had just suffered through losing a child, which is the hardest pain for any mother to endure. And rather than letting that pain break her, she was trying to rebound and move forward in life with a new baby. It was a beautiful, courageous thing for her to do, yet there I was mumbling about all the ways an infant would impede my lifestyle. So I realized at that moment that no, I did not have a choice. My only choice was to support my wife 100 percent in finding a beautiful little girl.

## PREPARE FOR THE PROCCESS

When Joey told me that he supported my decision to adopt a newborn, it really felt like we had turned a corner. But one of the things I've learned about adopting a baby is that it can be a very slow process. You don't just decide you want to adopt and then go pick up your baby. There is a lot of work you must put in before that day eventually comes.

I can't lie, the paperwork is the biggest headache. It felt like there was just so much of it. You have to provide your adoption agency with all sorts of medical and financial records. Then your family must undergo a very extensive background check that includes getting your fingerprints taken. After you pass those tests, you must schedule several home visits, where a representative from your adoption agency interviews your family in an effort to evaluate whether you'd be an appropriate family for adoption. Believe me, all of those steps require a ton of time and energy. And to keep it funky, they also cost a lot of money. I don't like to talk about amounts, because to me that's like putting a price tag on your baby. But for a lot of people, the cost is really something that has to be taken into consideration.

And once you pass all those tests and are approved by your agency, you still have to wait some more before you can get your baby. There are false starts where you think you're going to get a baby, only to have it fall through at the last minute for whatever reason. That happened to us several times. We learned the hard way that it's very important not to build yourself up too much when you're in line for a baby. Because no matter what they tell you, there's a good chance that that baby might not have truly been meant for you.

I'm not sharing all this information in order to discourage anyone, or to try to scare people away from adopting. I just want anyone who's considering adoption to understand that it's a very long process. That there are going to be moments where your soul feels tired, when you begin to think that adoption will never work out for you.

But as we learned, when you finally do bring your baby home the first day, it's like all the paperwork, all the interviews, all the phone calls with your lawyer, and all the waiting never even happened. All you'll be thinking about is the incredible little bundle of joy that you're welcoming into your home.

## SHE FEELS LIKE SHE CAME OUT OF ME

We ended up getting Miley almost a year to the day after we lost Victoria. And while it was definitely a long and trying process, now that Miley is here, the positive effect she has had on this house has been incredible.

To say that Miley has blended into our family would be an understatement. I think we all had some fears that Miley wouldn't feel "real," like she was truly part of our family. But nothing could be further from the case. Just today Diggy came up to me when I was feeding Miley and said, "Mom, she really feels likes ours." And everyone in the house says the same thing—that when they hold her, it just feels so right. In fact, I sometimes even have to remind myself that she didn't come out of me. Just as how sometimes I have to remind myself that I'm not Vanessa, Angela, and JoJo's biological mother. It feels the same way with Miley.

In fact, Miley is blending in so well that she's already getting her own nicknames. Her nanny Kristin calls her "Peanut" because she thinks she looks like a little nut. And JoJo calls her "Miley Davis," which is his little play on Miles. In fact, I should probably take a moment here and explain why we choose the name "Miley." After Miley was born, she lived with a wonderful foster family for one month who named her "Emily." While we wanted to give her our own name, we also wanted to respect the time she spent with them. We were playing around with ideas when someone said, "What about 'Miley'? It's her own name, but it's still got 'Emily' in it." That felt right to me, so I said, "OK. It sounds like a very happy name." And when my boys heard, they went crazy because it turns out that "Miley" is the name of the actress who plays the lead character on the Disney Channel's *Hannah Montana*, one of their favorite shows. Even JoJo liked it, though he had been pushing for "Josephine" since that's a combination of "Joseph" and "Justine."

## WHEN'S THE RIGHT TIME TO EXPLAIN?

Now that I'm no longer asking myself, "Is she the right one for us?" or "Is she going to feel different?" the biggest issue I have to confront is when to let Miley know that she's adopted.

Judging from all the research I've done, it's important to explain to your child that they're adopted very early in life. Essentially, when you're teaching them the basics like "1,2,3" and their names, you should also be starting to explain to them that they're adopted. That way by the time they're old enough to really understand the concept, it already feels like a very fundamental part of who they are. It's similar to how we plan to approach prayer with Miley.

But while I understand conceptually that telling them early is the right way to do it, in my heart I can also understand why people go years and years without saying anything. After only a few months, I'm already forgetting that Miley's adopted. I could understand not wanting to bring it up by the time she's three or four. In fact, Russy just told me that he doesn't want us to *ever* tell Miley that she's adopted. When I asked him why, he said, "Because telling her might hurt her feelings. And if she feels hurt, then she might want to leave." I had to explain to him that while it was very sweet that he was worried about her feelings, in the long run it would probably hurt her more to not let her know she was adopted.

Ultimately, I think what would really be painful for your adopted child is learning that you kept an important truth hidden from them for so many years. That would have to make them think, "Wow, this person I trusted so much was actually keeping me in the dark all this time." Run's partner DMC only found out that he was adopted a few years ago, and it was really a staggering blow to him. To the point where his pain was so great that he was thinking about taking his own life. He ultimately recovered from that blow, but I don't think there's any question that he would have preferred that his parents had told him when he was a young child. In fact, if you haven't seen it yet, you should check out his documentary, *My Adoption Journey*. When you see the incredible pain and confusion he felt at discovering he was adopted as a grown man, it will help you understand why as heartrending as it might be, adopted children need to hear the truth as early as possible.

## LETTING HER GROW

Another reality I'm going to have to come to terms with is that one day Milcy might want to learn who her birth mother is. I'm not gonna lie: Even though that day is probably years, maybe even decades, away, it still hurts for me to think about it. No matter how well Miley blends into our family, if she does decide to look for her mother, in the back of my mind I'll be thinking, "What does this mean? Is she looking because I haven't been a good mother? And if she finds her birth mother, is she going to want to stay with her?" But as scary as those thoughts might feel, the bottom line is that if I truly love Miley, then I can only take care of her the best that I can now and then support whatever decisions she makes in the future.

I do want to take a moment and praise Miley's birth mother for the difficult but courageous decision she made. When we talk about the adoption process, we tend to overlook how great these birth mothers must be. The truth is, it takes an incredibly strong person to carry a baby for nine months (and trust me, having gone through it three times, it's no joke), go through the agony of a delivery, and then, once you finally reach the finish line, to then say, "Here, take my baby." We try to act like a mother who does that must be messed up, or irresponsible, or cold-hearted. But the truth is, a mother who can look at her situation and say, "I can't do right by this child where *I* am in life right now, but I do want to give *her* a better life," is freaking amazing. That's not the action of someone who doesn't care. That's someone making the ultimate sacrifice of motherhood. So I always want Miley to know her biological mother is an awesome lady. If Miley asks about her mother, I'll tell her, "It's not that she didn't love you. It's just that she wanted better for you." And hopefully as a family we'll eventually prove that her decision was the right one.

## CELEBRATING ADOPTION

I want to end this section by addressing all the talk that's been going on lately about celebrities like Madonna or Angelina Jolie who adopt African-American (or in their cases, African) babies. I know some people, especially in the African-American community, have suggested that these stars are only adopting those babies because it's the cool or trendy thing to do these days. But without knowing Madonna or Angelina personally, I feel pretty comfortable in saying that isn't the case. Having experienced the process myself, I know that there's no way you're going to go through all the emotional ups and downs that come with adoption just to be trendy. Just like you're not going to go through all the diaper-changing and feeding and crying and burping just to earn some Liberal brownie points. When Angelina adopted that little girl in Africa, it could have only been because she fell in love with her. That little girl must have just run up and jumped into Angelina's arms and felt so great that Angelina's mothering instincts took over. She probably fell in love and just wanted to try to give that girl a better life.

Personally, I don't have any problem with these stars going to Africa, or Asia, or wherever they go and trying to give these beautiful babies a better life. Uncle Russell actually encouraged us to go to South Africa and adopt there, but we felt more comfortable going through the process closer to home. We felt that there are so many babies right here in America that need a better home that there was no reason to look overseas. That was our choice, but I think adopting a baby is a blessing no matter where you do it, or who's doing it.

Interestingly enough, it was a white foster family that first took care of Miley when she came home from the hospital. And when we came to pick her up from their house, the father became very emotional and admitted that he was going to have a very hard time saying good-bye to her. Even though she had only been with them for a month or so, he said he'd developed a very close bond with Miley, closer than he's ever felt for any of the babies that have stayed with them. And before we left, his wife took me aside and told me that they were actually thinking about adopting an African-American baby. But they were concerned that a black child might have issues growing up in a white household. They were worried that the baby might feel alienated, or left out, and they wanted to hear what I thought about it.

So I told her that while I thought it was great that she was trying to be so sensitive to the baby's needs, she shouldn't worry too much about adopting an African-American child. While it's true that a child in that situation will most likely have moments where they feel strange or different, the very same thing could happen with someone's biological children. JoJo definitely went through a period where he felt left out in our family, when he alienated himself and stayed in his room most of the time. Eventually we were able to pull him out of it, but he felt that way as an African-American child in an African-American household. Which is why I told her that while there's always a chance that any child, biological or adopted, is going to have their issues, as long as you give that child all the love that's in your heart, you'll eventually be able to help them get through it. So while we don't know how Miley is going to end up, we don't know how Russy is going to end up, either. We can raise both of them to go right, and they could still both end up going left. That's the chance you take with children, biological or adopted. As we'll explain in the next chapter, children don't come with guarantees. You can only do your best and then forget the rest.

## RUN'S TAKE BACK

Taking back your home from the bad feelings, mistrust, and misunderstandings that often come with having a blended family can be one of the most difficult things you'll have to do as a parent. And to do so correctly, you must rely on what I like to call the "Two Cs": confrontation and compassion.

I say "confrontation" because most children aren't going to feel comfortable talking about what they're feeling when their parents break up, or when it's time to move in with a new mommy or daddy. If they're uncomfortable around their new mommy, or resentful of their new daddy, they're most likely going to keep those feelings inside. But as a parent, you can never correct what you don't confront. That's true for this lesson in particular and really for everything I'm promoting in this book.

So before you can fix that resentment, you must confront it first. If your daughter has been talking back to her stepmother, then you've got to take her on a walk and ask her what's really bothering her. If your girlfriend is about to move in with you, you've got to call a family meeting and make sure you're kids are OK with the situation. If you sense your daughter is hanging out with the wrong crowd when she stays with your ex, then you've got to pick up the phone and make that call, no matter how uncomfortable that conversation might be. I know it would be a lot easier to sweep those kinds of issues under the rug, but you've got to confront them if you want the blended thing to work.

After you face those blending issues head-on, the next step

5

is to make sure that your confrontation is always dripping with compassion. As my wife said, these kids didn't ask to have a new mommy. They didn't ask to have to go live with a new daddy. Any drama they're feeling is really drama that we've thrust on them. So when confronting it, it's always important to keep reminding them, "None of this is your fault. No one's mad at you for feeling the way that you do. We're going to work through this together."

You're going to need so much compassion to take your kids back from the pain that they're going to feel at times. In fact, Will Smith might have said it best when I asked him how he made his kids comfortable with having a blended family. "Every day," he told me, "I just try to let them know that it's OK." And that's really the key. If your kids feel torn about having two mommies, you've got to let the kids know it's OK. We're going to work it out together. If your ex-husband feels uncomfortable about having his kids spending time with your new boyfriend, you've got to try to let him know it's OK. That you respect what he's feeling and you're going to try to find a solution that works. If your new wife is worried about overstepping her bounds with your kids, you've got to let her know it's OK. That you've got her back and that she should just follow her heart. Sometimes you've even got to remind yourself that it's OK. When you begin to worry about what's right for your kids, or how your new wife is going to react around your old wife, or what you're going to say to your ex's new man, just remember, "It's OK." There's no easy way to deal with a blended family. But if you always put your love for your children first, you'll eventually be able to take back your home from the drama that can drive blended families apart.

## CHAPTER 9

# Do Your Best and
# Then Forget the Rest

Hopefully Justine and I have been able to provide you with some guidance on how to take back your family from a variety of the dangers and distractions that threaten its happiness. But while we believe that every parent is capable of taking back their family, we want to end this book with a short chapter addressing those families who, despite a parent's hard work and unwavering commitment, are dealing with a child who still *seems* to be lost.

When we speak of these situations, we're not referring to the kind of physical loss we experienced with Victoria. Instead, we're referring to the sense of emotional loss that too many parents feel as their children begin to grow older. We know of so many parents who've committed themselves to raising their child the right way, only to see that child seemingly reject that guidance and instead insist on following a seemingly reckless and rocky path. As a parent, it's heartbreaking to feel that despite your best efforts and even better intentions, your own flesh and blood has gone astray. That's why we'd like to begin this chapter by reminding parents that while it is true that most children desire a greater degree of independence as they grow older, it is not inevitable that they will go astray. It *is* possible to maintain your influence over a teenager and even a young adult. And the way to do so is to remember that the older your kids get, the more involved *you* get. If you can manage to not only maintain, but even increase your presence in your children's lives as they grow older, the prospect of "losing" your child will become much less of a fear in your mind. And even more importantly, your increased guidance will prove invaluable to your child as they attempt to navigate young adulthood, one of life's most challenging periods.

However, we also want to keep it real: Sometimes even increased parental presence is not enough to keep certain children in line. If, despite all your efforts and prayers, your child still seems to be intent on taking the wrong path in life, please do not believe that that child is "lost" for good. While we understand how frustrating and scary it is to watch your child go off track, you must have faith that one day that child will return to the principles under which he or she was raised. If you have done your best by your child and taught them important principles like kindness, honesty, and hard work, even though they might seem to be forever out of your reach, there is a strong likelihood that they will one day return to the life that you had envisioned for them.

## THE OLDER THEY GET, THE MORE INVOLVED YOU GET

In our society, there seems to be a perception that a parent's responsibilities' lessen once their children reach eighteen. It's almost as if once they see that high school diploma hanging on the wall, Mommy and Daddy are allowed to take a well-deserved break from parenting. And while there have certainly been times when Justine and I wished that were the case, the hard truth is that if you really want to insure that your kids stay on the right path, then you're going to have to put that vacation on hold for a little bit longer. I'll say it one more time: The older your kids get, the more you have to get involved in their lives.

You must remember that at seventeen or eighteen years old, your children are on the verge of making some of the biggest decisions of their lives. They're often about to pick a college, a choice that will most likely end up determining what sort of career they follow, what sort of friends they will take with them into adulthood, and, for some, even who they will marry. It's also the age at which they're able to vote for the first time, which in our house is a very big deal. And if they're not going to college, it's also the age at which they can join the armed forces without your consent.

And as these kids get older, the temptations and pressures increase, as well. Whereas before they might have said, "No thanks, I'm good," when somebody offered them weed at a party, now it becomes a little more likely that they might say, "Yeah, let me hit that." Whereas before they'd be afraid to go to a party and get a lift home from someone who was drinking, now they might feel a little bolder about accepting the ride. This is also the age when they're most likely to go out with a boy that you wouldn't approve of, or start dating a girl that might expose them to bad influences. That's why this is also the time you need to be right there, ready to jump in when you sense some foolishness starting to brew. Don't put in all that hard work and then just fade into the background when they need you the most. Become even more involved!

For example, when I first heard that Angela was conflicted about dating Bow Wow, my reaction wasn't, "Well, she's getting grown now. She'll figure it out on her own." Nope, when she told me about her dilemma, I tried to give her even more guidance and become an even bigger part of her decision-making process than I did was when she was still a teenager. Similarly, when I heard that JoJo was running with a crowd that was a little too fast for him, I didn't say, "Well, he's almost a man now. He's old enough to choose his own friends." Instead, I went up into his room, pulled up a chair, looked him in the eye and said, "I hear some of those knuckleheads you've been running around with like to smoke weed. You know how I feel about that, so as long as you want to drive the car I bought you, then you can't be hanging around them anymore."

The fact is, I'm going to pour my authority over JoJo even thicker now than I did when he was only fifteen or sixteen. Because if I turn a blind eye to what JoJo's doing now, he's most likely going to take that freedom and run with it. And I'm probably not going to like where he ends up running to. At first, he might only run with some kids who smoke a little weed. But then it might progress into running with a crew that exposes him to even more dangerous elements. Soon he might find himself up in clubs where he doesn't belong. Where he'll be around people that smile in his face, but who are secretly plotting on his jewelry, or his car, or his money. There are simply too many temptations, and too many traps, for an eighteen-year-old boy out there, especially one who's on MTV every Thursday night. So even though I know I'm sounding a bit like one of those "overprotective" parents I used to make fun of when I was Jo-Jo's age, I'm not going to back off. I might take a few baby steps backward every now and then so I don't give the appearance of being too overbearing, but I'm always going to stay within striking distance. I don't care if he's living down the hall from me or in a dorm room, or even in his own apartment—I'm more prepared than ever to pounce and take JoJo back the second I suspect the world is pulling him, or any of our kids, in the wrong direction.

## SLOW AND IN CONTROL

When I try to keep JoJo (I'm using him as an example now, but again, this applies to all of our kids) out of the clubs and away from the wrong elements, what I'm really trying to do is slow him down. I know that one day he'll probably end up in those clubs anyway, but my hope is that that day won't come until he's mature enough to handle it. When he can go to a club and enjoy the music and chill out with his friends without making the wrong choices. When he's mature enough to know that even though he's only had "one drink," he'd still better not put his butt behind the wheel. When he's mature enough to say that even though the girls he just met are pretty and the party they're inviting him to back at their friend's place sounds like fun, there's still no way he's going to go to some stranger's house in the middle of the night with a bunch of people that he's never met before. When he's mature enough to come into contact with folks who don't have his best interests at heart, but instead of potentially falling under their influence, just giving them a pound and keeping it moving. I know JoJo will get there, but I just have to protect him until he does. Because right now, he's not ready.

And while right now the issue might be JoJo being in too much of a rush to get out on the scene, the truth is that all of my kids, and pretty much all kids in general, are in a rush. They're in a rush to grow up. To make their own decisions. To make their own money. To create their own look. To experiment with sex. That constant sense of rushing is why before you can become more involved in your child's life, you must slow it down a bit first. As a parent, try to view becoming more involved in an older child's life like trying to get into a boat that's already started to leave the dock. If the boat is already moving too fast, you're just going to end up in the water. But if you can make sure that boat is pulling away nice and slow, then you'll be able to jump aboard and still have some say in where it's going.

In our family, we employ a lot of strategies to slow our kids down. One of the most basic is making sure that there's always a string attached to whatever we give them. So while we let JoJo have a car, we also told him that he couldn't drive it at night. He didn't like that at first, but it definitely slowed him down a bit. Or while Diggy and Russy were allowed to have their own rooms when we moved into our current home, they weren't allowed to have locks on their doors. That way they won't try to move too fast with their independence by going to Web sites they shouldn't be on or watching movies that aren't age-appropriate. They can have their own space, but they also know they'll always be accountable for what happens in that space. And that accountability definitely slows them down a bit.

You can also slow your kids down by controlling the flow of money they get from you. If you're paying your children's college tui-

tion, or their car note, or their rent, or giving them a monthly sti-
pend or *any* kind of financial support, please don't be afraid to hold
that weight over their heads. A lot of parents will give their children
money no matter how they behave, but we believe that your children must understand that as long as they're willing to accept your
money, they're going to have to respect your rules and wishes, too.
So JoJo knows that if he keeps hanging with that crew that I told
him to stay away from, the car is going right back to the dealership.
Just as Angela knows that if she doesn't live up to the level of conduct I expect from her, that credit card I gave her will say "declined"
the next time she tries to buy some shoes. And that's true for Vanessa, just as it will be for Diggy, Russy, and Miley one day, too. Like
most parents, I love my kids and I want them to have the finer things
in life. Yet I will not hesitate for a second to take any of those things
away if I sense they are moving too fast in the wrong direction. And
that knowledge definitely helps keep them moving at the right speed.

On a more philosophical level, we've also found that you can
slow down your children by introducing meditation into their lives.
My brother Russell is a very strong believer in the power of meditation, and thanks to his influence, we've begun to make it a part of
our family's routine, too. When you walk into our home, the first
room you'll see is what I call my "Zen Room," an open room with a
waterfall, low lights, and soft music playing, where I like to spend
some time every day either reading, in prayer, or in meditation. I
think it's very important for my kids to see me spending time in that
room and putting such an emphasis on meditation and tranquillity.
Because while so far Vanessa is the only one who's started meditating (she calls it "quiet moments"), the peacefulness that that room
projects still has a calming influence on the entire house.

I realize that not everyone has an extra room in their home that
they can devote to meditation, but try to set aside some sort of space
in your home that will promote peacefulness and tranquillity. Even
if it's only a corner in your living room, it can make a difference.
Take a few chairs, turn them away from the TV, and establish a sepa-

rate space where you can spend a few minutes every day either meditating or reading. I know extra space is hard to come by, but I truly believe that when your children see you taking the time to slow your life down a bit, it will encourage them to slow down theirs a bit, as well.

## LOST, THEN FOUND

As much as my wife and I try to slow our kids down and keep them on the right path, we also live with the knowledge that despite our efforts, there is always a chance that these kids will go astray. There is a chance that no matter how hard I counsel him to stay away from them, JoJo might fall under the influence of the bad seeds out there. That no matter how much I encourage Vanessa to reject roles or magazine spreads that I think are too risqué, there could come a time where she stops accepting my advice and begins to lower her standards in order to gain more exposure. Just like one day I could tell Angela that I don't approve of her boyfriend, but then she not only keeps dating him, but moves in with him, too! Or down the line, Russy might want to drop out of school, or Diggy might want to move far away from the family and join a cult. And while any of those scenarios would hurt Justine and me very deeply, it's important that we remember that even though our child might have strayed from our authority for the moment, the positive foundation we spent many years building for them, and then spent even more years reinforcing, will ultimately be strong enough to keep them out of irreversible trouble and bring them back home.

I've seen many examples where a child has cut themselves off from their parents' program and chosen a lifestyle that seems to be in direct opposition to how they've been raised. And while those children have caused their parents tremendous pain and worry, I've also seen most of the children not only eventually return to the family fold, but also make their families tremendously proud. Even though those parents were convinced that they had lost their children's hearts and minds forever, in the end their relationships turned out to be stronger than they had ever been. One of the most inspiring examples of this scenario that I know of is the relationship between Kid Rock and his father.

Rock grew up in Michigan, where his father was a very successful car salesman. His father's dream was to see Rock follow in his footsteps, and he invested a lot of time trying to teach his son about the trade: how to brand your product, how to close a deal, and how to manage a staff—all the elements that go into being a successful businessman. But despite the long hours he spent learning the family business, the idea of eventually taking over that dealership didn't interest Rock one bit. All he wanted to do was run around with black kids and make rap music. And the more his father tried to push him toward the family business, the more dedicated Rock became to hip-hop. They couldn't see eye-to-eye, and eventually the tension became so great that Rock left home when he was sixteen in order to pursue his dream of being a rapper. And when Rock left, it was almost as if he had died in his father's eyes. The old man just couldn't understand why his son, who was in line to inherit this incredible opportunity, was prepared to throw it all away in order to be a rapper.

Of course, Rock didn't end up throwing his life away—he went on to become one of the most successful artists in the music game today. But Rock will tell you himself that one of the main reasons he was able to survive in the music industry all these years is because of the lessons his pops taught him back in the day. Sure, Rock was talented and ambitious, but there are plenty of talented and ambitious musicians out there who never make it. One of the qualities that sets Rock apart from the pack is his business savvy and his ability to understand the marketplace. They were the same lessons his father had taught him, just applied in a different industry. So while his father had assumed that all the work he had put into Rock had been lost when he left home, those lessons in fact helped propel his son to the incredible heights that he's reached today.

Now the father and son who seemed so far apart twenty years ago have a closer relationship than ever. In fact, the old man can't help but cry every time he sees his son, he's so proud of what Rock has accomplished. The son he was so sure he had lost has not only returned to the family, but is now making the family extremely proud.

I also saw a similar story play out between my parents and my brother Russell. Today my brother is one of the true legends of the music business, a great inspiration not only to me, but to the entire hip-hop generation. Yet there was a time when my parents, especially my father, were also concerned that Russell was wasting his life away. My parents were college graduates who very much wanted their sons to receive a similar education and go on to find success as professionals. Maybe as doctors, or educators, or even working for the government. For a while Russell tried to follow their vision, enrolling at the City University of New York, where he majored in communications. But even though Russell was getting good grades, college wasn't inspiring him. What was inspiring him was the hip-hop music he was hearing on the streets and at the discos all around the city. Instead of focusing on school, he poured all his energy into throwing hip-hop parties and trying to make a name for himself as a promoter. Soon he was skipping classes and pouring the money he was supposed to be using for tuition and books into his parties. Needless to say, my parents were not pleased. They knew their son was intelligent, and that with good grades could go on to graduate school and then a respectable, well-paying career. Instead, he was throwing that bright future away in order to promote a type of music that no one had even heard of before. And to make matters worse, he was losing money throwing all those parties. Because Russell was still just a kid, the people who owned the bars and clubs where he'd throw the parties used to rip him off, taking a bigger cut of the profits than they deserved. After every unsuccessful party, Russell used to come back to Queens and beg my parents for more money, claiming that the *next* party was the one that was going to put him on the map. I can remember that every time Russell would come back home with his hat in his hands, my father would just look at him and say, "I've got a son that don't cut no grass, don't shovel no snow. Just wanna go outside and disco." My father was a poet who liked to speak in rhymes a lot, but essentially what he was saying was, "This kid won't get the education he needs to succeed in this world. He won't even get an honest job. All he wants to do is take our money and waste it on this crazy music."

But even though my father thought he had lost Russell to the discos of New York City, eventually those discos helped Russell become exactly the type of man that my father had always dreamed he would be. Not only has Russell become a financial success, but he has used his celebrity to support countless charities and social causes, which made my father particularly proud. And while he may not have graduated from college, he speaks at countless schools around the country every year, encouraging young people to have the courage and determination to follow their dreams, too. So while it might have seemed that Russell was a lost cause when he was failing out of school and losing all his tuition money, he ended up making our entire family very proud. Even my hard-to-please father. In fact, when he was on his deathbed, I can remember my father saying, "I'm just happy that all three of my boys turned out so good."

## TAKING THEM BACK BY LETTING THEM GO

Since my wife and I have spent the better part of this book encouraging you to take back your children, it might seem surprising that we're going to end it by suggesting that sometimes you just need to let your children go. But one of the great ironies of parenthood is that it is often necessary to let your children go off into the world before it seems like your principles have taken hold. As many positive examples as you provide, as many guidelines as you set, your child might still have his or her heart set on tasting some of the forbidden fruit out there. Rather than fighting that urge to the point of destroying your relationship, at a certain point it is better to let them find out for themselves just how bitter that fruit can really taste.

Let me clarify one point, though. When I say, "Let them go," I'm not suggesting that you abandon your child. I'm not suggesting that you refuse to answer the phone when they call or cut off all ties with them. I'm not talking about letting them spend the night in jail instead of bailing them out. All I'm talking about is relaxing the parental leash a bit, not letting it go entirely. Let them take a few steps that you might not approve of, or think they're ready for. "Letting them go" means giving them the taste of independence they crave, while still remaining engaged in their lives. Perhaps not to the degree that you would like, but to a degree that at least allows you to monitor their situation, if not control it. Independence for your children and parental engagement do not have to be exclusive of each other.

Of course, the obvious question is, "When is the right time to let a child go?" Ultimately, that's a question that every parent must answer for themselves. As a parent, you must be honest with yourself and ask if you truly did your best by your child. Did you look the other way when your child broke the rules, or did you enforce them and teach them that there would always be a consequence to their actions? Did you set a good example for your child, or did your actions run counter to what you expected from them? Did you make yourself available to your child at all times, or were you distant, both emotionally and physically? Did you always tell them how much you loved them and how proud of them you were? Not only when they did well, but when they were struggling, too?

If you're not happy with your answers to those questions, then it's probably a little too early to let your child go. Instead of pulling back a bit, try to refocus on your parenting and see if you can't improve in some of those areas. Dedicate yourself to giving your child more time, more affection, more discipline, and a better role model to look up to. Truly commit yourself to the principles we've discussed in the book and see if that doesn't improve your relationship with your child. And, perhaps most importantly, remember that it's *never* too late to reinvent yourself as a parent. No matter what mistakes you've made, no matter what you've said, no matter how daunting the challenge may seem, you always have the power to do better. Don't become panicky and convince yourself that your parenting skills will never change. They always can, as long as you put in the work.

But let's say that your answers to all of those questions was a resounding "yes"; you've truly been the best parent that you know how to be for your child. If that's the case, and your child still continues to chafe under your authority, then you might have to resign yourself to letting them go for the time being. I wish I could say that there was a certain age, or a certain moment, or a certain sign that would always let you know when you've reached that point, but I can't. I believe that different people can bear different weights, and that what might be too heavy a burden for one might be manageable for another. But what is true for all of us as parents is that we don't want to fight our children so hard over their choices and lifestyles that in the process we build up a wall that can't ever be torn down. You must go hard as a parent, but not so hard that you destroy the relationship between you and your child in the process. Before you do that, it's better to let them go.

I realize that the idea of letting a child "go" seems like an incredibly frightening proposition for most parents. And I'm certainly no exception. Let's say that one of my boys kept getting into little scraps with the law—things like shoplifting, speeding, or underage drinking. Let's say I tried to set curfews, but they didn't work. Taking away his car didn't work. Holding family meetings didn't work. Consulting with Bishop Jordan didn't work. Even sending him to military school didn't work. At a certain point, when the weight of trying to maintain my authority over my son felt like it was about to bring the entire family down, I would have to resign myself to letting my son go.

But as scary and painful as it is to even write those words about a hypothetical situation, I also have faith that if a situation like that were to occur, it would only represent a temporary loss. That's because I believe that as long as you've truly committed yourself to teaching your children the principles and values that are important to you, they will always return to those values in the end. As it is written in Proverbs 22:6, "Train up a child in the way he should go: and when he is old, he will not depart from it."

Because of my belief in that Scripture, if one of my children were to go astray, I would never feel like it was a permanent departure. I would miss my child, I would worry a bit about that child, and I would pray that the child would find the guidance out on the street that he or she was no longer receiving at home. But I would not become despondent, nor would I let my wife become despondent, over the possibility that that child had forsaken us forever. Because I really do believe that if you train a child right, they will not depart from that training. In my eyes, that's the final piece of the parenting puzzle. Knowing that I've put the time into teaching them principles like kindness, hard work, respect, compassion, and faith, if they stray a bit, I ultimately know that they'll never live too far from those lessons. Or from their family.

In fact, my deep faith in that principle is why I'm comfortable saying, "and then forget the rest." I truly believe that no matter what sort of issues we face as a family, as long as I've applied myself to that situation as best I could, when the day is over, I can go to sleep without worrying about tomorrow. In fact, before I turn off the lights at the end of every day, I always say these words: "I can sleep tonight because God is awake!" I can rest easy because I know that as long as I've done my best, then I can forget the rest. That might sound glib to some people, but to me it just sounds like God.

# Acknowledgments

Rev Run and Justine would like to thank their beautiful children Vanessa, Angela, JoJo, Diggy, Russy, and Miley Simmons; as well as Jillian Manus, William Shinker, Lauren Marino, Amanda Walker, Brianne Ramagosa, and the team at Gotham Books; Jason Carbone, MTV, and the entire *Run's House* team; and Bishop Jordan and Zoe Ministries.

Justine would like to thank her mother, Susan Young, Gramps, her stepmom, Daisy, her father, Dave Jones, all her brothers and sisters, and her mentors Leroy and Jessy Burnette. Also, thanks to Jillian for believing in her and to Chris for being a great writer and now a friend.

Rev Run would like to thank his dad, Dan Simmons, and his mom, Evelyn Simmons, plus his brothers Russell and Danny Simmons, for being the first family he met! :-)

Chris Morrow sends his love to his daughter, Nissa Feng Morrow, who was born during the making of this book, and his wife, Peggy Cheng. He'd also like to thank Rev and Justine, William Shinker, Lauren Marino, and the crew at Gotham Books, Akasha Archer, Phil Braddock, Jillian Manus, John Morrow, Russell Simmons, and Michelle Tessler. And of course, Bill and Judi Morrow, for teaching him about the importance of family.